D0601461

The
Male
Chauvinist's
Cookbook

The Male Chauvinist's Cookbook

by Cory Kilvert

WINCHESTER PRESS

To all members of the stronger sex. May this book ease and hasten your triumphs—in the kitchen as well as elsewhere.

Copyright © 1974 by Winchester Press
All rights reserved

Library of Congress Catalog Card Number: 74-84074
ISBN: 0-87691-158-0

Illustrations and design by Marilyn Grastorf

Published by Winchester Press
460 Park Avenue, New York 10022

PRINTED IN THE UNITED STATES OF AMERICA

Contents

Introduction

WOMEN OF THE WORLD, take heed—men have arrived in the kitchen. And not just to watch or get trapped into drying the dishes. Somewhat like Caesar, we have come, we have seen, and we are about to conquer—you.

While we recognize the fact that your meat loaf isn't bad, we're pretty sure we can do better. So there's no use in your trying to dismiss us with an imperious wave of your wooden mixing spoon. We are here to stay.

If you'll just give it a little thought, you'll have to agree that we're long overdue. After all, we have a habit of succeeding at whatever we put our hands to. Since the dawn of mankind males have set and also changed the course of history. We have built empires, led entire nations to the pinnacle of civilization, sailed the Seven Seas, and scaled mountains to heights the girls have yet to approach. We have developed industry, nourished the world with the crops we've grown, and yes, we have walked on the moon. In short, we have proved our superiority in every walk of life with the sole exception of giving birth, and there are even a few of us around who are working on that.

Naturally, these and other interests have placed a premium on our time. We can't be everywhere at once. But even with all our myriad pursuits, we have managed to achieve a significant representation in the culinary arts—with Escoffier, Savarin, Beard, Soulé, and other masters of fine food. Just go into any French or Italian or Greek or German restaurant—when you step into the kitchen to compliment the chef, whom do you find yourself addressing? A woman? Certainly not. You find a man, a chef. These two words are synonymous. Cooks, on the other hand, are women, and this title never had—nor will it ever have—the prestige or panache of "chef." Yes, with all the millions of practicing housewives in the world, the greatest kitchens are still run by men. And with good reason. Man is the superior being.

Clearly, then, we all have what it takes to turn out a magnificent meal, whether it's baked beans or *beef bourguignon*. It's simply a matter of getting started and then sticking to our guns. To do this, however, we must first overcome several thousand years of misunderstanding with regard to man, society, and the kitchen.

You see, for some reason the kitchen has always been off-limits to men. Despite the individual triumphs of the great chefs, males as a team have failed to conquer this final fortress of feminine fascism. Of course, the problem has not been in achieving *success* so much as *access*. And my guess is that things got off on the wrong foot back in the Garden of Eden. When Eve served up that first rotten apple, an unfortunate precedent was set—women became identified as the premier preparers and profferers of food. Through the centuries, this original sin was allowed to expand, as males devoted their energies to bringing home the bacon, not frying it, to winning the bread, not baking it. In man's absence from the kitchen woman rushed to fill the vacuum, and now she stands bleating about an expertise to which she can lay claim not by achievement but by *default*.

Yet, we men have not complained. It is the ladies, in fact—"the world's only discriminated-against majority"—who have done all the whining. They claim that they have become prisoners of their sex, chained to the kitchen stove. Well let me tell you something—if society has somehow locked women into the kitchen, it has just as certainly locked men *out!*

Since childhood we've been told that we didn't "belong" behind a burner or in front of a salad bowl. We were encouraged to run along and play, and most of us did just that, never to return unless summoned by a dishtowel that heralded the start of another daily chore.

Oh sure, an occasional steelworker may rise up in wrath some evening and shout that he's eaten his last dish of soggy spaghetti. The trouble is, he's never put his own hand to the task of turning out a better product. He still believes what his mother told him. As a result, he's resigned himself to hundreds of lackluster meals and the general malaise that follows them.

Furthermore, the belief that he doesn't belong in the kitchen has fostered a fiction in man. He has rationalized that if indeed he has no place there, it must follow that there's something that adversely affects his manliness if he so much as picks up a spatula, let alone bastes a roast.

This is nonsense. There is not a damn thing effeminate about preparing good food. It is, in fact, an art, and is in many ways the last challenge facing the superior sex. Besides, the man who is truly confident of his virility will not give a second thought to donning an apron. Manliness is a state of mind, not of dress.

So take up your paring knives, men, and don't be shy about this undertaking. The ladies have been heard from on the subject—the mouse has roared. And now it's time for you—yes, you—to assert yourself in the only room in the house where you don't already reign supreme.

Now that you're fired up and ready to go (or at least you *should* be) let's get one thing straight. This book is not intended to be a manual on how to embarrass women—God knows they're fully capable of doing that themselves. This is a cookbook, and with it you will be able to prepare meals for two—yes, for you and for one more person—hopefully a *female*.

Surprised? Don't be. If you think about it, women *do* have their place in the scheme of things. And where would male chauvinism be without them? Women are to be loved and enjoyed—and so is cooking. This book will show you how to derive more pleasure from both.

They say that the way to a man's heart is through his stomach. But what about a woman's heart? Can't it be reached through the same avenue? Of course it can—and you're just the guy who can do it.

The rewards here are unlimited, and if you think you're lucky with women now, you haven't seen the half of it. (After all, if you can cook a woman under the table, think of where you can take her from there.) Women are impressionable. Unlike men, they feel instead of think. Furthermore, they basically want to be conquered—not only on the couch but in the kitchen, too. All their running around in pursuit of equal rights has obscured this fact, but it can still be seen amid the forest of placards that aim to discredit us for doing what we do better than they do—succeed.

So move aside, Betty and Gloria, Germaine and Billie Jean and Kate, and take your rhetoric with you. We men have work to do. And don't all you girls worry about the results. We'll be using our culinary skills not to put you down but to soften you up. War is still war, however, and the best *man* is going to win.

Cory Kilvert
New York City
September 30, 1974

Chapter 1

Success Depends on What You Have and How Well You Use It

NOW THAT YOU'VE DECIDED to take the plunge and become a chef, be certain that you stock your kitchen carefully. Cheap equipment only leads to second-rate results. This is true no matter what interests you pursue.

You wouldn't buy inferior tools to use on your vintage XK120 Jaguar or dress for a nightclub in clothing supplied by Goodwill Industries. Class takes cash, and you may as well face up to the fact that this dictum is just as valid in the kitchen as it is anywhere else. That's why you'll want to buy good cutlery, pots and pans, and whatever else you'll be using in the course of preparing all those memorable meals for all those willing women.

A sharp knife is the single most important kitchen implement. So you should purchase one or two top-quality carbon steel types, preferably by Sabatier. This French firm also makes stainless steel knives which won't rust but which unfortunately won't hold much of an edge either. Stainless knives—particularly those with serrated edges—are okay for slicing tomatoes and bread, but they won't hold up well for carving roasts, steaks, and poultry.

Carbon steel blades, on the other hand, can be honed to a fare-thee-well, although you'll have to dry them right after each washing if you want to keep them in the best of condition. Applying a thin coating of oil to them from time to time will prevent rusting and preserve them for whenever they're needed. Stains can be removed with steel wool and cleaning powder. A couple of quality knives will also save you the need for investing in gimmicky tomato and egg slicers, parsley choppers, apple corers, cabbage shredders, and all those other worthless toys that are hustled each night by slick pitchmen on The Late Late Show.

While you're at it, invest in a butcher's sharpening stone, and put a new edge on your knives when they show signs of getting dull. Just be certain that you squirt a few drops of 3-in-1 oil onto the stone before each sharpening. This will protect the blades from being cut too fast, a process which prevents them from attaining that serpent's-tooth quality you're after. A new sharpening stone soaks up oil like a wino on the underside of a muscatel bottle, but once it ages, it will require less and less lubrication to do a good job.

You'll also need good pots and pans, heavy aluminum ones that are sold in the kitchenware section of reputable department stores. If you try to make do with cheap substitutes you'll lose, because anything with a thin bottom will prevent heat from dispersing evenly and will probably burn whatever is in it. You may know how to prepare a particular dish, but if your pots and pans don't, you may as well reserve two stools at McDonald's for all the impression you'll make on Rosemary or Ann.

Cheap enamel pots tend to chip, and this can be dangerous if the chips end up in your mashed potatoes—which can be even worse if Elinor ends up behind a fluoroscope in the emergency ward. A well-enameled pot will hold up, however, and is far better for boiling eggs since it won't stain the way aluminum pots often seem to do.

Cast iron is the best material for frying pans and pots. (It must be because that's what the French use.) So investigate the ones made by Le Creuset. They may seem more costly than they're worth, but they'll still be in service after you're on Medicare.

The following list should serve you well in devising the downfall of dozens of delightful damsels who come to your place for food and frolic. You may later find the need for other things, too, but don't rush out and buy armloads of esoteric kitchen aids until you're sure of exactly what you need.

Basic Equipment List

Frying pans, 2, of heavy aluminum or iron (one 10-inch diameter, one larger)

Sauce pans, 3, of enameled cast iron or heavy aluminum (1-quart, 2-quart, and 3-quart capacities, with lids)

A double boiler (one saucepan that fits into another containing boiling water—for slow-cooking sauces, scrambled eggs, etc.)

A kettle, aluminum with a tight lid (about 6-quart size)

A casserole, metal or oven-proof ceramic with a tightly fitting lid

A loaf pan, metal or oven-proof glass (about 5 x 10 inches)

Roasting pans, aluminum or oven-proof glass (one 8 inches square, one about 10 x 13 inches)

A roasting rack (to fit in the above rectangular pan and hold meat and fish up out of their juices)

A pie plate, metal or oven-proof glass (8 inches)

A griddle, metal, often teflon-coated (about 10 x 16 inches). Buy this if you are confident that you'll be cooking lots of breakfasts for two. A griddle this size will fit over two burners, and can pan fry several foods at once: bacon at one end, scrambled eggs in the middle, fried eggs at the other end, and a few tomatoes on the side. All food, from pancakes to sauté bananas, is easier to flip over on a large griddle than on a not-quite-large-enough frying pan.

A carbon steel chopping knife (8-inch blade)

A stainless steel paring knife

A stainless steel slicing knife with serrated (5-inch) blade

A stainless steel bread knife with serrated edge

A swivel bladed paring knife (for peeling potatoes, apples, etc.)

A grapefruit knife

A sharpening steel for the carbon knife (or knives if you get ambitious)

A chopping board or butcher's block, solid hardwood (absolutely essential—no knife will stay sharp if you are slicing through soft vegetables onto hard formica or metal)

A pancake turner, metal, slotted (buy a plastic one if you have a teflon-lined pan)

A fork with long handle and two prongs

A spoon with long handle

A spoon with long handle and slots (for lifting eggs, vegetables out of water)

A soup ladle

Measuring cups, oven-proof glass (1-cup, 2-cup, and 4-cup sizes)

Measuring spoons, metal or plastic (a standard set from ⅛ teaspoon to 1 tablespoon)

Mixing bowls, oven-proof glass or stainless steel (a nest of 3 or 4 in graduated sizes)

A rubber spatula (for scraping the last sticky remnant out of the above bowls)

A can opener, hand or wall mounted (only a weak-wristed woman needs an electric one)

A "Handyaid," a 5-inch round rubber disc (guaranteed to help you grip and remove the stubbornest jar top. I bought mine for about $1 from the Vermont Country Store in Weston.)

A beer-can opener (it's also a tomato juice can opener for the bloody marys, of course)

A corkscrew (get a good quality one; otherwise you'll find pieces of cork floating in the wine. No girl looks attractive when she has to keep spitting at the table, however delicately, and you don't want to get turned off.)

A grater (preferably one with 4 sides and several different sizes of holes)

A colander (for draining spaghetti, rinsing food such as small berries)

A strainer, medium-sized (for eliminating tea leaves, lemon pips)

Funnels (a big one and a small one are useful)

A rotary beater, manual or electric (for everything from scrambled eggs to whipped cream)

A wire whisk

A blender, electric (makes you an instant expert at mayonnaise, home-made soups, etc.)

A food mill or potato ricer (an elaborate strainer or sieve, for puréeing)

Tongs, a pair

Scissors (the easiest way to "chop" fresh parsley and dill, to open unopenable plastic packages, etc.)

Wooden spoon(s) (for stirring—they don't get hot)

A salad basket, French wire (for washing lettuce. The easiest way to dry it is to go out on your terrace, or hang out of the window, or even step into the shower if there's room, and swing the filled basket rapidly round in circles at arm's length. If that's too athletic for you, the contraption doubles as a steam basket for vegetables when balanced in a saucepan just above the boiling water.)

A coffee pot and coffee bean grinder

A tea pot (if you/she likes tea)

A toaster, electric

A tea kettle, electric

Pepper mills, 2 (one for black peppercorns, one for white. You can't buy little tins of dried pepper powder if you aspire to being a Real Cook. Pepper mills on the table will impress Mimi, anyway.)

A garlic press (another impressive item, also much easier to use than chopping a clove of garlic into minuscule particles)

A cannister set (for storing flour, sugar, salt)

Containers for leftovers, good-quality plastic, in graduated sizes

An oven thermometer (essential—the control knob of every oven I ever met is inaccurate by about 50 degrees)

A meat thermometer (jab one end in the roast, so you know when it's really ready)

A basting syringe (an easy and somewhat sexy tool for getting the juices out of the pan and over the meat without slopping it everywhere)

An apron, dark blue with white pin stripes (in case you slop, anyway. Every professional chef uses one. Avoid the cute ones that read "Chief Cook." You know you're the Chief, whatever it is you're doing.)

A dish-draining rack (for the inevitable)

A waffle iron (see Chapter 10)

A hibachi (see Chapter 6)

Metal skewers, about 6 (for shish kebab on the hibachi, but also useful for trussing turkeys, etc.)

A tray, for serving breakfast in bed

Extra ice-cube trays

Now that you have acquired all the gear for cooking up a storm, let's start to think about buying food and stocking up your cupboards and refrigerator. There are a few ways of economizing on food, but none of them involves buying supplies of inferior quality. Such a maneuver usually costs more in the long run, and in fact you are always better advised to buy good-quality meat and produce because you will waste far less.

If you live or spend weekends in the country, you can grow your own vegetables. On the whole, food is cheaper in the country, whether you grow it or buy it. You can learn to cook without waste by making soups and using leftovers imaginatively. Perhaps the best way to economize is to buy a deep-freeze, which can be an expensive way to start, but pays off in the long run. It will save you both time and money.

If you are making beef bourguignon, you make double the quantity and put half in the freezer. If you come home with a brace of mallards, cook one and freeze one. If you fancy cranberries when it isn't Christmas time, freeze several pounds of them. If the supermarket has a special on double-loin lambchops, buy a dozen and freeze them. If you bake bread, freeze several loaves. Once you've spent a little time stocking up your freezer, you'll be able to produce marvelous dinners at very short notice (thawing out time) with an absolute minimum of shopping. But most important is what you eat. Eat real food, not garbage food. Real food means fresh meat, fresh vegetables, fresh fruit, milk, butter, eggs, cheese, and real bread. (Real bread means bread full of texture and flavor, whole wheat bread, oatmeal, rye in a dozen varieties, pumpernickel, and many others. It does not mean that sodden white tasteless pulp that has been foisted upon the public for so long.)

Don't waste your money on instant this and instant that, and packets of pre-mixed drink powder. If you're too enfeebled to squeeze a real lemon, then you're too weak to squeeze a real woman, and you might as well stop reading this book right now. Eat real breakfast cereals, too, not the crisp air they sell in big boxes. The only nourishment that stuff contains is in the fruit and sugar you anoint it with. You'd be just as well off sitting down to a bowlful of chopped cardboard. *Real* cooked rice, leftover from dinner, may be used cold in the morning. With a little milk and some brown sugar this is an excellent, economical, and nutritious breakfast.

Stocking the Cupboard

Salt, try sea salt for more flavor
Pepper, black, whole, for use in pepper mill No. 1
Pepper, white, whole for use in pepper mill No. 2
Sugar white, granulated
Sugar, white, superfine, for fruit
Sugar, light brown
Sugar, dark brown
Maple syrup (buy the real thing, not flavored sugar syrup)
Vinegar, red wine
Vinegar, white wine
Vinegar, cider
Oil, olive (good quality French or Italian)
Oil, corn or other vegetable
Flour, white, all-purpose
Rice, long grain white—*not* instant
Rice, brown
Noodles, egg
Spaghetti
Lentils
Oatmeal and/or Cream of Wheat
Potato, instant mix (a rare exception to the no-instant rule)
Crackers and biscuits and cookies
Croutons
Tea
Coffee, fresh

Coffee, instant

Cocoa powder

Baker's chocolate

Worcestershire sauce

Tabasco sauce

Soy sauce (buy a Chinese or Japanese brand)

Jam, jelly, marmalade

Chicken bouillon cubes

Beef bouillon cubes

Canned soups, concentrated (tomato, oyster stew, clam chowder, black bean, green pea, cream of mushroom, beef bouillon, consommé)

Canned tomatoes, Italian plum variety (for spaghetti sauce)

Canned tomato purée

Canned pork and beans

Canned red kidney beans (for chili)

Canned: sardines, rolled stuffed anchovies, anchovy fillets, crabmeat, shrimp, tuna (several), salmon, ham, smoked oysters, smoked clams, caviar

Herbs: basil, thyme, marjoram, oregano, chervil, bay leaf, dill, rosemary, tarragon, summer savory, dried shredded green onions, dried parsley flakes, dried onion flakes, garlic powder

Spices: cinnamon, whole cloves and powdered cloves, nutmeg, ginger, allspice, paprika, curry powder, chili powder, cardamom, saffron, turmeric, poppy seeds, cumin

Colman's dry mustard powder

Onion juice

Vanilla extract

Lemon extract

Toothpicks

Miniature bottles of: kirsch, Cointreau, cherry brandy, Cognac, triple sec, curaçao, brandy, sherry, pear liqueur, etc. (for flavoring desserts and fruit)

Beer and mixers of your choice—keep a small variety of imported beers and ales; if you pride yourself on your taste in Scottish malt whisky, keep spring water or Perrier for it; also, try keeping a bottle of Danish aquavit in the freezing compartment

Milk

Half-and-half (for coffee)

Fruit juices (fresh and frozen)

Butter and/or margarine

Eggs

Bacon
Bread, muffins, etc.
Fruit, fresh
Salad fixings: lettuce, tomatoes, cucumbers
Cold cuts
Mayonnaise, Hellman's is the best, or make your own (a large jar)
Pickles
Chutney
Mustards, a variety, some really hot—always include one good French
    Dijon mustard with white wine
Cream cheese
Frozen chopped chives
Lemons (and limes in season), parsley, and onions

A Few Preliminaries—Hints and Warnings

Before trying anything: Read and absorb Chapter 1. Read any recipe you choose to try carefully once or twice and make sure you have everything you need on hand. Check any unfamiliar terms in the list of definitions in this Chapter.

Seasonings: It is neither always possible nor desirable to give exact amounts in recipes for seasonings. These are matters of personal taste. Always season food very lightly to begin with. You can always add more later, but it is not easy to rescue a dish that has been oversalted. Stop and taste frequently. Don't hesitate to omit a flavor you dislike and substitute one you prefer.

To separate an egg (the yolk from the white, that is): If you have ever seen it done, it's simplicity itself. If not, a little explaining is in order. For some recipes you need only egg yolks or only whites, and since eggs come ready-mixed you have to separate them. Provide yourself with two cups, one for yolks and one for whites. Crack the egg against the edge of the cup destined for whites, and instead of opening it downwards so that the egg drops into the cup, open it upwards so that the egg yolk stays in half the shell and probably a good bit of the white in the other half. Dump the white into the cup, and then using the two pieces of egg shell as if they were cups, gently transfer the yolk from one to the other and back again, each time leaving as much of the white behind to be dropped into the cup as possible. Then drop the yolk into the other cup.

To peel potatoes: If you have new potatoes or if the peel looks generally fresh and young, just scrub the potatoes with a brush under running cold water and don't bother peeling them at all. But if you are dealing with a tough old customer who requires peeling on esthetic grounds, let him boil for a couple of minutes and then hold him under the cold tap and peel. The skin will come right off.

To make a salad: Put the lettuce in the sink and take the head apart under cold running water. Separate the leaves and make sure that each one is rinsed clean of mud and sand and sometimes little flies. Discard tough or wilted outer leaves. Dry the lettuce leaves with paper towels or with a clean dish towel, and put them away in the refrigerator to crisp or "freshen," as they say. Drying the lettuce is important because wet lettuce will not crisp successfully and it will dilute your salad dressing. If possible, toss the lettuce in a little oil before adding the salad dressing.

To increase a recipe: If you want to double or triple a recipe, go ahead, but *NEVER* double the seasonings, above all the salt. Use the same amount, and then carefully add a *little* more, tasting it as you go.

On Making Coffee

Instant coffee is definitely a no-no, but on certain occasions there is no other choice. At these times, instead of shoveling a teaspoon of the stuff into each cup, shovel four or five into a big pot or glass server, pour boiling water into it, and stir. For some reason, it tastes better that way, probably because the water doesn't cool as quickly as it does in a cup.

Coffee-making, however, is a serious business and at times an art. Really good coffee depends on a series of variables: the innate quality of the coffee bean itself, how freshly-ground it is, and how well it is prepared.

You'll have to choose between drip pots, percolators, electric percolators, and filter coffee makers. If you're a real coffee freak, maybe you'll want to buy a small espresso machine. Drip machines aren't bad. Nothing beats the smell of coffee from a percolator, whether normal or electric. But the best coffee is filtered. There are a variety of simple devices for making filtered coffee on the market. They vary in size from 1 cup to a dozen. Buy yourself about an 8 to 10 cup job. I will explain the method and virtue of filtered coffee.

The coffee grounds (ground fine) sit in the filter paper and you pour water through them. It drips into the pot below. The first important thing is not to use boiling hot water. The water should be below the boiling point, at about 185° to 195°, before it touches the coffee. The most accurate way to achieve this is with a thermometer. The easiest is to let a kettle of water boil and then throw in a cup of cold water. Then pour it through the coffee grounds. Reason? Simple. At the boiling point, a bitter fraction is released from the coffee grounds. You won't notice it immediately, but if the coffee sits for a while or if you warm it up later, you will notice a bitter and/or sour taste. Never pour boiling water on your coffee, and you will be able to reheat it later and even the next morning without disastrous loss of flavor. Similarly, never let coffee boil when reheating it. One brand of filter coffee maker comes with an optional water bath for keeping the coffee hot or reheating it without boiling it.

Two other details lead to good coffee making: store coffee, especially if it has been ground, in the refrigerator, and keep your coffee maker scrupulously clean.

Choose a breakfast blend and another richer one for after-dinner coffee. You cannot beat the flavor (or the smell), of freshly ground coffee, so consider investing in an electric coffee grinder. You can buy one for less than ten dollars.

There are a number of variations you might like to try when serving after-dinner coffee. Serve it black with a twist of lemon peel. Serve it with dark brown sugar instead of white. When making the coffee, add a pinch or two of ground cardamom seed to the grounds.

A Word About Sauces

Many people are intimidated by the very idea of making sauce. Foolish. There is no mystique, no mystery.

Here is the very simplest sauce you can make for meat or fish, roasted or fried: when you have finished roasting or frying the fish or meat, you will discover a reddish-brown substance stuck to the bottom of the pan. Many people regard this substance as a nuisance which is difficult to clean off the pan. Alas. Much of the flavor of the meat or fish is in this substance, and it is not in the least difficult to get off. Remove the meat. Find a wooden spoon and a cup of cold water. Leave the pan over a low heat. Pour in a little cold water. Stir around with the spoon. The substance will begin to loosen and look like sauce and smell good. Continue scraping and stirring with the wooden spoon and adding a little cold water (don't drown it) until all the stuff is off the pan and dissolved. Taste the sauce, and add a little salt if necessary (unlikely). Behold! A delicious sauce, and a practically clean pan. This works on frying pans as well as roasting pans and saucepans. Mind you, if you have burnt whatever it was you were cooking, forget the sauce, but use the method for cleaning the pan.

The next simplest sauce is the traditional thickened sauce. It is invariably composed of three ingredients: a fat, meaning butter, oil, lard, fat off a roast; a thickener, meaning flour (white or whole wheat or corn flour); and a liquid, meaning water, milk, wine, juice from a pan as described above, fruit juice, in fact *any* liquid.

The basic principle upon which the sauce works is that you cannot add the thickener after the liquid because it will make lumps. You start with the fat, fairly hot in a pan. You add the thickener with a spoon and stir it into the pan, being careful not to scorch it. This mixture of fat and thickener is called a *roux*. You let the roux cook for a minute or two, stirring and blending it with a wooden spoon. Then you add the liquid, pouring it gradually into the roux and mixing it constantly. The proportions are 1½ tablespoons of fat, 1½ tablespoons of thickener, 1 cup of liquid. As the sauce comes to the boil, it will begin to thicken. If it is too thick, add more liquid. If it is too thin—but I said you cannot add the thickener after the liquid, and you cannot. There is a way, however. Put a little bit of thickener (say, a teaspoon or two of flour) into a jar with a tight lid, and add a little liquid to it—enough to thin the sauce. Shake it up vigorously until all the flour is well mixed into the liquid. To be on the safe side, pour the resultant mixture into the sauce through a strainer to get rid of any lumps.

Therefore, to make roast beef gravy, use the pan juice made as described in the first paragraph as the liquid, plus the fat you can pour off. Add flour to the fat, and then add the juice. Test for seasoning and add salt or pepper or wine or what you will.

Now you can make sauce. So let us turn to some of the famous ones.

BÉCHAMEL SAUCE–1½ tablespoons butter, 1½ tablespoons flour and 1 cup milk

MORNAY SAUCE–as above, plus a little grated cheese

NORMANDY SAUCE–as above, but use water instead of milk, and after cooking, add some heavy cream

SAUCE SUPREME–to a Normandy Sauce, add a little beef extract

SAUCE AURORE–to a Normandy Sauce, add a little tomato purée

All of the preceding sauces have to be cooked long enough for the flour to cook. Raw flour does not taste very nice. Cook them over a low heat so that they just bubble gently for at least ten minutes. And stir them pretty regularly to make sure they are not sticking. If you refused my advice and bought a cheap, thin-bottomed saucepan, here is where you will regret it.

Of course, you must add salt and pepper to taste to these sauces. But you can go on from there and invent your own. Add any herbs you fancy, depending on the purpose of the sauce. Dill in a sauce for fish, for instance. And also for fish, how about using ½ white wine and ½ water? Or half wine and half milk for a richer sauce? Suppose you have a ham steak. Put some dry mustard into your thickener before adding it to the fat—actually the mustard acts as a thickener itself. You can turn the basic Béchamel sauce into a curry sauce by adding curry powder and other Indian spices to the thickener. Have fun.

BASIC FRENCH DRESSING

Buy:

Olive oil, French or Italian, best-quality (1 large bottle)

Corn oil, or safflower oil (1 large bottle)

Wine vinegar, red and white (1 large bottle of each)

A selection of pepper and herbs (see list, p. 7)

In a measuring cup, put oil and vinegar in the proportions of 3 parts oil to 1 part vinegar. Add salt and freshly ground black pepper to taste. Mix well. Make fresh dressing each time you need it.

You may prefer to use olive oil exclusively. Good olive oil has a very light, smooth flavor, but inferior brands may taste strong or even rancid. Some people prefer a mixture of olive oil and another oil. Others prefer corn oil or safflower oil alone. Experiment a little and discover your own preference.

As far as vinegar is concerned, you can use cider vinegar or plain white vinegar, but their flavor is very strong and they are very acid. Wine vinegar is really much better. Its flavor is good and its mildness helps bring out the flavors in the salad itself.

Once you have made the basic dressing, you can proceed to season it in many different ways. But remember that the simplest is often the best. You may add a little crushed garlic, or you may prefer to rub the garlic on the salad bowl. Add a very small amount of salad herbs, such as parsley, thyme, chervil, basil, marjoram. Try them one at a time until you get to know their individual flavors, and then try a few modest combinations.

FRENCH MUSTARD DRESSING

Buy:
French Dijon mustard with
    white wine (1 pot)

Check Cupboard for:
Olive oil   **Wine vinegar**

Put 1½ heaping teaspoons of Dijon mustard into a measuring cup and add 1½ ounces of wine vinegar. Mix them together thoroughly. Then add olive or corn oil very slowly, beating constantly with a fork. Pour the oil in a thin stream, and continue beating until the mixture begins to thicken to the consistency of mayonnaise. You can add enough oil to fill ½ to ¾ cup. Then season the mixture with salt and pepper, and add herbs or garlic if desired. Make this dressing at the last minute. Warning: do not try to make this dressing with any other kind of mustard; it won't work.

MAYONNAISE

Buy:
Eggs   **Lemons**

Check Cupboard for:
Olive or corn oil   **Mustard, dry**
Cayenne pepper

Mayonnaise is composed simply of oil and egg yolk, flavored with a little lemon, salt, and pepper. It is made possible by the fact that an egg yolk, if beaten thoroughly, can be persuaded to absorb oil. If the egg yolk is cold, it will absorb less oil than it will if it is at room temperature. At room temperature, 1 large egg yolk will absorb ¾ cup of oil. For some reason, it is easier to make mayonnaise with some other oil then olive; olive oil is more likely to cause the mayonnaise to separate. Lemon juice is added to mayonnaise to thin it and add flavor.

Have ready the following: the juice of 2 lemons, 2 egg yolks in a bowl at room temperature (if the eggs were in the refrigerator, run hot water into the bowl to warm it, and dry it before putting the egg yolks into it), a large measuring cup containing 1½ cups corn or olive oil, an egg beater, a tablespoon for measuring.

Add to the egg yolks, ½ teaspoon of salt, ½ teaspoon of dry mustard, less than a pinch of cayenne. Mix thoroughly. Then add, stirring constantly, 1 tablespoon of lemon juice.

Now the secret is to add the oil to the egg yolks a drop at a time while beating constantly until about 1 tablespoon of oil has been absorbed; then you can speed up a little and add the oil 1 teaspoon at a time, still beating. Keep going until the mixture is about as thick as whipped cream. Make sure that all the oil is completely mixed each time before you add more. When you have added all the oil, stir in one more tablespoon of lemon juice. If the mayonnaise is still too thick, add a little more lemon juice until the mixture is the desired consistency.

If the mayonnaise should separate (probably because the oil was added too quickly), all is not lost. Put a brand new egg yolk in a bowl and add the separated mayonnaise to it, beating it in gradually.

Basic mayonnaise is delicious as it is. You can, however, vary the flavor for different purposes. To serve with chicken or chicken salad, flavor the mayonnaise with a little curry powder. To serve with fish, flavor with dill or tarragon. To serve with seafood, flavor with tomato paste or chili sauce. For a particularly good variation, add up to ¼ cup chopped fresh parsley or other fresh herbs.

BASIC INFALLIBLE RICE

Buy:

**Rice, long-grained (1
    package)**

Check Cupboard for:

Oil   **Chicken bouillon cubes**

Using chicken bouillon cubes, make 2½ cups of chicken bouillon and keep it simmering and ready to add to the rice.

Put 1½ tablespoons of oil into a medium-sized saucepan and heat it gently over a low to moderate heat. Add one cup of rice to the oil and stir it with a wooden spoon so that the rice becomes thoroughly coated with the oil. Let it heat for a minute or two, and then add 2½ cups of boiling chicken bouillon. Let the rice and bouillon return to the boil, then turn the heat down so that the water is just simmering. Cover tightly and cook until all the liquid is consumed. You can judge this by tipping the saucepan to one side.

If you plan to use the rice with a beef dish, use beef bouillon cubes instead of chicken. Needless to say, you can cook the rice in plain boiling water too. Or in diluted beef bouillon or consommé from a can.

Some Definitions for the Male Chauvinist Cook

Al dente: Italian term meaning cooked until done but not over-cooked. Usually applied to pastas (spaghetti, macaroni or noodles) which should have some "bite" or resilience.

Bake: To cook by dry heat in the oven. Called roasting when applied to meat.

Baste: To moisten meats by spooning melted fat or drippings over them during roasting.

Batter: Not the man on the baseball diamond, but a mixture of flour and a liquid (and some other ingredients), thin enough to pour.

Beat: To mix by stirring rapidly with a fork, whisk, or rotary beater.

Bind: To use one ingredient to hold together other ingredients. For example, to use mayonnaise as a binding agent for tuna salad.

Blanch: To scald, nuts in particular (or fruits), by placing in boiling water for 1 to 5 minutes, in order to loosen skins.

—15—

Blend: To mix 2 or more ingredients until smooth, using a wire whisk, rotary beater, or electric blender.

Boil: To cook in liquid at boiling temperature (212° F).

Braise: To brown meat or vegetables in fat, then simmer them with a small amount of liquid in a covered pan over a low flame.

Bread: To cover or coat food with bread crumbs or meal, by first dipping it into milk or slightly beaten egg, then into the crumbs.

Broil: To cook exposed to direct heat, on a rack placed under the source of heat, or over an open fire.

Brown: To cook partially and quickly until color (and flavor) of food changes. Browning can be done in a frying pan, hot oven, or broiler.

Capers: Pickled flower buds, usually of a Mediterranean shrub, used as a condiment.

Caramelize: To heat sugar slowly in a heavy, shallow pan over moderate heat until it melts.

Casserole: An oven-proof earthenware, glass, or metal covered dish in which food can be baked and served. Also: the type of dish cooked, often using meat, vegetables, potatoes or rice, sauce, etc.

Chill: To allow to become thoroughly cold, but not frozen.

Chop: To cut into small bits with a knife on a board or in a chopping bowl.

Chutney: A spicy relish made of fruits, spices, and herbs.

Coat: To cover the entire surface of food with flour or bread crumbs.

Coddle: To cook gently (particularly an egg) by heating in water just below the boiling point. Similar to "cuddle," to handle gently below the boiling point, too.

Combine: To mix together.

Condiment: A seasoning or relish, such as pepper, mustard, spicy sauce.

Court Bouillon: French term for a quickly prepared stock in which to cook fish.

Cream: To mash in a bowl with a wooden spoon, until mixture (of butter and sugar, for example) is smooth and has the consistency of heavy cream.

Crisp: To heat foods (such as crackers or cereal) until they re-

	gain their original crispness. Or, to soak vegetables in cold water in order to make them firm (see "Freshen").
Croutons:	Toasted or fried bread cubes.
Cube:	To cut into small squares.
Curdle:	To coagulate (accidentally) a sauce or other liquid into small clots, so that it is no longer smooth.
Curry:	A powder prepared from turmeric, cumin, coriander, and many other pungent spices and herbs. Used as a seasoning in cooking, especially rice dishes from India and the East.
Dash:	Less than a sprinkle of a dry ingredient, or several drops of a liquid. Also: one of the essential qualities of a male chauvinist.
Dot:	To place small pieces of butter, cheese, etc. here and there on the surface of food for added flavor and decoration. (Dorothy's nickname.)
Dredge:	To cover food thickly with flour, meal, or sugar.
Drippings:	Fats and natural liquids that accumulate in the pan when meat is roasted or broiled.
Dust:	To sprinkle lightly.
Epicure:	A person with refined taste in food and drink; one devoted to sensuous pleasure and luxurious living; a male chauvinist (see "Gourmet").
Escalope:	French spelling of escallop or scallop, a thin, boneless slice of meat (often applied to thin cutlets of veal).
Fillets:	Strips of boneless steak, fish, or meat, cut into sizes for serving. To fillet is to remove bone.
Fold in:	To add ingredients by gently bringing a wooden spoon down and through a mixture with a cutting motion, then back up to the surface, folding the mixture over. Purpose is to avoid loss of air, especially when adding whipped cream or beaten egg whites.
Freshen:	To soak vegetables in ice water to revive their appearance. To soak salt fish or meat in cold water long enough to take out some of the salt.
Fry:	To cook in a small amount of hot fat over direct heat. (Only in "deep frying," as with doughnuts or french-fried potatoes, is the food covered by fat).
Garnish:	To add decorative foods to a prepared dish to improve appearance and taste. For example, parsley, lemon wedges, hard-cooked egg slices, tomato wedges,

	chopped olives. Put dark garnishes on light foods (parsley on eggs), light garnishes on dark foods (grated cheese on green vegetables). Be imaginative and show her your artistic side.
Glaze:	To make a golden-brown crust form on some foods by placing them briefly under the broiler.
Gourmand:	One who delights in eating well and heartily—that's Doris, all right.
Gourmet:	A connoisseur of fine food and drink; a male chauvinist epicure, probably.
Grate:	To cut food into shreds or particles by rubbing against a grater.
Grill:	To broil.
Herbs:	Small green aromatic plants used (dried or fresh) as seasoning.
Hors d'oeuvre:	French term meaning "outside the main work," i.e., appetizer(s) served before dinner.
Jell:	To make liquids set into semi-solids by adding gelatin.
Julienne:	Descriptive of vegetables such as carrots or potatoes cut into thin strips.
Marinade:	A mixture of oil and vinegar (or lemon juice or wine), usually with added herbs or condiments, in which meat, fish, or vegetable salad is soaked for added flavor and tenderness.
Marinate:	To soak food in a marinade, anywhere from 1 to 48 hours, so that it absorbs flavor and becomes tender.
Melt:	To dissolve with heat. Try it with Betty Jane, as well as with the butter.
Mince:	To cut into the smallest pieces possible.
Mix:	To combine ingredients until they are evenly distributed, by stirring or beating.
Mold:	A container decoratively shaped so that food cooked or jelled in it will have a pleasing form (you should be good at judging this). Also: the green fungus that will grow on your abandoned leftovers unless you clean out the back of the refrigerator once in a while.
Mousse:	A French frozen dessert of whipped cream, egg white, sweetening and flavoring, sometimes with gelatin added. Also certain hot dishes of a creamy smooth texture.
Pan broil:	To cook meat uncovered in a shallow, heavy pan over

	direct heat, with low temperature, pouring off excess fat as it accumulates.
Pan fry:	Same as "fry." To cook in a frying pan in a small amount of fat. Meat (and other foods) is usually added when fat is hot but not smoking.
Parboil:	To boil food until partially cooked by dropping it for a few minutes into rapidly boiling water to tenderize it. Cooking is usually finished in some other manner.
Pare:	To cut or trim away the rind or skin of potatoes, apples, etc.
Pâté de foie gras:	A French paste (pâté) usually made out of poultry livers.
Peel:	To cut or pull away the outer skin of tomatoes, onions, oranges, etc.
Peppercorn:	The dried berry of the black pepper plant. You grind peppercorns in your pepper mill to produce powdered pepper.
Pimiento (or pimento):	A sweet red pepper preserved in oil.
Pinch:	You know how this is done. Using usual method, pick up a substance between thumb and forefinger. It will amount to ⅛ teaspoon or less. If it's female, it will yelp or giggle or retaliate.
Poach:	To cook slowly in simmering (not boiling) water, or in a small pan over simmering water (in an egg poacher, for example). Except when eggs are being poached, the liquid should not be deep enough to cover the food.
Preheat:	To heat an oven or cooking pot to desired temperature before placing food in it for cooking. Your dinner alone should do this to Mary Lou.
Purée:	A thick mixture made by forcing cooked food and liquid through a wire strainer or sieve, using the back of a wooden spoon (a food mill or an electric blender makes the job easier). Also, to make such a mixture.
Reduce:	To boil a liquid until some of it has been carried off as steam. This is what What's-Her-Name may need to do after several of your Dozen Dinners.
Roast:	To cook meat by baking in an oven.
Roux:	A blend of butter or other fat and flour, generally cooked together briefly before adding a liquid to produce a sauce.

Sauté:	The French term for "fry." To cook quickly in a frying pan using a small amount of fat.
Scald:	To heat milk or liquid to just below boiling point (until bubbles form at the side of the pot). In the case of milk, a thin skin forms over the top. Also, to pour boiling water over or to rinse with boiling water.
Score:	To cut shallow slashes along the edges of a steak to prevent it from curling up; to cut shallow slashes in the skin of some roasts, such as leg of pork, so that they baste themselves. Also: what the male chauvinist cook attempts after every meal.
Scramble:	To cook eggs by mixing the white and yolk together, adding milk, salt and other seasonings. Use fork, egg beater, or whisk.
Sear:	To brown pieces of meat or poultry on all sides very quickly over high heat in a skillet. Cooking is finished in some other way.
Separate:	To remove the yolk from the white of an egg.
Shallot:	A small, green plant of the onion family having clustered bulbs and resembling garlic, but milder in flavor.
Sherbet	A frozen dessert made of fruit juice, sugar, water, milk, and egg white.
Shortening:	Butter, lard, other animal fat or vegetable oil, used to make cake and pastry light or flaky.
Shred:	To cut or tear into thin strips or pieces.
Sift:	To put fine dry ingredients (such as flour, sugar) through a sieve to remove any lumps.
Simmer:	To cook in liquid kept just below boiling point.
Skewer:	To pierce or fasten meat or poultry with long, wooden or metal pins to keep them in position during cooking. Also, such a wooden or metal pin.
Skillet:	Frying pan.
Sliver:	To cut or chop a food such as almonds into thin bits or strips.
Spices:	Substances such as seeds, certain nuts, dried berries, bark, and roots of plants which are ground and used as seasonings (pepper, ginger, nutmeg, etc.).
Spit:	A thin, pointed rod or bar on which food is impaled and held over a fire.
Steam:	To cook food over, but not in, boiling water: the food is usually held in a specially designed sieve. The con-

HAM ROLLED UP

Buy:

Ham, sliced, good quality (¼ pound)
Cream cheese (1 small package)

Horseradish, the hotter the better, from a deli

Check Cupboard For:

Hot mustard, preferably imported from France

Mash up the cheese with a fork, having left it out of the refrigerator to get soft and therefore easy to mash. Add some horseradish teaspoon by teaspoon, tasting as you go, until you like the flavor. (Don't finish it—just taste it!) Or, instead of horseradish, use hot mustard. Spread this mixture on the slices of ham, then roll up the ham and fasten it with a toothpick. You may want to trim the ham to a smaller size either before spreading it with cheese of after rolling it up. Arrange on a plate.

If there is any cheese mixture left over, eat it on crackers. Likewise the ham.

SMOKED SALMON SPLURGE

Buy:

Smoked salmon—Scottish is best if you can find it or afford it (¼ pound)
Parsley

Black bread or good quality brown bread, in thin slices
A lemon

Check Cupboard for:

Butter

This one is easy. Cut the bread into moderate-sized pieces. Butter it. Lay slices of salmon on it. Sprinkle a little chopped parsley on it. (Chopped parsley?? Use a pair of scissors.) Cut the lemon into three or four wedge-shaped pieces. Arrange it all on a plate. Each of you can then squeeze a little lemon juice onto the smoked salmon—very cosy—and very delicious.

SUMMER SAUSAGE AND CHEESE

Buy:

Summer sausage or salami, thinly sliced, from the deli (¼ pound)

Green onions, fresh, also called scallions (1 bunch)

Cream cheese (1 small package)

Check Cupboard for:

Jar of dried shredded green onions, in case you can't find fresh ones

Toothpicks

If you are using fresh onions, trim off the roots and part of the green tops, peel off the first layer of skin, and chop them into small pieces.

Next, lay out your slices of summer sausage. Spread the cream cheese on the sausage and sprinkle it with dried or fresh onion. Then roll up the sausage slices and nail them with toothpicks. Dead easy, really, but tasty and quite impressive. Serve them on a plate.

MARINATED ARTICHOKES

Buy:

Artichokes packed in a marinade (1 jar) or plain (1 can)

Check Cupboard for:

Toothpicks

If you managed to find marinated artichokes, just dump them into a bowl, and serve them with toothpicks or forks and paper napkins—they drip.

If you bought a can of plain artichokes, make a simple French dressing (see p. 12). Measure how much you need by determining the amount of liquid in the can of artichokes, and then make a little more than that. Put the artichokes and enough dressing to cover them into a jar with a lid, shake them up a little (gently, or they'll break), and put them in the refrigerator to marinate for several hours. Serve as described above.

Note: Real French dressing is not that orange glop they sell in bottles.

STUFFED CELERY

Buy:

Celery, 1 bunch

Stuffing of your choice (see below)

Check Cupboard for:

Paprika

Mayonnaise

Wash and trim the celery, and as you trim, inspect the celery to see if it has long, tough strands. If it has, peel them off. Cut the celery into inch-long bits. With a knife, fill them with whatever stuffing you think she might like.

Possible Stuffings: cream cheese sprinkled with paprika, cream cheese mixed and mashed with a little blue cheese and sprinkled with paprika; a little mayonnaise and a bit of anchovy; some of your home-made paté (see p. 33) or some paté out of a can; sardines mixed up with mayonnaise. Consult other lists of flavors in this chapter. Arrange the stuffed celery on a plate.

CREAM CHEESE DIPS

Buy:

Cream cheese (1 small package)
Light cream (½ pint)

Flavor of your choice from list of variations below

Leave the cream cheese out of the refrigerator for several hours; it is easier to mash at room temperature. Mash it in a bowl with a fork and thin it little by little with the light cream until you get the gooey consistency that will cling to a cracker. Then mash in whatever it is you are using to make this particular dip and adjust the consistency with more cream if necessary. Add salt, pepper, and seasonings to taste. Sprinkle chopped parsley or chives or paprika on top.

Flavor Variations: blue cheese or Roquefort; anchovy paste; chopped olives; minced clams; mashed avocado with a little minced onion and a little lemon juice; a few chopped smoked oysters; canned shrimp; chopped radishes, chopped chives, and lemon juice; red or black lumpfish caviar.

Serve in a bowl with crackers or potato chips on the side.

SOUR CREAM DIPS

Buy:

Sour cream (1 ½-pint carton)   **Flavor of your choice from list of variations below**

Surely by now everyone knows how to make the dip that consists of sour cream mixed with dried onion soup mix. It is, nevertheless, a good one. You can vary the flavor a little by adding a little lemon juice, or a little Worcestershire sauce, Tabasco, or paprika.

Flavor Variations: minced clams, seasoned with dill or tarragon; red or black lumpfish caviar; chopped onions and a variety of herbs, fresh or dried; chopped shrimp or crab or lobster.

Serve in a bowl surrounded by crackers, potato chips or whatever you like. You might add a plateful of bits of celery, strips of carrot, and florets of raw cauliflower.

SLICED CUCUMBER

Buy:

A cucumber   **Tidbits of your choice (see below)**

The cucumber is a fine substitute for a cracker, especially in summer, and being wet already, it never gets soggy. Just wash it, trim off the end, and cut it into regular slices about ⅛ of an inch thick.

Now you can park all sorts of things on your slices. A small shrimp on a blob of mayonnaise, a lump of cream cheese with a smoked clam on it. Anything, in fact, that you can park on a cracker parks equally well on a slice of cucumber. In many supermarkets these days you can find, usually refrigerated, small tins of Swedish or Danish herring tidbits. They are just the right size and come marinated in a variety of delicious flavors: wine, dill, lemon, tomato. And by now you can think of lots of other things, too. Arrange it all on a plate, and decorate with good old parsley.

STUFFED EGGS

Buy:

Eggs (½ dozen)   **Flavor of your choice (see below)**

Check Cupboard for:

Mayonnaise   **Wine vinegar**
Lemon   **An onion**

Remember, 1 egg yields 2 stuffed halves, or 3 stuffed thirds if you are any good at cutting eggs in three. So unless your date happens to be a lumberjack, ½-dozen eggs are more than enough to stuff at one time.

Stuffing eggs is easy. Boiling them has two pitfalls, both easily avoided. If you are not careful they crack or burst in the water, or else the shell clings to them and you get a pock-marked mess when you try to shell them.

To avoid cracking, start them in cold water over a moderate heat. If they come to the boil too quickly, they are apt to crack. Ten minutes boiling is enough to produce hard-cooked eggs.

To prevent the shell from sticking, put the eggs under the cold-water tap as soon as they are cooked. Peel them as soon as they have cooled off a little.

Then cut each egg in half carefully (the long way, that is), and even more carefully remove the yolks and put them in a bowl. The point is not to mangle the white. Add several large tablespoons of mayonnaise, depending on how many eggs you are stuffing. One tablespoon per egg is about right. Add a few squirts of lemon juice, salt and pepper, and use just a litle wine vinegar to thin the mixture. It shouldn't be any thinner than thick mayonnaise when you have finished mashing it all together. This is your basic stuffing. Now add your choice of the following: minced onion, chopped parsley and/or chives, and capers; curry powder; anchovy paste; Worcestershire sauce; dry mustard (go easy); finely-chopped cold ham and gherkins; mashed sardines; crabmeat; a little paté; lumpfish caviar; left-over chicken chopped up, etc. Note that some of these things will combine, others won't. Be bold. Experiment. And garnish with fresh chopped parsley!

EGG, ANCHOVY, AND MAYONNAISE APPETIZERS

Buy:

Eggs (½ dozen)
Anchovy fillets, rolled, with capers

Parsley, fresh

Check Cupboard for:

Mayonnaise
Green onions, dried

Crackers, round

This one is easy. It is a matter of assembly rather than preparation.
Hard-cook one or two eggs. (For directions, see the previous recipe.)

Shell them and leave them in the refrigerator for a while so they'll be easier to slice, although they are always difficult to slice.

You can slice them (carefully) on a chopping board, but I think it's easier if you hold them in your hand. Hold the egg in your left hand, and slice crossways with your right—the point being to produce evenly sliced rounds of egg with the yolk still neatly inside each round. Caution: the yolk is usually not in the middle where you would expect it, but lurking on one side, so you have to proceed carefully so as not to break the white at its thinnest point.

Place a round of egg on each cracker, a dollop of mayonnaise on each egg round, a rolled anchovy fillet on each dollop of mayonnaise, and once over lightly on top with the chopped parsley or dried green onion. Arrange them on a plate.

These are quite filling, and excellent with a little vodka into which you have introduced a sliver of lemon peel.

CHICKEN LIVERS AND BACON

Buy:

Chicken livers (½ pound,   **Bacon (½ pound)**
unless you can find a
smaller container)

Check Cupboard for:
Toothpicks

Turn the oven on, set at 350°, before you begin. Then have a short drink to make sure that it reaches 350° by the time you are ready to use it. While you are having the drink, decide how many chicken livers the two of you can eat.

If you are going to cook 10 chicken livers, cut 5 pieces of bacon in half. Put the bacon in a frying pan over a *low* flame. When it has produced a little fat, add the chicken livers. Turn them until they are slightly cooked on all sides, keeping a careful eye on the bacon so that it remains limp.

Turn off the stove, remove the frying pan, and set everything aside to cool down until you can touch the bacon and liver without getting burned. Then wrap a piece of bacon around each piece of liver, nail it together with a toothpick, and put them all into a pan and into the oven (350°) to finish cooking—about 15 or 20 minutes.

Don't forget to salt and pepper them when they are done. A squirt of fresh lemon juice is good on liver too. Sprinkle with a little parsley, if you feel up to it.

PICKLED MUSHROOMS

Buy:

Mushrooms, whole, small (1 small can or 1 box of fresh ones)   **Parsley**

Check Cupboard for:

Oil, preferably corn oil   **Toothpicks**
Wine vinegar

This recipe came about because once, years ago, I bought a small glass jar of cocktail mushrooms in a great hurry and at an exorbitant price. They were quite good, but were merely packed in a little olive oil with some herbs. Later in a quieter moment, I thought, "Hell, I can make more and better ones for half the price." I did. The recipe follows.

Drain or wash the mushrooms, depending upon what kind you bought. If fresh mushrooms look clean and really fresh, you probably needn't bother peeling them. Rinse them gently, and spread them on a couple of layers of paper towel to drain and dry.

Then make French dressing (see p. 12), or for even better effect make it into a vinaigrette by adding chopped parsley, chopped fresh green onions, and any other fresh herbs in season. Dill is particularly nice with mushrooms.

Slice the mushrooms, or, if they are really small, leave them whole. Put them in a jar or anything with a lid, cover them with the dressing, and leave them in the refrigerator for several hours or better still overnight.

Serve with toothpicks and *paper napkins*—they drip.

COOPER'S LIVERWURST
or
YOUR VERY OWN PATÉ MAISON

Buy:

Liverwurst, best quality (½ pound)
Cream cheese (small package)
A lemon

Red wine (get something decent and drink the rest with dinner)
An onion

Check Cupboard for:

Mayonnaise
Worcestershire sauce
Curry powder

Nutmeg
Butter

This paté is genuinely easy to make. You merely assemble all the parts and mash them together.

Leave the liverwurst and the cream cheese on the kitchen table so that they will be at room temperature and therefore malleable when you start work.

Put the liverwurst and the cream cheese in a bowl. Range all the other ingredients around it. Get out your smallest saucepan and put 1½ tablespoons of butter into it. Put it on the stove at the very lowest heat you can contrive, and keep an eye on it. Melted, not black, butter is the object.

Now add all of the following ingredients to the liverwurst and cheese: a good squeeze from ½ the lemon, 2 tablespoons of mayonnaise, 1 tablespoon of finely chopped onion, 1 tablespoon of Worcestershire sauce, ½ teaspoon of curry powder, 1 pinch nutmeg, and 2 tablespoons red wine (add more if the paté seems very thick). Save the melted butter for the end. When everything has been added, mash and mix it all together. A wooden spoon is best.

Smooth the top with a knife to make it look tidy, sprinkle some good old parsley on it, and put it away in the refrigerator to cool. Serve with a knife beside the bowl and crackers or bits of buttered toast.

RAW BITS AND DIPS

An arrangement of raw vegetables is colorful and attractive to the eye and tastes fresh and clean and crisp. This leaves the other three senses up to you.

Buy:

Ingredients for one or two of the dips described in this chapter	**Green pepper**
	Cauliflower
	Tomatoes
The smallest quantities you can find of some of the vegetables listed below	**Onions, green**
	Asparagus
	Cucumber
Carrots	**Zucchini**
Radishes	**Mushrooms**
Celery	

Make any dip or dips described in this chapter. Wash, slice and trim the vegetables, and arrange them on a large plate, board, or platter.

Alternate Dip: Use mayonnaise, flavored with any of the following: a little garlic, parsley, chives, or grated onion; anchovy paste or Worcestershire sauce or curry powder; chopped olives, perhaps, or capers. Use your imagination, but do add a few drops of fresh lemon juice and a little freshly ground black pepper, and salt to taste.

SARDINE SNACKS

Buy:

Sardines (1 tin)

Check Cupboard for:

Mayonnaise	**Crackers, or bread for**
A lemon	**making toast rounds**
Onion juice	

Do not despise the sardine. In some circles it is considered a true gourmet delicacy. There is even such a thing as a vintage sardine, and the true fancier lays down tins of dated sardines and turns them over lovingly several times a year until he considers that they have reached the peak of excellence. A little shopping will reveal to you that a large variety of sardines is available and that they come from many different places—Norway, Portugal, Denmark, France. Try several varieties and brands, and compare their flavors.

Mash the sardines with the juice of half the lemon (if it is juicy) or all (if it is not), and ½ teaspoon of onion juice. Then add a little mayonnaise to make it all stick together—a teaspoon or so. Add pepper if you like, but taste the mixture before adding salt.

You can make toast rounds by cutting rounds out of bread slices with a small glass or jar or jar lid. Toast them and butter them, and spread the sardine mixture onto them. For extra panache, put a little piece of cheese on top of each, and heat them in the oven until the cheese melts. Or simply serve the mixture in a bowl with a knife and crackers on the side.

SHRIMP SNACKS

Buy:

Shrimp (1 tin)

Swiss cheese, grated (smallest quantity you can buy)

Check Cupboard for:

Mayonnaise
Onion juice

Crackers, or bread for buttered toast rounds

First rinse the shrimp thoroughly under cold running water. This will help restore a fresh flavor. Then chop them into small bits. Add 2 teaspoons of onion juice and 2 tablespoons of grated cheese. Then add enough mayonnaise to stick it all together and give it the consistency of a spread. Season to taste with salt and pepper.

Sprinkle with fresh parsley, or dried green onions, or paprika, or fresh or dry dill. Serve in a bowl with knife and crackers on the side, or else spread on buttered toast rounds.

Variations: Use crab meat or lobster instead of shrimp.

A PLATTER OF TASTY BITS

Buy:

Oysters, smoked (1 can)

Olives, large or small, green or ripe, stuffed or plain, in oil or brine, Californian or Greek or Italian or Syrian or Armenian

Salami and related sausage—choose from dozens of varieties (¼ pound)

Shrimp, fresh, boiled, ready to serve

Lemon, to slice and serve with the shrimp

Prosciutto (Italian ham), sliced **very thin** (¼ pound)

Carrots (just a few)

Celery

Radishes (1 bunch)

Eggs, to stuff, if you wish

Pickles, gherkins or dills, sweet or sour or spiced or garlicked, cucumber or onion or tomato or banana or pepper

Arrange it all on a tray or platter, some of it in small bowls perhaps, and garnish with the ever-popular parsley. A small bowl of mayonnaise in the middle is useful.

BEEF TARTARE

Buy:

Top round or sirloin (½ pound) (ask the butcher to put it through the grinder TWICE for you— hamburger will **not** do)

Check Cupboard for:

An egg

A lemon

Thyme

Worcestershire sauce or Tabasco

Simply put the beef in a bowl and season it *to your taste* with: an egg yolk, a spoonful of minced onion, a squeeze or two of lemon juice, a little

Worcestershire or Tabasco sauce, a pinch of thyme, and salt and pepper. Mix it all with your fingers.

Experiment a little with other seasonings if you like, but be careful not to overseason or you will spoil the good taste of the meat itself.

Serve in a bowl with a knife and crackers on the side.

AVOCADO DIP

Buy:

An avocado, large and ripe   **An onion**
Orange juice, fresh or frozen   **A tomato, large**

Check Cupboard for:

Tabasco   **Crackers**

Cut the avocado in half, remove the seed, and scoop the fruit into a bowl. Later you can offer the seed to the lady and ask her if she'd like to take it home and grow you a splendid house plant with it. Mash the fruit with a fork. Add 2 teaspoons of orange juice, 1 teaspoon of finely minced onion, the tomato peeled and finely chopped, salt and pepper, and a dash of Tabasco to taste. Mash and mix it thoroughly.

The Tomato: Tomatoes are easy to peel if you put them in a bowl and pour some boiling water over them. After peeling, let them sit for 2 or 3 minutes before pouring off the water. Cut them in half and shake or squeeze the excess moisture into the sink. You will now find them easy to chop.

Serve in a bowl with a knife and crackers on the side.

Cheeses of Champions

Cheeses are as simple as an appetizer can be, and are also a suitable substitute for any dessert. But before you go bananas in your local specialty shop and buy up several different kinds, keep an important consideration in mind: cheese is expensive and perishable. So limit yourself to a maximum of four types per occasion.

Cheeses are divided into two distinct categories—real and fake. The latter are sold widely in bright foil wrappers, glass jars, tubes, and "stoneware" crocks, and often have "whiz" or "spread" somewhere in their names. This simply means they've been processed to the point where flavor has been sacrificed on the altar of spreadability.

Real cheese, on the other hand, is cut from large wheels or is packaged in small squares or rounds. Of these, both medium-to-hard and soft types abound, in which the first sub-category is well represented by certain cheddars and related English cheeses, the small Dutch cheeses in their wax covers, and Scandinavian and German cheeses such as Jarlsberg and Münster.

Soft cheeses are often of French origin and include Camembert, Brie, Pont L'Evêque, and Coulommiers. If in doubt about the age of what you're about to buy, give it a quick sniff. Since you can't do this in a supermarket where everything is packaged, do your shopping in a cheese store where sniffing rights will quickly reveal the tell-tale ammonia odor of anything that's over the hill and on the brink of spoiling.

To cover all the bases with your date, buy both hard and soft cheeses. Good suggestions include a slice of Swiss Emmenthaler (far superior to the better-known Gruyere), a Boursault (which is *very* rich), a creamy Banon (courtesy of a continental goat), a small Dutch Edam, a ripe American Limburger (whew! but delicious, too), a Norwegian getøst, a piece of English Stilton, and a Canadian Oka (which is strong enough to open all eight sinus cavities, but also perfect with fresh apples or pears).

Regardless of your choices, see that you remove them from the refrigerator about four hours before serving. If you plan to provide crackers, go with something bland that won't compete with the flavor of the cheese which in some cases will be delicate. This removes from all consideration all those pizza- and garlic-flavored bombs that in their artificiality stand as monuments to chemistry.

Although hard cheeses can be enjoyed without crackers, soft cheeses generally demand some sort of support between plate and palate. English water biscuits are good if you can find them. You probably can't in Jawbone Junction, Nevada. Scandinavian flatbrot is also fine. Stoned Wheat Thins from Canada are a cut above U. S. Saltines and Ritz crackers, but the latter two are still sufficient.

Fresh French-type bread is always a good choice with cheeses, but don't be suckered into buying imported real French bread. By the time you get it, it will be as hard as a Louisville Slugger.

Warning! Watch Her Liquor Level

Keep in mind throughout the cocktail hour(s) that your object is to make her mellow, not so juiced up that she lapses into a catatonic state. Since you want her to appreciate your obvious good taste, talents, and ultimate tactics, you'll have to be the judge of when she's had enough booze.

Don't cut her off too soon, though. Somewhere between complete sobriety and total insensibility is that perfect balance where she starts to toy with the suddenly intriguing thought that just maybe you'll take her out to dinner or—better yet—prepare something for her yourself. When that balance point is reached, you'll recognize it. Then strike like the tiger that you are. Insist on her staying, sweeping aside all the hackneyed objections which by this time she'll only half believe herself. (What to do now? Whip up a pot-luck meal—there are plenty to choose from in the next chapter.)

Yes, yes, you know she's supposed to call her college roommate about going to the movies. But she can call her tomorrow, can't she? She can pick up her laundry then, too. And speak to her landlord about screens for the windows. And . . .

"And I really do mean it, Mary Lou darling. Your legs are so much sexier than the ones on that babe in *Penthouse*."

Chapter 3

Pot Luck Meals
(and Other Quickies)

IT'S THE FINAL QUARTER. The two-minute warning is about to be given, the Redskins have been pushed back to their own eleven, and it's first and ten for the Giants. Who knows? Maybe they'll win this one after all.

And then the damned doorbell rings. Who can it be? What unfeeling barbarian can possibly be afoot in the final moments of a game like *this*? There it goes again. "Okay, okay, okay," you chant in a testy monotone as you stumble toward the door, keeping both eyes glued to the tube. Throwing it open, you're about to berate this insensate fool, this idiot, this . . .

And there she is. All five feet four of her. With those dark brown eyes, that soft blonde hair, and the wildest pair of . . .

Naturally, you ask her in to enjoy the closing moments of a game which suddenly seems rather dull and meaningless. She's absolutely ravishing! And that Southern accent!

"Georgia," you wonder out loud.

"Nawth Ca'lina," she drawls instead, her big, bovine eyes following yours as she sinks slowly into your upholstered chair in front of the TV. Her mouth forms a smile that immediately turns your knees into jellied consommé.

Okay. So much for the first impressions. Where do you go from here and how do you get her to go along with you? She tells you she just moved into the building this morning and there's something wrong with her stove.

"It won't what? Oh, it won't go *on*. Well, gee, that's great! I mean . . ."

What you're trying to say, you dummy, is that you were about ready to whip up something in your own kitchen and wouldn't she like to linger over a little pot luck? After all, you ask her while your toes curl up in your shoes, what are neighbors for?

By the time she discovers what *this* neighbor is for, it will be just a tad too late. But surely you want to conquer her in style, and this implies that you offer her a mint julep or whatever southern belles enjoy after a hard day of laying carpets and toting tables.

Ask her to select a record and show her how to work your stereo. No, she's not putting you to any trouble. Does she like Roberta Flack? Wonderful! She can put on her latest album. Nothing quite matches the sheer thrill of having a young thing contribute to her own decline and fall.

As for you, you'd better get busy in the kitchen. Being the rotten schemer that you are, you're not entirely unprepared for damsels in distress. You know well that on these occasions, if there is nothing to put in the pot, then you will never get lucky. So your refrigerator is stocked with a good supply of staples. Now is the time to impale a few of them on toothpicks or spread them on crackers and serve them to that little unexpected surprise. These, together with that stiff drink, will keep her busy for five or ten minutes, which is all you should need to prepare an impressive pot luck meal for two.

Pot luck meals are bound to be as unpredictable as the guests, but you'll almost certainly come to rely on a few basic items. Make a point of having these standbys on hand at all times:

Canned soup (several varieties)	**Spaghetti**
Tomato purée (several small cans)	**Canned corned beef hash**
	Canned tuna fish
Canned whole tomatoes (preferably Italian plum varieties)	**Canned beans (a variety)**
	Egg noodles
	Rice

This list is not to suggest that you serve merely a plate of wet noodles or the heated contents of a can of hash. The diner around the corner can serve her these nonmemorable meals that one might normally expect to find in a life-raft survival kit. Instead, your aim should be to embellish these basics or to use them to add special effects to meat, chicken, eggs, fish, and a variety of vegetables. The simple pot-luck recipes in this chapter will show you how. Follow them carefully, use a little of your own imagination, (and perhaps another drink or two), and you'll be well on your way to transforming this damsel in distress into a disdressed damsel.

However, the recipes in this chapter are not all for pot-luck meals—some are for *quick meals,* which are a course of a slightly different color. Quick meals are legitimate repasts for which you have planned ahead, knowing full well that you won't have time to prepare them at the last minute.

There are all sorts of reasons for planning quick meals. One of them is Joanne, that stewardess who keeps insisting that you fly her. Well, on Tuesday she's scheduled for a four-hour stopover in your city and she wants to kill the time at your place. She'll arrive at 6:30 and depart at 10:30. Naturally, you'll want to use these four hours to your best advantage, which means a minimum of kitchen activity and a maximum of the other kind.

Your best bet is a quick meal, which you can plan and prepare almost entirely the day before. This way, you can get home at six, take a shower and dress, and while you're doing so the stove can be putting the finishing touches on dinner. By 6:30 both you and your meal will be ready to put the finishing touches on Joanne.

For a list of foolproof quick meals, turn to page 52.

Pot Luck Meals

Soups

You will find that soup is the cornerstone of most pot-luck meals. When you are buying soup in the supermarket, remember that it comes in both cans and packets, and that canned soup comes in two varieties, condensed and ready-to-serve. To the dry mixes you usually just add water. The condensed kind may be combined with milk, water, or a combination of the two. Ready-to-serve soups are just that—they require nothing more than heating.

There are shops and elaborate delis that stock a range of gourmet and imported soups you might like to try. As for the old favorites, try raising them above the ordinary by following these tips.

TOMATO SOUP: Use a can of condensed tomato soup, and dilute it with half milk and half water. Add a little chopped onion and basil, turn the fire down low, and simmer until the onion is almost cooked. Top with a generous dollop of sour cream.

BLACK BEAN SOUP: Dilute as directed. Serve with sour cream and a slice of lemon, or add a little chili powder before heating.

ONION SOUP: Use a dry mix and prepare it as directed. Then float a stale slice of French or Italian bread on top of each bowl and sprinkle with a mixture of grated Gruyère and grated Parmesan cheese. Put the bowls in a moderate oven and heat until the cheese melts. (You must use *both* kinds of cheese, or you won't get that marvelously gooey consistency for which real French onion soup is famous.)

FAST BORSCHT: Mix one can of consommé, one can of V-8 juice, and one can of beets. Add a little chopped onion, a little lemon juice, and some salt and pepper. Heat and simmer gently until the onion is cooked. Serve with sour cream.

BULL SHOT: Perhaps this is the place to remind you that consommé is the one that jells if you leave it in the refrigerator and bouillon is the one that just gets cold. So put some bouillon in the refrigerator to just get cold. Pour it into a glass with an ice cube, a lemon slice, and a shot of vodka. Presto—drinks and first course all in one glass—a great concept if you're really in a hurry.

You can expand your soup-making repertoire greatly if you try combining two different canned soups to make a new soup. (The tastes are intriguing, and you can always say that it's an old recipe requiring hours of preparation and that you just happened to have prepared a batch yesterday.) A selection of hybrid soups follows.

TOMATO AND GREEN PEA: This is really called Purée Mongole and is very good. Just combine a can of each of the soups and dilute according to directions. Add a bay leaf.

TOMATO AND CREAM OF CELERY: Combine a can of each and dilute. A little basil adds a nice flavor. Sprinkle with croutons.

TOMATO AND CREAM OF ASPARAGUS: Combine one can of each and dilute as directed. A squeeze of lemon juice is nice with this one.

CREAM OF CHICKEN AND CREAM OF MUSHROOM:
Combine one of each and dilute. Add a little white wine and a sprinkling of nutmeg.

CHICKEN WITH RICE AND CREAM OF TOMATO: Combine one can of each and dilute. Mix ½ teaspoon of curry powder with some of the water you used for diluting until it makes a paste without lumps, and add it before you start heating the soup.

CHICKEN WITH RICE AND GREEN PEA: Combine a can of each and dilute as directed. Add a bay leaf.

NEW ENGLAND CLAM CHOWDER AND CREAM OF CELERY: Combine one can of each and dilute. Add a little thyme.

A shot of wine, especially sherry, will liven up most soups. You should also consider any and all of the following garnishes: chopped hard-cooked egg, grated cheese, slivers of ham, frankfurter or chicken, slices of avocado or lemon, chopped parsley, onion, chives, or dill, paprika, basil, thyme, croutons, sour cream, yogurt. Just use common sense, i.e. don't top cream of mushroom soup with sour cream or sprinkle chopped onions on onion soup.

BAKED CORNED BEEF HASH

Check Cupboard for:

Corned beef hash (1 1-pound
  can)
A potato, large
An onion, small

Cream, milk, a can of
  bouillon, or a bouillon cube
Butter

Preheat the oven to 325°.

Peel and chop the spud. Peel and chop the onion. Throw the chopped spud into a pot with some water and salt and start it boiling. Fry the chopped onion very gently in about a tablespoon of butter. When the spuds have boiled for about ten minutes, drain them. Find a casserole and put into it the can of hash, ⅓ cup milk or cream or bouillon, the spuds, the onion, and salt and pepper to taste. You may want to flavor it with a little Worcestershire sauce or some herb or other. Mix it all together thoroughly in the casserole and stick it in the oven for about half an hour. Leave the lid off to let it crisp on top, but keep an eye on it to make sure it doesn't burn.

Serve it from the casserole.

LUCKY NOODLES

Check Cupboard for:

Egg noodles (1 package)

Preheat the oven to 325°.

Cook the noodles according to the instructions on the box.

Meanwhile, check the refrigerator for leftovers which could be mixed with the cooked noodles and heated briefly in the oven with some Parmesan cheese on top. Leftover beef stew? Splendid. A lump of cooked steak from the hibachi and some peas? Also good. Slice the steak thin. Nothing in the icebox? Try the cupboard. A can of clams? Perfect! Canned chicken or ham would do too. If you are managing well, there ought to be something better than hash and canned spaghetti sauce.

When the noodles are cooked, drain them in the colander, and put them in a casserole with a generous lump of butter, lots of grated Parmesan, and some poppy seeds if you have any. Mix in the clams (beef stew, sliced steak, and peas, or whatever) and put it all to heat in a medium oven. No need to cook it; just make sure the added ingredients are hot through. And don't forget the salt and pepper.

ANN'S BEANS

Check Cupboard for:

Baked beans, 1 can **Hot tomato ketchup**
Dry mustard **Dark brown sugar**

Preheat the oven to 325°.

Put the beans in a small casserole and add ¼ teaspoon dry mustard, a good shot of ketchup, and 1 heaping tablespoon of dark brown sugar. Stir well and heat in covered casserole for 20 minutes to half an hour.

HOT LUCK SANDWICH

Check Cupboard for:

Eggs (2)
Bacon (2 slices)
Onion (2 slices)

Cheese preferably a sharp
   cheddar (2 slices)
Bread (2 slices)

Cut the bacon into little pieces with the kitchen scissors, and fry it until it's nearly crisp. Drain off the excess fat and spread the bits of bacon evenly around the frying pan. Break two eggs into the pan, keeping them whole and apart. Break the yolks with a fork, and park a slice of cheese on each egg and a slice of onion on top of that (not too thick or it will never cook). Cover the frying pan and let things cook.

Make a couple of slices of toast, butter them, and keep them hot. When the cheese has melted and the onion looks transparent, divide the eggs and put one egg plus cheese and onion on each piece of toast. Salt and pepper to taste—you won't need much.

Serve with cold beer.

CURRIED EGGS

Check Cupboard for:

Eggs (4)
Butter
Flour
Milk
Curry powder
Thyme

Cinnamon, powdered
Clove, powdered
Cumin, ground
Ginger, powdered
Yogurt, plain (optional)

Hard-cook four eggs (boil them for 10 minutes, place under cold water, crack, and peel).

Mix together the following dry ingredients: 1½ tablespoons flour, 1 teaspoon curry powder, ¼ teaspoon each of thyme, cinnamon, and cumin, ⅛ teaspoon each of clove and ginger.

Put 2 tablespoons of butter into a saucepan, melt them, and add the dry ingredients to the butter, mixing them well with a wooden spoon. Gradually add 1 cup of milk, and cook the sauce over a low heat stirring until it thickens. Salt and pepper to taste.

Quarter the eggs and pour the curry sauce over them.

Serve with some yogurt in a side dish. Serving yogurt with curry is a Pakistani custom, and has a pleasant, slightly salty, and cooling effect.

Spanish and Other Ethnic Rices

SPANISH RICE

Buy:

Rice, long-grain (1 package)
Tomatoes, fresh, chopped (1 or 2) or canned (1 small can)
Peppers, green or red, chopped, (1 or 2)

An onion, small, chopped
Peas (part of 1 frozen package)
Anchovy fillets (1 or 2)
Olives, green or ripe

Check Cupboard for:

Oil
Turmeric (or saffron)
Capers

Consommé (or bouillon or bouillon cubes)

To prepare basic rice, see page 14. The move from basic to Spanish Rice occurs when you add the liquid (boiling water, bouillon, consommé, or combinations plus a little wine) to the rice and oil. Along with the liquid you add as many of the items listed above as you can. If you use canned tomatoes, pour in the canning juice too. Add seasonings, including garlic, to taste. When the rice is cooked, as in basic rice, so is everything else.

Variations:

If you can prepare Spanish Rice, you can also prepare Spanish Rice with Chicken (add leftover chicken), Spanish Rice with Tuna (find a can of tuna in the cupboard and add that) and Spanish Rice with Clams (find a can of whole or chopped clams and add that—the dish now almost qualifies as a paélla—almost).

Suppose that what you have left over is hamburger or bits of cold steak or roast beef. Cut up or crumble the beef (or lamb or pork), find some things that will go with it into the rice, and create one of the following dishes.

INDIAN RICE

Use Leftover:
**Beef or lamb or pork or all
  or two, chopped**

Buy:
An onion, small	**An apple**
Peas (1 frozen package)	**Rice, long-grain (1 package)**
Raisins or currants	

Check Cupboard for:
Curry powder	**Clove powder**
Thyme	**Oil**
Garlic	**Consomme or bouillon or**
Cinnamon	**bouillon cubes**

Add to the cooking liquid the chopped beef, 1 teaspoon of curry powder, the onion, chopped, half of the package of peas, the apple, peeled and chopped, a handful of raisins or currants, ¼ teaspoon of thyme, a crushed clove of garlic, ¼ teaspoon of cinnamon, and ⅛ teaspoon of clove powder. The result is almost a curry. Almost. Use more curry powder if you like it hot. Season to taste and serve with a bottle of chutney if you have one. A pot of yogurt on the side is the perfect accompaniment.

BEEF RISOTTO

Use Leftover:
Beef, chopped	**refrigerator or freezing**
Vegetables (any in the	**compartment)**

Buy:

Tomatoes, as in Spanish Rice

An onion

Check Cupboard for:

Garlic
Bay leaf or other herbs

Worcestershire sauce

As usual, add everything to the rice and liquid, and it will all be ready together.

By this time you should be able to improvise. For a fabulous seafood dish, just simplify Spanish Rice by leaving out everything except a little tomato, some chopped peppers and onion, and turmeric or saffron. Then add 1 can each of shrimp, lobster, and crab. When the rice, etc. is cooked, stir in a little sour cream.

Quick Meals

The success of the quick meal depends more on time-and-motion expertise than it does on cooking skills. And it requires a little practice so that you know precisely what you are doing. If you have to stop in the middle and search through every drawer in the kitchen looking for the garlic press, or if you forget to put the water on to boil or turn the oven on in time, then the quick meal turns into a long annoying drag—and so does your evening with Joanne.

You *have* to think about it the day before, or if it is not a working day, the morning before. Buy the necessary items. Give the menu some thought. Apportion your time. If the main course is going to consist of cold meats laid out on a plate, then you will have more time for a quick soup or a dessert. Conversely, if preparing the meat is going to require most of your attention, choose for soup a jellied consommé and the simplest dessert possible.

What can you do ahead of time? Lay the table. Have the kitchen tidy, organized, and ready to go. Trying to cook in a mess is one of the most miserable, frustrating, and generally cross-making experiences I know. You can't find anything and there is nowhere to put it down even if you do find it!

—49—

Put the white wine in the refrigerator to chill. Take out the pots and pans you are going to use and sit them on the stove. Lay out the knives, chopping board, measuring cups and spoons, and other utensils you are going to use. Are you going to need lemon slices? Slice them now, wrap them in aluminum foil or plastic wrap, and put them in the refrigerator. Chopped parsley? Chop a whole bunch of parsley and store it in a little plastic container in the refrigerator. Jellied consommé? Put it in the refrigerator 24 hours ahead of time. In brief, look critically at the recipe for each dish you mean to prepare and decide what you can do in advance, even if it's only taking the package of noodles off the top shelf and setting it on the kitchen table.

Vegetables for Quick Meals

Fitting vegetables into your quick meal need not be a hassle. If you can read (and presumably you can, unless someone has been reciting this book to you), you can prepare with ease the endless variety of frozen vegetables. Most of these can be improved greatly if you boil them in chicken bouillon instead of water. This involves nothing more complicated than crushing a bouillon cube in a pot of heating water. Then just dump in the beans, spinach, peas, asparagus, or broccoli, and you'll be in business in just a few minutes.

When they're done (and whatever you do, *don't* let them boil any longer than the instructions say), drain off the water and add a bit of butter to the contents of the pot. Shake in some salt and pepper and a short burst of lemon juice. The juice works wonders; it's almost as useful in seasoning food as salt, and it improves the taste of just about everything but a cup of coffee.

Frozen vegetables are fine, but they're no match for the real thing, and what many people don't know is that fresh vegetables (or most of them) are no more difficult to prepare than their frozen counterparts. Some of them, in fact, such as spinach and zucchini, are easier.

Spinach usually comes in a plastic bag already washed. For two people you will need one bagful. Don't be alarmed by the amount. Spinach is the opposite of rice. It shrinks unbelievably when you cook it. To cook it, put about half a cup of water in the bottom of a pot big enough to hold the spinach, salt it slightly, and add the spinach. Put it over a moderate heat and press the spinach down a little from time to time. It will reduce itself to about a quarter, if not less, of its original size. As soon as it has done this and is sitting in the bottom of the pot looking like dark-green cooked spinach, it is done. Drain off the water, add butter, and season to taste (a pinch or so of nutmeg is delightful).

Zucchini takes even less time to cook than spinach. Buy two. Trim off the ends and slice them in rounds about ⅛th of an inch thick. If you slice them too thin, they come apart. Put them in enough boiling salted water to cover them, and cook them for about 2 or 3 minutes. That's all. Drain, season, butter. You can sprinkle a little grated parmesan cheese on them (out of a jar). Zucchini can also be fried (delicious) in just as little time. Put a little butter and a little crushed garlic in a frying pan or on a griddle, spread your sliced zucchini all over it, sprinkle with a little salt, turn once, allow about 10 minutes for the entire cooking process, and there you are.

Tomatoes, the original love apple, are fresh and delicious and add a cheerful color to any plate. Serve them raw, sliced, with a drop or two of olive oil on each slice, and a little basil. Serve the little cherry tomatoes whole. Bake tomatoes in the oven (for about 20 minutes at 350°) with oil, garlic, breadcrumbs, salt, pepper and parsley on top. When you broil a steak, put halves of tomatoes under the broiler too for the last ten minutes before the steak is done. When you are frying bacon, put a couple of whole cherry tomatoes in the pan as well, or slices of larger tomatoes.

Potatoes for Quick Meals

Boiled new potatoes have two endearing qualities. One, they're delicious—better, I think, than any other kind. And two, *you don't have to peel them.* Buy a pound, selecting the smallest ones you can find. Wash them by scrubbing them with your hands under running cold water. Put them in a pot of cold water, salted, and let them come to the boil. Once they are boiling, they take about ten minutes to cook, but you will have to judge this yourself by dint of poking them with a fork to see whether they are done. When they are done, drain off the water, clean off the film that makes a rim around the pot, and put a couple of knobs of butter into the pot. Add the potatoes, and turn them in the butter over a low heat, adding chopped parsley, pepper, and salt.

Fried potatoes are much easier than many people think. Just peel and slice as thin as you can a couple of ordinary medium-sized spuds. Put some oil in your deepest frying pan (don't use butter). When it is smoking, put in the potatoes for five minutes, turning them occasionally. Take them off. Then let the fat heat up some more until it is smoking abundantly. Put the potatoes in again for two minutes. Take them off. Sprinkle with salt and serve.

Now that you know how to deal with vegetables, you have all the basics—everything it takes to put together a real meal for two. From here on, it's just a matter of timing, of getting everything started (and finished) within a smooth and unhurried progression.

Well, I've taken care of that part. Here are six three-course meals for luncheon or dinner. Preceding each trio of recipes is advice on how and when to begin each part of the meal so that it's all coordinated perfectly. Follow these timetables carefully, and your courses will arrive and depart so efficiently that even Joanne the stewardess will be impressed. She may even decide not to show for that ten-o'clock flight.

QUICK-MEAL MENUS FOR LUNCHEON OR DINNER

Menu #1
Smooth Creamy Tarragon Soup
Cold Meats and Green Salad
Strawberries and Sour Cream

Menu #2
Cold Cucumber Soup
Minute Steak
Vanilla Ice Cream and . . .

Menu #3
Jellied Consommé with Sherry
Escalope of Veal with Noodles Parmesan
Chilled Fruit with Yogurt and Brown Sugar

Menu #4
Half a Grapefruit
Adam and Eve Pork Chops
Vanilla Ice Cream, Coffee Flavored

MINUTE STEAK

Buy:

**Minute steak, ½″ thick (1
    pound)**

**Green beans, frozen (1
    package)**

Check Cupboard for:

Butter

Potatoes (1 big or 2 medium)

Put the minute steak into a heavy frying pan with just a little fat so that it won't stick. Cook 5 minutes per side for medium.

For green beans and potatoes, see general cooking instructions on page 50.

VANILLA ICE CREAM AND . . .

Buy:

Vanilla ice cream (1 pint)

Topping (see below)

Try the following and think of some more: a little slightly thawed frozen orange juice; canned or fresh fruit; a little marmalade; a little applesauce; booze—sample the following:

Cointreau, curaçao, Grand Marnier, Triple Sec, Kirsch, Cherry brandy, Drambuie, Crème de Menthe, Crème de Cacao, Anisette, Cognac, Benedictine, B & B.

Try combining some of the liqueurs with the fruits mentioned above, e.g. Cointreau with an orange flavor.

Here is where your stock of miniature bottles of liqueur comes in handy—ask Joanne the stewardess to bring some with her.

Menu #3
Jellied Consommé with Sherry
Escalope of Veal with Noodles Parmesan
Chilled Fruit with Yogurt and Brown Sugar

The Day Before:
Make the soup, store in refrigerator.

Before Joanne Arrives:
Chill the fruit.

Just Before Joanne Arrives:
Begin heating the water for the noodles.

JELLIED CONSOMMÉ WITH SHERRY

Buy:

Consommé, undiluted (1 or 2 cans)
Sherry (1 bottle)

Lemons
Parsley

Open the cans of soup and put them in a bowl. Add two or three jiggers of sherry. Put the bowl in the refrigerator overnight. It will jell. Spoon into individual bowls, and garnish with wedges of lemon and chopped parsley.

ESCALOPE OF VEAL WITH NOODLES PARMESAN

Buy:

Veal escalopes (2)

Parmesan cheese, grated (2 or 3 ounces)

Check Cupboard for:

Egg noodles (1 package)
Butter

Flour

Prepare the noodles according to the directions on the package. When cooked, toss with butter and add some grated parmesan cheese.

Put some flour onto a large plate.

Put the frying pan over moderate heat with a lump of butter.

Seize one of the escalopes of veal and press it into the flour using your fingers to press the flour into the meat on both sides. Repeat with the second escalope. The butter should be beginning to smoke. Lay the escalopes into the pan and let them cook for exactly 2 minutes. Turn them and cook them for exactly 2 minutes on the other side. Turn them again and let them cook for 3 minutes.

There is a reason for this timing and turning. If you don't do it, the meat juices will soak into the flour, the flour will come off and stick in the pan, and the meat inside won't brown properly.

When the escalopes are golden brown, take them out of the pan, salt them, and put them on a hot plate. Pour a little water into the frying pan and let it boil, making a delicious brown sauce. Pour this over the escalopes and serve them with the buttered noodles.

Variations:

Add a spoonful of canned tomato purée to the brown sauce in the frying pan and mix well. Heat for a minute and pour over the escalopes.

Add some paprika to the brown sauce for a Hungarian version (never add pepper when you use paprika).

Add a tablespoon of good thick cream to the brown sauce.

Add a teaspoonful of capers to the brown sauce.

In another frying pan, cook some thinly sliced mushrooms in butter and add some coarsely chopped ham. When it is thoroughly hot, add it to the brown sauce.

CHILLED FRUIT WITH YOGURT AND BROWN SUGAR

Buy:

Natural yogurt (1 or 2 pots)   **Fruit**

Check Cupboard for:

Brown sugar

Use any kind of fruit you like, fresh or canned. Frozen is all right, as long as you remember to take it out of the freezer the night before. There is no point in buying it on the way home because it won't thaw out in time, and if you jab at it with an ice pick, you'll just end up with a mess.

Put the fruit in dessert bowls, top with the yogurt, and sprinkle a little brown sugar on top.

This works very nicely with white seedless grapes.

Menu #4
Half a Grapefruit
Adam and Eve Pork Chops
Vanilla Ice Cream, Coffee Flavored

Before Joanne Arrives:
Prepare the grapefruit halves, chill in the refrigerator.

Just Before Joanne Arrives:
Cut up the apples, put them on to boil.

HALF A GRAPEFRUIT

Buy:
**Grapefruit (1, or as many as
    you like)**

Check Cupboard for:
Sherry (optional)   **Brown sugar**

Cut the grapefruit in half. With a grapefruit knife, loosen fruit from rind, and cut out the center core. Loosen the membranes between the sections. Pour in a little sherry, or brandy, or rum. Add a little brown sugar.

ADAM AND EVE PORK CHOPS

Buy:

**Pork chops, about ½-inch
   cuts (2 or 4)**

**McIntosh apples, hard red
   ones (2)**

Check Cupboard for:

Butter

French mustard

Peel the apples and remove the cores and seeds. Dice them and put them into a saucepan with perhaps 1½ tablespoons of water, no more. Cover them and bring them to a boil. They will make their own water and will cook in 5 to 10 minutes. Add a pinch of salt.

Heat your *heavy* frying pan, and put in a small lump of butter and the pork chops. The fat from the chops will mingle with the butter. If the chops are thin enough, 5 to 10 minutes cooking on each side will be sufficient. If any part of the meat is still pink, or emits pink juice, cook longer. When they are done, surround them with the apples, and pour the fat from the pan over the apples. Serve with French mustard.

VANILLA ICE CREAM, COFFEE FLAVORED

Sprinkle vanilla ice cream with a teaspoon of instant coffee (the old kind that's powder, not freeze-dried crystals—they just don't work). This tastes so good that many people don't guess what it is they're eating.

Menu #5
Stuffed Eggs
Salad Niçoise
Melon Halves with Sherbet

Well Before Joanne Arrives:
   Boil the eggs for the hors d'ọeuvre, stuff them, chill in the refrigerator.

Boil the 2 eggs for the salad at the same time.

Cook the 2 potatoes for the salad, in time to chill and slice them. (Hot salad is nasty when it isn't intended to be hot.)

Wash the lettuce, dry, store in the refrigerator in a plastic bag.

Just Before Joanne Arrives:

Cut up the potatoes, eggs, tomatoes, and anchovies for the salad.

Halve the melon, and scoop out the seeds.

STUFFED EGGS

Buy:

Eggs (6)

Boil the eggs, peel and halve them, then add stuffing of your choice (see p. 29) to the yolk.

SALAD NIÇOISE

Buy:

Romaine lettuce (1 small head)	**Eggs (2)**
Anchovies, flat fillets (1 small can)	**Potatoes (2 small ones)**
Tuna (1 can)	**Olives, ripe (2 or 3 ounces)**
	A tomato (medium-sized)

Check Cupboard for:

Parsley	**Tarragon**

Wash the lettuce, separate the leaves, dry them (discarding outer, tough, or wilted leaves), and store in the refrigerator until required.

Make a French dressing (see p. 12), and add to it ½ tablespoon of chopped parsley, ½ teaspoon tarragon, and ½ teaspoon chervil.

Cook the little potatoes. If they are small, they will cook in about 12 to

15 minutes in boiling water. Start them in cold water. Hard-cook 2 eggs (in the same water as the eggs you're going to stuff for appetizers). Cut the tomato into small bite-sized pieces. Slice the chilled cooked potatoes. Cut the anchovy fillets in half or quarters.

Arrange a bed of lettuce in the bottom of the salad bowl, and sprinkle a little French dressing over it. Then arrange about ½ the tuna and the potatoes on top of the lettuce. Arrange the tomatoes around the edge. Decorate the salad with the eggs, quartered, and the anchovies and the olives. Pour the remaining dressing over the salad and serve immediately.

MELON HALVES WITH SHERBET

Buy:

A ripe honeydew melon

Lime or lemon sherbet (½ or 1 pint)

Question: How do you tell when a melon is ripe? Answer: Pick it up and gently press your thumbs against the little mark where the melon was once attached to its stalk. It should be a little soft there. Sniff the same place. It should smell faintly sweet.

Chill the melon, if you can find the time. Slice it in half and scoop out the seeds with a spoon. Place each half on a plate and fill the hollow with sherbet.

Variations:

Fill the melon with fresh strawberries or raspberries. Some people like their melon plain with a little lemon, or just with sugar, or with sugar and ginger powder, and some (particularly in France) with a little salt and pepper!

Menu #6
Sliced Tomatoes Vinaigrette
Grilled Lamb Chops with Peas and Boiled
 New Potatoes
Fruit with Cheese

Before Joanne Arrives:

Make the vinaigrette dressing.
Make sure that the cheeses are at room temperature.
Chill the dessert wine.

Just Before Joanne Arrives:

Slice the tomatoes.
Heat water for the peas and potatoes.

SLICED TOMATOES VINAIGRETTE

Buy:

Tomatoes, ripe, perfect (2 or 3)

For recipe for vinaigrette sauce, see p. 214.
Slice the tomatoes, arrange on a plate, pour on the vinaigrette dressing.

GRILLED LAMB CHOPS WITH PEAS
AND BOILED NEW POTATOES

Buy:

Lamb chops, cut thin (4)   **Mint sauce or jelly (if you like)**

Check Cupboard for:

Mint (dried flakes) for the peas   **Butter for the potatoes**

Heat your *heavy* frying pan, and put just a little oil in it. Cook the lamb chops for 5 to 6 minutes per side. Check to see if they are done by making a tiny cut with a knife near the bone.

Serve with mint sauce or jelly (optional—and good).

For minted peas and boiled new potatoes, see general instructions for vegetables and potatoes, p. 50.

FRUIT AND CHEESE

Buy:
Cheese   **Wine**
Fruit

Buy 3 or 4 kinds of cheese, ¼ pound of each. Avoid processed cheeses, and try to find a pleasing variety. Some delis and specialty grocers stock a good selection of imported cheese. Choose a good sharp cheddar, preferably cut from a wheel, as a basic cheese. Then look for an imported Gruyere or Emmenthal, a ripe Camembert with no trace of an ammonia smell (apply the nose test), and then add something like a Bel Paese from Italy or a Port Salut from France or a real Edam from Holland.

Serve your cheese with thin crisp biscuits or French-style bread.

Buy 2 or 3 kinds of fruit. Grapes seem to be a particularly good accompaniment to cheese and so do ripe pears. Cherries are always delightful. Citrus fruits have rather a strong flavor, although tangerines might be mild enough. And of course, the combination of a hard, crisp, juicy McIntosh or Northern Spy apple and a piece of sharp cheddar is hard to beat.

Champagne is the perfect dessert wine, and a good white Burgundy comes close to it. With desserts *and* cheese, you can try the sweeter white wines, such as the Sauternes.

Chapter 4

A Super Bowlful of TV Meals

LURING LUSCIOUS CYNTHIA into your lair for an afternoon of filmed—and live—sports requires a considerable amount of organization and planning.

First of all, you've got to fend off that horde of slobs who descended on you last year and who now think they've got squatters' rights to grind potato chips into your carpets and burn your tables with cigarettes. It's not that you don't dig this crowd. You do. It's just that you don't want them to interfere with what promises to put as many points on your scoreboard as the Dolphins'. So they can do their drinking and yelling at the neighborhood gin mill while you enjoy two games to their one.

Circumstances strongly suggest that you keep things simple in the kitchen. Elaborate meals have no place in this game plan, since you'll miss out on all the action which will begin as soon as you see Cynthia framed in your front door.

By this time, you should have a few morsels ready that she can enjoy with her first drink. (See Chapter 2 for full details.) The recipes that follow in this chapter can all be prepared in advance and eaten with one hand—which offers all sorts of opportunities where occasional fumbles and passes are concerned, not to mention unsportsmanlike conduct if all else fails.

I once knew a guy who would invest a certain amount of time in the traditional social amenities. If this failed to produce the desired results with his date, he would wait until she left the room for a few moments and then strip off every stitch of his clothing, pushing it under the couch with his feet. Upon her return, she would find him wearing nothing but a broad leer. Of course, this sort of behavior can lead to a half-time trip to your local precinct house, but it can also lead to much more pleasant things. No one can possibly counsel you in these shady areas of the man-woman relationship.

Regardless of what your technique may be, you won't have much of a chance to exercise it if you fail to organize each event properly. You've got to feed this honey or hunger will force her to leave early. In addition, you can't expect her to be satisfied with several bowlsful of stale popcorn followed by a frozen TV dinner.

Plan ahead. A little preparation and thoughtfulness at the front end will reap its own rewards. This includes shopping a day early for the ingredients needed in whatever simple recipe you select from those suggested here. Have everything at least half ready by the time she arrives. Aside from making it easier on you, it will give you a chance to explain at least some of the fundamentals of the game to her.

It's probably hopeless, however. After all, she *is* a woman. Most women can't seriously be expected to understand what constitutes an off-side, safety, clip, or the various other fine points of the game. This becomes obvious just as soon as the whistle sounds for the opening kickoff.

"Why is that player knocking down that other man?" she'll probably ask, "He doesn't even have the ball."

"He's a blocker, Cynthia. He's supposed to do that so the guy with the ball can make the yardage needed for a first down."

"Oh, yes. I remember now. A first down is when one team carries the ball over the other team's baseline, right?"

"Not exactly, darling," you should answer with an approving smile, "but little girls with legs like yours shouldn't worry about such things."

You see? You've got problems as far as her understanding of the game is concerned, and you're going to need time to solve them. You won't be able to discuss anything with her, however, if you have to stand in the kitchen, staring balefully at a ham and yam casserole.

Fortunately, there's enough time between the quarters to check on whatever is in the oven or on the stove. While you're at it, get two trays ready with plates, silverware, napkins, and whatever else you'll need to polish off the meal. If you plan to go the wine route, pull the cork in each bottle at least an hour before use so that the contents can "breathe." White and rosé wines should be thoroughly chilled.

Figure things out so that you can enjoy your TV fare at half-time when the alternative would be to watch a high school marching band playing a medley of theme songs from Walt Disney movies. If you've operated according to form, she'll be just a little bit oiled by booze by then and will appreciate something good to eat. This also means you'll be able to sit with her through the second half, which opens up many enchanting possibilities which have nothing whatever to do with what's on camera.

Once the game has ended, you may want to explain more about football's finer points and perhaps give a few practical applications of illegal use of hands. However, don't forget that you've got a few pots and dishes to be done in the kitchen. If Cynthia offers to wash and dry them, protest. Briefly. Don't overdo it. Remember that this is woman's work. Just as every guy knows about football, so does every female know about cleaning up. It was all part of the Home Ec courses they took in high school.

While she's busy in the kitchen, you'll have a chance to shut off the TV which can only be a hindrance to what remains on your own schedule of coming attractions.

STUFFED AVOCADO

Buy:

An avocado, ripe

Shrimp, cooked, peeled (¼ pound)

Check Cupboard for:

Mayonnaise
Parsley

Lemon

Be careful when you buy the avocado, if you are not accustomed to buying them. The color of the skin doesn't have anything to do with the relative ripeness of the insides. Different species of avocado vary from bright green to nearly black as far as the skin color is concerned. You have to judge by touch. A ripe one is evenly soft all over. If it is squishy at one end, it's apt to be rotten. If it is hard, it will be inedible for several days until it ripens. And if you cut open a green one, you'll have to throw it out, because it won't ripen. If you are in doubt, buy your first few from a proper fruit and vegetable store and get the fruit man to help you until you get the hang of it.

Slice open your fine ripe avocado the long way, and remove the huge seed. Mix your fresh shrimp with enough mayonnaise to hold them together. Add a squeeze of lemon juice, decorate with a little chopped parsley, and spoon the mixture into the avocado halves.

SHIRRED SPANISH EGGS

Buy:

Eggs

Spanish sausage, "chorizo," if available (if not, use Polish hunting sausage, or any dry ready-to-eat sausage of similar size, including salami)

Spaghetti sauce, a very small can or jar (if you have some left-over homemade sauce, so much the better!)

Check Cupboard for:

Butter   **Oregano**

For this dish you need 2 oven-proof dishes, shallow, and about 6 inches in diameter. They can be glass or pottery.

Pre-heat the oven to 400°. Use one or two eggs per person, as desired. Break the eggs into the oven-proof dishes with a generous teaspoon of butter. To each dish, add a couple of slices of the sausage, removing the skin if there is one, and a tablespoonful of spaghetti sauce. Add salt, pepper, and a pinch of oregano. Bake in the oven until the whites of the eggs are firm and the yolks still liquid. About 5 minutes.

PUB SALAD

Buy:

A beefsteak tomato, huge
White wine, very dry, very good (1 bottle)

Parmesan cheese, freshly grated (2–3 ounces)

Check Cupboard for:
Olive oil, best quality

Carefully cut the core out of the tomato with a sharp pointed knife. Then cut the tomato in thick wedges. Put them in a deep bowl and pour a cup of white wine over them. Stick them in the refrigerator for 10 minutes to marinate while you do something else. Then remove them from the wine, sprinkle them with 2 tablespoons of Parmesan cheese and 2 tablespoons of olive oil. Attempt to toss them without dismembering them, and put them away to chill in the refrigerator for 45 minutes. Drink the rest of the wine.

CHEF'S SALAD

Buy:
Lettuce, romaine or Boston or Bibb or chicory (1 head)
Two varieties of lettuce make an especially good salad, so let the second be one of the following: endive or escarole or water cress or young spinach
Tomatoes
Cucumber
Green onions
Ham and/or chicken (¼ pound)
Cheese, Swiss or cheddar (¼ pound)
Anchovies, flat fillets (1 can)
Eggs

A chef's salad is a meal in itself—particularly in warm weather. You can make it ahead of time and add the dressing (French dressing is best—see p. 12) when you are ready to serve. Just store it in the refrigerator until zero hour.

Hard-cook two eggs.

Wash all the lettuce under cold running water and separate the leaves. Shake out the water in a wire salad basket if you have one (you ought to). If not, dry the lettuce with a clean tea-towel or with paper towels.

Wash the tomatoes and cube them, shaking out excess moisture. Peel and slice the cucumber (or part of it). Wash and trim the roots and tops off the green onions. Chop them. Slice the ham, chicken, and cheese into strips a couple of inches long by less than ¼ inch wide. These are called julienne strips. Quarter the hard-cooked eggs. Tear, do not cut, the lettuce into pieces, using the same amount of other greens as lettuce. Put it into a large shallow bowl. Add the tomatoes, cucumbers, and green onions. Scatter the meat, cheese, and anchovies on top. Add the dressing and toss at the table.

A chef's salad is also infinitely expandable and absorbs leftovers very well. Bacon left over from breakfast (unlikely), slices (very thin) of leftover steak, other bits of cheese, leftover green peas.

Other optional ingredients, all good: black olives, bits of red or green sweet peppers, sliced radishes, croutons, strips of salami, tongue, shrimp, artichoke hearts, capers, and anything else you can think of.

MACARONI SALAD

Buy:

Macaroni, small elbow (1 package)

Olives, ripe (¼ pound) (Try and get 'em from a deli which gets Greek olives by the tub—much better than canned.)

Tuna (1 can)
Eggs
Cabbage (1 small head)

Check Cupboard for:

Mayonnaise
Dry mustard

Vinegar

Cook ⅓ cup elbow macaroni in boiling salted water until tender. While you're at it, you might as well boil one egg in the same water. Drain the macaroni, rinse it well in cold water, and drain again, rescuing the egg meanwhile. Contrive to dry the macaroni a little by letting it drip in a colander or by using paper towels. Put it in a salad bowl with ½ cup of ripe olives, ½ cup canned tuna (drain it), and 1 cup finely shredded cabbage. In a measuring cup, combine ¼ cup mayonnaise, 1 teaspoon dry mustard, 1 tablespoon vinegar, ½ teaspoon salt. Mix well and pour over the salad, stirring it in lightly. This salad is better cold, so stick in the refrigerator for a while. Garnish with sliced, hard-cooked egg.

Oh, yes. Take it on a picnic sometime.

FAST PIZZA

Buy:

**A frozen pizza of the size
  you wish**

Check Cupboard for:

Olive oil
Salami
Olives, green and/or ripe
Anchovies
Parmesan cheese

Mozzarella cheese
**Sweet pepper, green or red
  (canned ones will do)**
Oregano or basil

Preheat the oven to 425°.

Get out your frozen pizza and start to redecorate it. Spread a little olive oil over the surface. There will probably be enough tomato sauce on it, but you can always add a little tomato purée if you like. Cut the salami slices into bite-sized pieces and distribute them. Remove the olive seeds and add the olives. Cut up the anchovy fillets into small bits and add them. Sprinkle Parmesan cheese evenly, and add pieces of mozzarella. Add pieces of chopped pepper. Sprinkle with oregano or basil.

Put it in the oven and bake it for as long as recommended on the frozen pizza package, and then for a little longer if the cheese hasn't melted sufficiently. It should be bubbling nicely.

Break out some beer and enjoy.

CAESAR SALAD

Buy:

**Lettuce, romaine, best
  quality (1 head)**
Anchovies, flat fillets (1 can)
Garlic
**Parmesan cheese, freshly
  grated (2 ounces)**

A lemon
An egg
**Bread, white, for making
  croutons (or a box of the
  commercially made kind)**

Check Cupboard for:

Butter

Olive oil

One of the world's truly great salads, the Caesar salad must be eaten immediately after preparation and never allowed to stand.

Croutons: Remove the crusts from 2 or 3 slices of bread and cut them in cubes. In a frying pan, put ¼ cup olive oil and a tablespoon of butter and the bread cubes. Add 2 cloves of garlic thinly sliced. Turn and toss the croutons over a medium fire until they are crisp and brown. Set them aside on paper towels to cool and drain.

Salad: Separate the leaves of the lettuce, wash them under cold running water—the colder the better. This freshens them. Drain them thoroughly, and roll them up in paper towels and put them in the refrigerator to crisp. Open the can of anchovies, and cut some of the fillets into small pieces. Squeeze a lemon and have the juice ready. Boil some water in a small saucepan, and keep it on the simmer until you need it.

Get out your big salad bowl, and arrange the ingredients of the salad nearby so they will be ready to assemble.

Rub the bowl with a garlic clove. Turn the heat up under the saucepan so that the water will return to the boil. Get the lettuce out, and break it into the bowl in manageable pieces. Next, remove the boiling water from the stove, put an egg in it and let it stand for one minute exactly. Pour a little less than ½ cup olive oil over the lettuce. Toss well. Then add croutons, anchovies, lemon juice, and freshly ground pepper. Toss again and add salt if necessary. Break the coddled egg into the bowl, and add 3 tablespoons of Parmesan cheese. Toss again and eat immediately.

BOB COLE'S SLAW

Buy:

Cabbage, white (1 head)   **A sweet pepper, green or red**

Check Cupboard for:

Wine vinegar   **Onion salt or a little minced**
Olive oil   **fresh onion**
Dry mustard   **Parsley**
Celery seed or celery salt

Shred the cabbage, enough to fill two cups. Chop half of the pepper.

Put ¼ cup olive oil and 1½ tablespoons wine vinegar into a salad bowl. Blend into the oil and vinegar the following seasonings: ½ teaspoon salt, ¼ teaspoon pepper, ¼ teaspoon onion salt, ½ tablespoon sugar, ½ teaspoon dry mustard, ½ teaspoon celery seed or ¼ teaspoon celery salt.

Add the cabbage and pepper and mix thoroughly into the dressing. Just before serving, sprinkle with chopped parsley.

NIGRO'S HAM AND YAM CASSEROLE

Buy:

Ham, cooked slice (¾ pound)
Yams in syrup, canned (look for a 12-ounce can, which holds about 1¼ cups)

Currant jelly

Preheat the oven to 350°.

Cut the ham slice in two and place in a shallow baking dish. Arrange the yams on the ham, cutting them into smaller pieces if necessary. Melt two tablespoons of currant jelly with one tablespoon of water and spoon over the yams. Bake in the oven for about 30 minutes or until the ham and yams are heated thoroughly.

BEEF AND POTATO CASSEROLE

Buy:

Ground beef (1 pound)
Apples, crisp (3 large or 4 small)

Potatoes, instant mashed
Lemons
Onions, (2 large ones)

Check Cupboard for:

Butter
Garlic
Nutmeg

Beef bouillon cubes
Parsley

Preheat the oven to 325°.

Prepare the package of instant potatoes according to directions on the package.

Peel, core, and thinly slice the apples. Squeeze the juice of half a lemon over them; this prevents them from turning brown. Peel the onions and slice them very thin. Then sauté them in a frying pan in 2 tablespoons of butter. Add to the onions the pound of ground beef, stirring it around and separating it until it has browned. Add to this mixture 1 clove of garlic chopped fine, 1 teaspoon of salt, a couple of shakes of pepper, and ½ teaspoon of ground or grated nutmeg. Then add 1 beef bouillon cube dissolved in 1 cup of boiling water. Add some chopped parsley, stir everything together thoroughly, and let it simmer for a few minutes.

Get out a good-sized casserole or baking dish and start to construct as follows: grease the bottom of the dish with a little butter or oil and then put in a layer of mashed potatoes, pressing them down thoroughly. Then a layer of meat from the frying pan. Then a layer of the sliced apples. Repeat the layers until you run out of material, ending with the potatoes. Dot the top with butter and breadcrumbs and bake for about 30 minutes.

This dish will serve more than two people and makes a fine leftover to be reheated.

BARBOUR'S TOUCHDOWN CHILI

Buy:

Ground round (1 pound)
Red kidney beans (1 can)
Tomatoes, whole (1 regular-sized can)

A sweet pepper, red or green
Onions
Sour cream (1 small carton)

Check Cupboard for:

Flour
Chili powder
Oregano
Thyme
Ground cumin or coriander

Dry mustard
Cayenne
Dried chili peppers
Garlic
Celery seeds

Since chili is the sort of dish you'll want to make from time to time, here is a shortcut to future chili making. You make up a good-sized jar of the dry spices and the next time you make chili you use a couple of spoonsful of that instead of adding spices one by one. Degrees of spiciness in chili vary a great deal. In Texas they range from one-alarm (mild) to five-alarm (éat with an asbestos spoon). You'll probably want to change the proportions of the ingredients to suit yourself. Add more chili powder, chili peppers, cayenne, and dry mustard according to taste. And remember that the shelf life of most herbs and spices is not long. Even a good hot chili powder tames down considerably after a year in a tin can or jar. Find an empty glass jar and make up the following in a convenient multiple:

Basic Chili Powder Mix:

2 tablespoons flour, 1 or more tablespoons chili powder, 1 teaspoon oregano, ¼ teaspoon thyme, ¼ teaspoon each of cumin and coriander (ground), 2 teaspoons dry mustard, ⅛ teaspoon cayenne pepper, ½ teaspoon celery seeds, lots of black pepper, a sprinkle of red chili peppers, crushed. This adds up to 4½ tablespoons of chili mix, so even if you have made 5 times this amount, whenever you make chili, just use 4½ tablespoons of the mix.

Find a big pot and the frying pan. Peel and chop a big onion and a sweet pepper. Put the beans and the can of tomatoes in the pot with the onions and sweet peppers over a low heat. Put the ground beef in the frying pan over a moderate heat and stir it and separate it as it begins to fry. When it is well separated, and beginning to brown nicely, dump in 4½ tablespoons of the chili mix, stir it into the grease from the meat at the bottom of the pan, and then turn the meat so that the chili is well mixed. Add a clove of crushed garlic. Transfer the whole business into the pot with the beans and tomatoes. Then put a little cold water into the bottom of the frying pan and heat it, stirring and scraping with a wooden spoon. All the bits of meat and chili stuck to the bottom will come loose and you can add this mixture to the bean pot as well. Add salt to taste. Cook the chili over a low heat and keep it simmering until the onions and peppers are done and the sauce has thickened a little.

When you serve the chili, put a dollop of sour cream in each dish.

MEAT LOAF

Buy:

Ground round steak (½ pound)

Ground pork (½ pound)
Bread crumbs (1 box)

Onions	**Tomatoes, fresh (2 or 3) or**
Celery	**canned**

Check Cupboard for:

Eggs	**Parsley**
Butter	**Tomato purée or ketchup or**
Bacon	**tomato sauce of any kind**

Once you have made one or two meat loaves, you will be able to branch off on your own and experiment and create delicious variations. But first, here are some basic truths about meat loaves: 1) Bake them for 1 to 1¼ hours per pound of meat. 2) Bread crumbs prevent the loaf from becoming too heavy and give a nice texture. You can also use rice, or oatmeal, or other cereals. 3) Most people base a meat loaf on ground beef, but veal and pork are very good too. Try mixing different proportions of two or three kinds of meat. 4) Herbs and spices, within moderation, work very well in meat loaves. Onion is a standard ingredient, and leftover vegetables of any variety add interest. 5) Lay a few slices of bacon on top of the meat loaf before you cook it. The bacon lends a nice flavor and bastes the meat. Bake without a cover.

Preheat the oven to 350°

Fundamentally you throw everything into a mixing bowl—except the onions, celery, and butter—and mix it with your bare hands.

In a frying pan, put 2 tablespoons butter, 1 medium onion finely chopped, and ½ cup of chopped celery. Cook this gently until it looks transparent and limp.

In a large mixing bowl, put the meat, 1 egg lightly beaten, ½ cup of bread crumbs or rice (cooked) or oatmeal, ½ cup of tomatoes (fresh or canned), up to ½ cup chopped parsley, ½ teaspoon thyme, 1 teaspoon salt, lots of freshly ground pepper. Add a shot of Worcestershire sauce and/or a shot of lemon juice. Mix it with your hands, adding the onion and celery when it is done.

If you have a loaf-shaped Pyrex oven pan or a casserole of suitable size, put your meat loaf into that, and top with a few slices of bacon.

If not, shape the mixture into a round loaf with your hands and bake it in any oven pan, including the frying pan. If too much fat accumulates in the bottom of the pan, pour it off carefully. There shouldn't be any left when the loaf is done. After cooking, let the loaf sit in a warm place for 15 minutes before serving.

A tomato sauce, such as you would use for spaghetti, is good on a meat-loaf.

Serve with beer or a hearty red wine.

Variations:

Flavor with a little nutmeg, or curry powder, or chili powder.
Add a little red wine.
Use peas, green peppers, corn.
Put a little cheese on top.

HAM AND MUSTARD SAUCE

Buy:

Ham steak, thick (¾ pound)

Check Cupboard for:

Dry mustard

Make a Béchamel sauce as described on p. 11, with this variation: mix 2 teaspoons dry mustard with the flour which you add to the melted butter. Add a little rosemary to the seasonings; it goes particularly well with pork.

Slash the edges of the ham steak to prevent it from curling. Bake the ham slice in a moderate oven (350°) for about 45 minutes.

Serve with the mustard sauce accompanied by boiled potatoes.

SAUERKRAUT MIT BRATWURST

Buy:

**Sauerkraut, fresh or canned
    (1 pound)
Apples, hard**

**Onions
Caraway seeds**

**Boiling sausages: do not buy
ordinary pork sausage—ask
for bratwurst, knackwurst,
weisswurst, and similar
sausages—two sausages (of
different kinds) are enough
for each person.**

**If boiling sausages are not
available, buy pork ribs,
country style (2 or 3 per
person)**

Check Cupboard for:

White wine (optional)
**Several kinds of mustard,
i.e. French Dijon mustard,
English Colman's prepared
mustard, German (tafelsenf),
French Moutarde de Meaux,
etc.**

Brown sugar
Parsley

Put the sauerkraut into a colander or sieve, prop it under running cold water, and wash it thoroughly. Leave it under the tap while you do something else. All sauerkraut needs this treatment or it will be unpleasantly sour.

Peel, core, and chop coarsely the apples (2 small ones or 1 medium); peel and chop coarsely 1 medium onion.

By now the sauerkraut has rinsed sufficiently. Drain it thoroughly, pressing out excess water with your hand, and put it in a large pot. Add the onions and apples and 1 teaspoon of caraway seed. Add 1 tablespoon of dark brown sugar, or more if you wish. Add freshly ground black pepper. Add a cup of fresh water or white wine and water mixed. Stir well, and place over a moderate flame until the water starts to boil, then reduce the heat so that it simmers. Stir from time to time, and make sure the liquid does not boil away, adding a little more if necessary. The sauerkraut should cook for at least 30 minutes and up to 45. Season to taste with salt.

If you have boiling sausages, heat them in a pan of hot water very slowly and very carefully. Do not let them boil—despite their name—or they will burst open. Depending on the girth of the sausages they require 15 or 20 minutes to heat through.

If you have country-style pork spare ribs, they will take longer to cook than the sausages, so start them before you tackle the sauerkraut.

Put a little oil in the frying pan. Sprinkle the ribs with a little flour and salt, and brown them on each side in the hot oil. When they have browned, pour off any excess oil and put ¼ cup of cold water in the pan.

Cover it with a lid and let the ribs simmer for about 35 minutes. The juice can subsequently be added to the sauerkraut when you serve it. Season to taste with salt and pepper.

Serve the sauerkraut with the sausages or the spare ribs, sprinkle with parsley, and set out a choice of mustards.

GARLIC SPARE RIBS

Buy:

Pork spare ribs (2 pounds)
(get the butcher to cut the
ribs into 2½-inch lengths
and to separate them)

Check Cupboard for:

Soy sauce   **Corn oil**
Fresh garlic   **Sugar**

If you have a broiler, cook the spare ribs under it on a sheet of aluminum foil. Oil the ribs lightly and sprinkle a little thyme and black pepper on them. Turn them frequently. Cook until the meat is no longer pink, and the outside browns but does not burn.

If you prefer to use the oven, cook the spare ribs in a roasting pan at 350° for about an hour, having oiled and seasoned them as described above.

In a frying pan, mix ¼ cup oil, ¼ cup Soy sauce, 2 teaspoons sugar, and 2 cloves of minced garlic. Heat this mixture until it bubbles. When the spare ribs are done, turn them in this sauce in the frying pan and then serve. Add a little salt if necessary.

VEAL AND MUSHROOM CASSEROLE

Buy:

Two veal chops, large
Mushroom soup, condensed
(1 can)

Check Cupboard for:
Sherry

Preheat the oven to 350°.

Put a little oil in the frying pan and brown the chops in it on either side. Then put the chops in an oven dish which has a cover. Put a little cold water in the frying pan, and heat it to make pan juices. Add them to the casserole. Pour ½ can of condensed mushroom soup diluted with 2 tablespoons of water and 2 of sherry over the chops. Cover and bake for about 35 minutes or until the chops are tender when poked with a fork. Add salt and pepper to taste and sprinkle with chopped parsley.

You may wish to experiment by adding a green herb such as rosemary or marjoram.

CORN AND TOMATO CASSEROLE

Buy:

Tomatoes, ripe, medium-sized (3)
Corn, whole, not creamed (1 can)

Cheddar cheese, sharp, aged (¼ pound)

Check Cupboard for:

Bread crumbs
Milk
Butter

Flour
Thyme

Preheat the oven to 350°. Put the kettle on to boil.

Make a Béchamel sauce as described on p. 11, adding a little thyme as well as salt and pepper.

Pour boiling water over the tomatoes and let them stand for about 20 seconds; then cool them under running water. This facilitates peeling. Peel, remove cores, and cut in thick slices.

Get out a casserole dish and butter the inside. Put a layer of corn on the bottom, about ½ cup. Pour over it ½ of the Béchamel sauce, and then make a layer using about ½ of the tomato slices. Repeat, finishing with a layer of tomatoes. Cover with ⅓ cup grated cheddar cheese and ¼ cup bread crumbs. Dot the top with butter, using about 2 tablespoons. A little parsley?

Bake for about 25 minutes, until the cheese bubbles and the dish is cooked through.

Variations:
Use basil instead of thyme.
Add a tablespoon of minced onion.

COLD BAKED APPLES

Buy:
Apples, firm and tasty

Check Cupboard for:
Brown sugar   **Flour**
Vanilla essence   **Butter**

Preheat the oven to 425°.

Core four of the apples and peel them halfway down. When you core them, don't make a hole in the bottom. Put them on a baking dish, peeled half up.

In a saucepan, melt 3 tablespoons of butter and add 2 tablespoons of flour and mix. Then add ½ cup of brown sugar and ½ teaspoon vanilla. Stir well and let the sugar melt. Then pour this mixture into the holes left by the apple cores and over the apples. Put them in the oven, and when they have acquired a crusty coating from the sauce, turn the oven down to 350°. Total cooking time should be about half an hour.

Let them cool, and then put them in the refrigerator to chill.

Serve with thick or whipped cream, if you like.

Chapter 5

A Loaf of Bread, a Jug of Wine and Pow!

PICNICS TAKE PLANNING—lots of it. And not only in the area of food and drink. Suitable site selection is crucial, since the object is to strand your date as far from civilization as you can get to in a day and back. This completely eliminates from consideration the use of those public tables along the nation's major roadways.

These are absolutely out! Why? Because Selma will have the obvious option of countering your caveman tactics simply by flouncing forth to the pavement and flagging down a passing motorist with her half slip. To avoid this, you have to head her into the tall timber or at least onto the fringe of a gentle wooded slope well beyond the sound of traffic and factory whistles. Once you arrive—complete with thermos bottles and a hamper full of good things to eat—you'll be in complete control of her immediate destiny. That will be mainly because the keys to your Mustang will be in the pocket of your Oleg Cassini slacks. If she wants to take them from you, she'll have to out-wrestle you, and that presents charming prospects of its own that are far beyond gastronomic considerations.

But figure it this way. By the time she spreads your blanket beneath an old willow tree, she'll be thirsty and hungry and more than ready to cut herself in for an equal share of the action—and let the potato chips fall where they may.

Once you're there, you'll encounter another problem—mosquitoes. These pests seem to attend virtually every picnic in force, especially on a day with little or no wind. Highly sensitive to scents, they'll be just as attracted to Selma's perfume as you are, but their attentions to both of you will be somewhat different from what you have in mind for her—which obviously doesn't include a dose of malaria.

That's why you'll want to bring along an aerosol can of insect repellent such as "Off" or "6—12." This will also discourage the persistent attacks of deerflies and horseflies, which strike wherever they sense body heat. And if all is going according to plan with Selma, your body will be getting warmer by the minute.

Basic woodlore is another important consideration. Do you know what poison ivy looks like? Better find out, because if you catch it, your social contacts will be limited for some time to blowing kisses to your mother.

With these considerations in mind, turn your thoughts to refreshments followed by some of the ideas for outdoor meals outlined in this chapter.

Consider buying a set of thermos bottles—one each for booze, soup, and coffee. If beer is your bag, you'll be able to use a thermos bag instead. This weighs much less than a portable ice chest, and its contents can be kept cool by one or more "ice-paks." These wondrous plastic containers hold a chemical which, once frozen, remains cold for 24 hours or more. Of course, thermos bags are also useful for keeping hot solid foods warm.

Salt and pepper shakers should be stoppered with wax paper seals beneath their tops to prevent spillage in transit. Include a roll of paper towels in your essentials, too. Their full value will be evident only if you forget to bring them along, but don't overdo the paper products if you plan on making a deep impression on Selma. This suggests that you pack china plates and mugs, an assortment of silverware and linen napkins instead of their counterparts in paper and plastic. Assuming you don't want this dally in the boondocks to be a replication of a utilities company fish-fry, you'll have to limit modern living's aids to plastic garbage bags.

Whatever you do, don't forget to bring along a can opener plus a corkscrew/bottle opener combination. Once you've established a soft, romantic mood with that young thing beside you on the blanket, you won't want to have to go Asiatic with a wine bottle by breaking its neck off on a rock.

If cold cuts are to be a feature of your alfresco frolics, be certain that you buy good brands. Those selections in blister packs at your local supermarket were probably sliced up and packaged shortly after the Whiskey Rebellion and are being kept in suspended animation by their preservative additives. A reputable delicatessen is a much better bet for bologna, salami, and related processed meats, and whatever you decide on will be sliced fresh to your order. The same holds true for cold roast beef. In a good deli you can watch your meat being sliced, and if the first slice looks a little elderly, you can just tell the butcher to start with the second. As for pickles, there isn't a bottled dill in the whole of Christendom that can match the class of one of those impressive "cukes" hauled from the depths of a barrel of brine at the neighborhood delicatessen.

Herring in sour cream and other cold seafood delicacies also make good picnic provender and so do cold lamb, veal, and roast or fried chicken. Of course, you'll need bread, too, as well as butter plus mustard or mayonnaise, or maybe both.

Salads are perfect for outdoor enjoyment. Just be sure that you carry the dressing in a jar and apply it *after* you reach your destination. Mix salad ingredients in a plastic container with a tight lid. Then all you'll have to do when you want to enjoy it is pour in the dressing, replace the top, shake, and serve.

After you finish eating, impress upon Selma the importance of resting for a few minutes—no bird-watching expeditions, no romps in sylvan glades. Tell her, if indeed you have to at this point, that what you both need is to lean back on the blanket and relax, just relax for awhile . . .

GAZPACHO ANDALUZ

Buy:

**Tomatoes, ripe, best quality
  (3 or 4 medium-sized)**
Peppers, sweet, red (2)
A cucumber, large

Celery, pascal (1 bunch)
An onion, red if available
Garlic
Croutons

Check Cupboard for:

Olive oil
Lemon
Basil

Parsley
Sherry

This marvelous fresh soup is well worth the cost of the blender you need to make it.

Using the blender according to directions, purée the tomatoes and cucumber without peeling—just cut them into chunks the blender can take. Remove stem and seeds from the peppers, and purée them. Peel and chop the onion coarsely and purée it. Throw in two cloves of garlic with the onion. Trim two or three stalks of celery and purée them with their leaves. Combine all the puréed material in a large bowl as you proceed.

Then add 2 tablespoons of olive oil, the juice of ½ lemon, ¼ cup of sherry (preferably dry), ¼ teaspoon of basil, and 1 teaspoon of parsley. Salt and pepper to taste. You can now adjust the flavor to your taste by adding a little more lemon or oil.

Put the gazpacho in the refrigerator and let it chill thoroughly. Prepare the traditional garnish for the gazpacho: small amounts of each of the main ingredients chopped into small pieces, i.e., tomatoes, cucumber, peppers, celery, onions. If you were planning to eat at home, you would set out little dishes of each of these and one of croutons. On a picnic, however, it is simpler to put all of the fresh diced vegetables into one plastic container with a tight-fitting lid and the croutons into another.

Put the gazpacho itself into a thermos which you have already chilled. It will probably be easier to serve it in mugs, but if this is a Picnic of Great Magnitude, soup plates are indicated.

ICED CHICKEN AND LEMON SOUP

Check Cupboard for:

Chicken bouillon cubes (5)	**A lemon**
Eggs	**Parsley**

This is a light and delicious Greek summer soup, called in Greek *αvgolémono*. The recipe is simplicity itself.

Put 4 measuring cups of water into a saucepan with 5 chicken bouillon cubes and heat to boiling.

Meanwhile squeeze a lemon and put the juice in a bowl. In the same bowl break two eggs. Using an egg beater, beat the eggs and lemon until they are well mixed.

When the chicken bouillon boils, remove it from the heat. Take a cupful of it and add it slowly to the egg-lemon mixture in the bowl by beating a little then adding a little and so forth until you have added the whole cup. Reason: if you add the eggs to the hot soup all at once, they will harden into shreds and bits. Then carry out the same process pouring the lemon-egg-soup mixture back into the saucepan with the rest of the soup, beating a little and adding a little. Place the saucepan over moderate heat, and continue beating. Do not—repeat—do not allow the soup to boil again. It will thicken slightly, and then it is done. Eggs will thicken soups and sauces *if* you keep the temperature at 144° or less. Add pepper; it probably won't need much salt. Let the soup cool, and then put it in the refrigerator to chill thoroughly. Pack in a pre-chilled thermos. Add a little parsley.

Note: This soup can also be served hot.

WINE CONSOMMÉ

Buy:
Beef bouillon condensed (1 can)   **Lemons**
Red wine, dry (1 bottle)

Put the bouillon in a saucepan and dilute with half a cup of water and half a cup of red wine. Heat it but do not let it boil. Then add a shot of lemon juice and pour it into a preheated thermos. Take along some garlic croutons.

MIDWINTER SOUP

Buy:
Clam juice or clam broth (1 can)

Check Cupboard for:
Chicken bouillon cubes   **Tabasco**
Tomato purée   **Parsley**
Sherry, dry

Although its name implies anything but a picnic in July, this is a good restorative on a cold day and travels well to football games.

Combine in a saucepan the clam juice, 2 cups water, 3 chicken bouillon cubes, and ½ tablespoon of tomato purée. Simmer for 15 to 20 minutes. Then add ¼ cup dry sherry, a dash of Tabasco, and 1 teaspoon of chopped parsley. Pour into a preheated thermos.

RADISHES AND SWEET BUTTER

Buy:

**Radishes, preferably the
long red and white ones (a
bunch or two)**

**French bread or crusty rolls
Butter, unsalted (½ pound)**

This is a favorite first course in France.

Wash and trim the radishes and put them in a plastic baggie in your food cooler. Pack the butter so that it will keep cool too.

Some people butter the bread and some butter the radishes. Just don't salt them.

SEASONAL RAW VEGETABLES

Buy:

**Cherry tomatoes
Celery
Cucumber (slice it the long
way into 2-inch lengths
and remove the seeds)
Carrot sticks
Radishes**

**Green onions
Cauliflower florets
Fennel slices
Zucchini slices or strips
Sweet green or red pepper
sticks**

Instead of hors d'oeuvre, take along an assortment of washed and trimmed raw vegetables which you can eat with your fingers. All you need is a little salt and pepper and perhaps a container of chilled mayonnaise. A mustard mayonnaise is also good with raw vegetables, and may be made by adding 1 tablespoon of French Dijon mustard to 1 cup of mayonnaise.

ANGELICA'S EGGPLANT

Buy:

An eggplant, medium size

Check Cupboard for:

Onions   **Lemon**
Olive oil   **Garlic or garlic salt**

Preheat the oven to 350°.

Put the eggplant, whole, onto some sort of baking dish, stick it in the oven and leave it there until it gets quite soft. Then take it out and wrap it up in some old newspaper—this allows it to cool slowly—and let it cool to the point where you can handle it easily and without burning your fingers. Then peel it, mash the inside part in a bowl, and set it aside.

In a frying pan cook ½ cup of minced onion in ¼ cup olive oil, slowly over a low flame. When the onion is soft, add the mashed eggplant, stir well, and allow to cook for another 5 or 10 minutes. Then add a tablespoon of lemon juice, and season with salt and pepper and garlic salt or fresh garlic to taste. Cool and then chill in the refrigerator. Pack into a plastic container with a tight lid. Serve with slices of cucumber and bread and butter.

HARD-COOKED EGGS WITH GUSSIED-UP MAYONNAISE

Buy:

Eggs

Check Cupboard for:

Any spices required for the
type of mayonnaise you
choose from the
suggestions below

Prepare as many hard-cooked eggs as you need; two per person is generous.

Choose one of the mayonnaise variations given below which have been selected because they are particularly good with eggs.

> *Green mayonnaise:* This is a mixture of fresh herbs in season added to mayonnaise. Either chop the herbs or mix them in a blender. Combine ½ cup of mixed herbs with

one cup of mayonnaise. Use as many as possible of the following: a few leaves of fresh spinach, 1 tablespoon fresh tarragon, 1 tablespoon chopped chives or green onion, 1 teaspoon chopped dill, 1 teaspoon minced marjoram or parsley or both.

Curry mayonnaise: Add 1½ teaspoons (or more if you prefer) of curry powder to 1 cup mayonnaise.

Caper mayonnaise: To 1 cup of mayonnaise add 2 tablespoons capers and 1 teaspoon grated or finely minced onion. Add a little paprika for the color.

Mustard mayonnaise II: Add 2 teaspoons dry mustard and 1 teaspoon wine vinegar to 1 cup mayonnaise. (For another mustard mayonnaise, see p. 13.)

Red mayonnaise: To 1 cup of mayonnaise, add ¼ cup red caviar, and 1 teaspoon lemon juice.

For basic homemade mayonnaise, see p. 13. (Hellman's is the best commercial mayonnaise on the market.) But no matter what kind you use, remember that mayonnaise on a picnic *must* be kept cold and eaten the same day.

Picnic Sandwiches

A few tips about sandwiches for picnics. When you are traveling with sandwiches be sure to avoid the kinds that dry out or leak liquids. Don't use lettuce that wilts easily—stick to romaine or iceberg varieties. Be careful of mayonnaise unless you have facilities for keeping either all the sandwiches that contain it or a jar of it well cooled. If you want to make an early start, make sandwiches the night before—leaving out the lettuce and mayonnaise—and stick them in the freezing compartment of your refrigerator. If you remove them in the morning and pack the picnic, they will be thawed out by noon and will be fresh and cool in the bargain. Freeze them inside plastic bags.

When packing sandwiches, wrap them individually in wax paper; if you have made several different kinds, it helps to label them. You can also buy plastic boxes designed to fit sandwiches. If you have to store sandwiches for more than six hours at home, freeze them.

You'll find a great many sandwich ideas on pages 126-130. However, the following pages include recipes for a few more sandwiches that are particularly good company on a picnic.

CHEESE AND GREEN PEPPER SANDWICH

Buy:

Cheddar cheese, sharp, aged (½ pound)
Pepper, green, sweet (1 large)

Green onions (1 bunch)
Pimientos, red (1 small jar)
Lettuce, iceberg (1 head)

Check Cupboard for:
Mayonnaise

Grate enough cheese to fill 1⅓ cups firmly packed. Mince enough green pepper to fill ½ cup. Mince enough pimiento to fill a heaping tablespoon. Chop enough green onion to fill another heaping tablespoon. Mix cheese, pepper, pimiento, onion, and add enough mayonnaise to hold them together.

This should make about 4 sandwiches. Use any bread you like, but keep the sandwiches cool until ready to eat.

CHINESE TUNA SANDWICH

Buy:

Tuna, canned (1 7-ounce can)
Chutney (1 bottle)

A green pepper, small
Green onions

Check Cupboard for:
Mayonnaise

Drain the can of tuna and put it in a bowl, separating it with a fork. Add 4 tablespoons of chopped chutney, 3 tablespoons of minced green onions, and ½ cup mayonnaise. Season with salt, pepper, lemon juice, and a little thyme. Chill the mixture before making the sandwiches, and keep them cool until you are ready to eat.

NORWEGIAN SANDWICH

Buy:

Cream cheese (3 oz.)
Smoked salmon, thinly
   sliced (¼ pound)

An onion, sweet, red
Bagels, dark rye, or even
   French or Italian bread

Check Cupboard for:

Eggs (3)
Dill

Lettuce
Butter

Hard-cook 3 eggs and slice them. Slice the onion as thin as you can. For a picnic, take all the ingredients with you and build the sandwiches on the spot. Spread the cream cheese onto the bread and season it with a little salt and pepper. Then lay slices of smoked salmon on the cheese, and alternate them with egg and onion slices. Sprinkle with dill and top with some lettuce.

LIVERWURST & ONION SANDWICH

Buy:

Liverwurst (about 8 oz.)
Horseradish, hot (1 jar)
A cucumber

An onion, large, red (1)
Lettuce
Dark rye bread

Check Cupboard for:

Butter

Set some butter (about ¼ pound) out to get soft, and then mix it with ¼ teaspoon of horseradish, drained. Spread this mixture on the bread. Then make a layer of sliced liverwurst, sliced cucumbers, and thinly sliced onion. Top with freshly ground black pepper and a lettuce leaf. Makes 4 sandwiches at least.

SOMERSET SANDWICH

Buy:

Cheddar cheese, sharp, aged
(about ¼ pound)

Chutney (1 jar)

Check Cupboard for:

Eggs
Lettuce

Whole wheat bread

Hard-cook 2 eggs.

Leave the cheese out of the refrigerator for a couple of hours. Then slice it very thin (with a cheese slicer if you have one). Lay the slices on buttered bread, spread a little chutney on top of the cheese, and lay sliced egg on top of the chutney. Top with lettuce.

Picnic Salads

POTATO SALAD

Buy:

Potatoes, medium-sized (3)
Bacon
Capers
Pepper, green, sweet

Parsley
Green onions
White wine, dry (1 bottle)

Check Cupboard for:

Olive oil
Mayonnaise

Garlic salt, or fresh garlic
Eggs

Boil the potatoes in their jackets until just tender, then peel them while they are still warm and cut them into chunks. In a small saucepan heat ¼ cup of wine with a dash of garlic in it until it is warm but not hot. Pour this over the still-warm potatoes and they will absorb the wine—(turn the potatoes gently to facilitate this.)

Fry two slices of bacon until crisp; drain them on paper towelling. Hard-cook 1 egg, peel, and slice it.

Chop 2 or 3 green onions, ½ the pepper, and 1 tablespoon of parsley.

Make a mixture of crumbled bacon, onions, pepper, parsley, 1 tablespoon olive oil, 1 tablespoon of capers (drained), and add all of it to the potatoes. Pour over them enough mayonnaise (½ cup) to bind everything together. Season to taste with salt and pepper.

Pack it into a pre-cooled wide-necked thermos, or into a container to go into your portable icebox. Pack the sliced egg separately, and add to each serving when you sit down to eat.

If you take this salad on a picnic, it *must* be refrigerated.

LENTIL SALAD

Buy:

Lentils, brown (1 box— usually 1 pound)

Green onions (1 bunch)

Check Cupboard for:

Olive oil
Wine vinegar
Worcestershire sauce

Lemon
Garlic
Thyme

Put half the box—or ½ pound of lentils—into a big bowl, just cover them with water, and let them soak overnight.

Next day, rinse them under cold running water and put them in a good-sized saucepan with enough fresh water to cover them. Add salt—about ½ teaspoon—to the water. Bring them to the boil, turn the heat down, and let them simmer until tender—perhaps 15 or 20 minutes. Drain them and let them cool in a colander. (If you are into soups, then save the water the lentils cooked in—it makes a very good soup stock.)

Make ½ cup of French dressing (see p. 12) and add to it a couple of shots of Worcestershire sauce, 1 clove of crushed garlic, ¼ teaspoon of thyme, and the juice of ½ lemon.

Chop four or five green onions. Then put the lentils into a bowl, add the onions, pour in the dressing, and mix well. Adjust the seasoning to your taste.

Variations:

Add some chopped green or red peppers or celery. Substitute other herbs for the thyme.

TUNA SALAD

Buy:

Tuna, first quality (1 can)   **Parsley**
Green onions and/or a
   sweet pepper and/or celery

Check Cupboard for:

Lemon
Mayonnaise   **Thyme**
Paprika

Put the tuna in a bowl and flake it with a fork. Chop a total of about 2 tablespoons of the vegetables you are using. Chop some parsley. Add to the tuna. Add 1 teaspoon of lemon juice, ¼ teaspoon of thyme, a sprinkling of paprika, and salt and pepper to taste. Then add enough mayonnaise to bind it all together. Pack in a container and keep it cool. Serve with a garnish of black olives and sliced tomatoes if possible. This salad is an excellent sandwich filler too.

Optional: Give it a shot of Worcestershire sauce.

MIXED BEAN SALAD

Buy:

Kidney beans (1 can)   **Pimientos (1 small jar)**
Lima beans, frozen (1 small   **Green onions (1 bunch)**
   pack)   **Celery (1 bunch)**
Green beans, frozen, not   **Parsley**
   French cut (1 small pack)

Check Cupboard for:

Oil, olive or corn   **Tarragon**
Wine vinegar

Cook the lima and green beans according to the directions on the package, but be particularly careful not to overcook. Cook the kidney beans, if necessary (see label on can), and let them cool.

Chop 2 stalks of celery (take the rest of it along washed, for nibbling with salt or cheese). Chop 5 or 6 green onions, and a couple of teaspoons of parsley. Chop the pimientos.

Make a French dressing (see p. 12) and add ½ teaspoon of tarragon to it.

Combine all the ingredients and let them marinate in the dressing for several hours or overnight in the refrigerator. Pour off excess dressing and pack in an air-tight container in your picnic cooler.

Fowl Play

BREAST OF CHICKEN ZAGROBA

Buy:
Breasts of chicken (2)

Check Cupboard for:

Olive oil	**Pepper**
Lemons	**Green onions, chopped,**
Thyme	**dried**
Garlic salt	

Preheat the oven to 350°.

Put the chicken breasts in a roasting pan and pour over them first a little oil—make sure that they are coated—and then some lemon juice. Sprinkle them with thyme, green onions, and freshly ground black pepper. (Salt them after they are cooked.) Roast them for 35 to 40 minutes, basting from time to time. When the skin has turned golden and is beginning to crisp in places, they will be done. Let them cool, and wrap them in wax paper.

HOT OR COLD BROILED
ROCK CORNISH GAME HENS

Buy:

Rock Cornish Game Hens (2)

White wine, dry (1 bottle)

Check cupboard for:

Butter
Lemon
Onion

Parsley
Thyme

You have three choices: 1—Cook them at home and take them with you cold: 2—Cook them at the picnic on a grill or hibachi; 3—Cook them partially at home and finish them at the picnic on a grill or hibachi.

At Home: Preheat the oven to 375°.

Mince the onion and parsley until you have 2 tablespoons of each. Melt ⅛ pound butter (i.e. ½ of a quarter-pound stick) in a small saucepan and add to it 3 tablespoons of white wine, the juice of ½ lemon, the onion and parsley, a pinch of thyme, and some freshly ground black pepper—add salt after cooking.

Put the birds in a roasting pan and pour this mixture over them. Baste them with it frequently, and cook them for 40 to 50 minutes. When the meat pulls away from the bone, the birds are done.

At the Picnic: Take the basting sauce with you and baste them little by little as they cook. They will take almost an hour to cook.

Half Home/Half at the Picnic: Follow the instruction for (1), cooking the birds for only 30 minutes. Finish them at the picnic, allowing extra time because of the fact that they will cook more slowly on a grill than in an oven.

Picnic Desserts

DESSERT FRUIT WITH A DIFFERENCE

First of all, here is a list of fruit just to refresh your memory and arouse your interest and hers:

Grapes, plums, cherries, bananas, raspberries, strawberries, blueberries, blackberries, black raspberries, loganberries, peaches, apricots, apples, melons—watermelon, canteloupe, honeydew, casaba, pineapples, pears, oranges, grapefruit, tangerines, kumquats, ugly fruit, persimmons, and sometimes in some places—papaya, mangoes, custard apples, fresh figs, nectarines.

A selection of these, fresh, cool and in their own pristine perfections, seems a perfect finish to any picnic meal.

There are, however, more elaborate and also delicious ways of preparing and serving fruit. A couple of these follow.

Melons: (all except watermelon). Take them to the picnic in a cooler, slice them open and serve them with one of the following: fruit sugar; fruit sugar and powdered ginger; white wine; salt, or salt and pepper.

Oranges and grapefruit: Peel them and remove inner skins and strings, but keeping whole sections of fruit. Marinate them in any orange liqueur (Cointreau, Triple Sec, Curaçao). Garnish them with toasted coconut and toasted almond slivers.

Peaches and Pears: Peel them and remove pits and stones. Slice them and marinate in brandy.

Berries: Marinate any kind in kirsch and serve them poured over lemon sherbet.

FRESH STRAWBERRIES

Buy:

Fresh strawberries in season
(1 or 2 little baskets)

Here you have a choice. If the strawberries are flawless and have a marvelous flavor, just rinse them under cool water and eat them whole, dipping them into fruit sugar and sour cream or sweet cream (buy whipping cream).

If they are less than perfect, rinse them, remove the stems, and slice them. Put them away in the refrigerator for a while with a sprinkling of sugar—they will make delicious juice. To this delicious juice you can add a little more juice from your collection of miniature bottles of liqueur. Try a little kirsch, for instance. Add it, however, just before serving the strawberries. Pack them in a leak-proof container for transportation and keep them cool.

THELMA'S FRUIT SALAD

This takes a little work, but it is absolutely worth the effort.

Buy:

**A selection of fruit,
  including oranges, apples,
  bananas, plums, peaches,
  grapes (the more the
  merrier)**

**Raspberries, frozen (1
  package)
Kirsch, 1 miniature bottle**

Peel, slice, remove seeds, and otherwise deal with the fruit, cutting it into small pieces and putting it in a bowl.

Let the raspberries defrost, and add them plus all their juice to the fruit salad. The juice is the secret ingredient, for it gives color and flavor to the whole salad. Add a miniature bottle of kirsch; refrigerate for a while before serving to allow the liqueur to permeate the fruit.

Don't buy too much fruit.

Variations:

Vary the flavor by using other fruit cordials, if you wish. The orange liqueurs are good and pear liqueur, cherry brandy, and cognac are all delicious.

WATERMELON AND VODKA

Buy:

**Watermelon, the best one
  you can find**

Vodka (1 bottle)

Cut a deep plug about two inches square in one end of the water-melon—a *deep* plug. Then slowly, slowly pour the vodka into the melon until it will not hold another drop. Carefully replace the plug and secure it with tape. Put it in the refrigerator for about 24 hours, turning it 4 or 5 times to make sure the vodka permeates the flesh of the melon.
  Serve as usual.

Variations: Instead of vodka, use light rum, brandy, champagne, or white wine.

SANGRÍA—ANDORRA STYLE

Buy:

**Red wine, respectable (1 or 2
  bottles)**

Oranges (1 or 2)
Peaches or plums (a few)
Lemons (1 or 2)

**Soda water (1 or 2 big
  bottles—equal in volume
  to the wine**

Check Cupboard for:

Sweet and dry vermouth

Brandy

Traditional sangría is closely related to a spritzer. It is meant to be a long, cool summer drink which you can put away in great quantities without bringing on collapse or alcoholic heat stroke.
  You must mix it to your own taste. Find a big pitcher or outsize thermos. Pour wine and soda water into it, a little more wine than soda, but vary it as you please. Add slices of orange and lemon with the rind, and slices of peaches and plums. Other fruits are good too, especially cherries, and apples. Then, for each bottle of wine, add a jigger of brandy and a jigger or two of vermouth. A dry sangría will have only dry ver-

mouth; a medium, a jigger of each; and a sweet, sweet vermouth only. Adjust the proportions to your taste. Serve it in tall, tall glasses with lots of ice.

MUSCOVY MOCHA

Buy:

Baker's chocolate, unsweetened (1 package)

Coffee, a strong after-dinner blend (1 pound)

Check Cupboard for:

Milk
Vanilla extract

Sugar

This one's for a cold day, but you can ice it as well.

Melt 1½ ounces of chocolate (it usually comes in 1-ounce squares) in ½ cup of water over a low heat, stirring until the chocolate melts and becomes smooth. Add a pinch of salt, 3 tablespoons of sugar, and 1 teaspoon of vanilla extract. Then add 1½ cups of milk slowly, stirring all the while. Take it off the heat, and beat it with an egg beater for a few minutes.

Then add 1½ cups of rich, strong coffee. Serve hot, with a dollop of whipped cream if you like, or chill it and serve it over ice cubes.

You may want to adjust the sugar to your taste, and you might always add a shot of dark rum or brandy.

LEMONADE

Buy:

Lemons (about 10)

Check Cupboard for:

Sugar (and gin)

Squeeze all the lemons. This should give you about ¾ cup lemon juice, or more.

With a paring knife peel the rind off two of the lemons (having squeezed them first). Put the lemon rind, 1 cup of sugar, and 1 cup of water in a saucepan and simmer it gently for about 10 minutes. Let it cool. Then add the lemon juice and about 4 cups of water, and set it aside to cool. Fresh mint leaves are a marvelous addition if you can find any. Grow your own. They grow like weeds in Staten Island.

MINTED ICED TEA

Buy:

Tea, not tea bags, a good	**A lemon**
Indian variety (½ pound)	**Oranges (2)**
Fresh mint, a handful	

Check Cupboard for:

Sugar	**Boiling water**

Squeeze the juice from the lemon and the oranges. Pare the lemon and orange rind into strips (removing the pulpy white inner side) and put them into a big bowl with 2 tablespoons of tea and 15 or 20 mint leaves. Pour over them 4 cups of boiling water, and let it all sit until the water has cooled. Then add the fruit juice and sugar to taste, and stir until the sugar dissolves. You'll probably need almost a cup of sugar. Chill and enjoy, whether at a picnic or at home.

On a really scorching day, iced tea is the most refreshing drink possible. As the heat diminishes and evening draws on, add a little light rum to it.

OTHER DELICIOUS THINGS TO DRINK

Fitz's Spritzer: Fresh grapefruit juice, an equal amount of soda water, a slice of fresh lime, a shot of vodka, and lots of ice.

Cold beer: Danish, German, Canadian, or English.

Lime and Lager: Half and half limeade and American beer. (Use frozen limeade.)

Spritzers: Red or white wine, soda water, and a slice of fresh fruit.

Kir: About the most beautiful and delicious pre-dinner drink in existence. Buy 1 bottle of a good white French Burgundy—one of the Pinot family, for instance. Buy a bottle of crème de cassis (black currant cordial). Chill the wine. Add 1 teaspoon of crème de cassis to the bottle. Superb.

Chapter 6

Rewarding Repasts for Backyard, Beach or Balcony

THE NAME OF THE GAME is charcoal—preferably in briquettes since these last longer than large chunks. They're also less likely to throw off cascades of sparks which can be disconcerting and even dangerous when you're bending over the beef or whatever else is being grilled.

But this is the only material that's common to all cookouts. What you put the charcoal in, what you place over it to be cooked, and how you prepare each meal is strictly a matter of taste—or lack of it.

Marty has one of those vast machines that looks like an early iron lung. Complete with a sliding hood, warming shelves, wheels, and a motorized rotisserie, it cost him well over 100 bills. The steaks he produces on it are like the charred upholstery of an Auburn. Burned to a cinder on the outside and virtually raw in the middle!

You'll never turn Becky on with this sort of fare. That's why you shouldn't be tempted to invest in a lot of worthless machinery just for the sake of looking organized. All you really need, in fact, is an inexpensive grill with enough top surface to accommodate a good-sized steak or whatever else you plan to prepare for your young friend.

This can range from one of those round units with a grill that can be raised and lowered to a Japanese hibachi. The latter is sold in several sizes and has the advantage of being built of iron for long service.

If your plans for Becky hinge on a country scene, you can even prepare a makeshift grill with a few rocks over which a simple gridiron can be placed. This is a cinch to set up along the seashore.

An excellent alternative to this approach is embodied in a Swaniebraai, the little-known African safari cooker which is made of three round sections of thin steel that fit on top of one another to form a bucket. This operates on an ingenious principle which replaces charcoal with six sheets of crumpled newspaper. When meat is placed over the burning paper, its fat drips into the fire, preventing the paper from burning up before the meat is cooked. Believe me, this can make you look a lot more experienced than Marty with his enormous grill, chef's hat, and apron with the imprint that proclaims an expertise he'll never attain.

A fireplace can also be easily pressed into service, although you'll be risking grease stains on the hearth, especially where porous bricks are concerned. But a little good management can prevent this. Just spread a length of cardboard over the hearth before you get started. Charcoal is the best thing to use here, but wood will suffice if you give it enough time to burn down to coals. Don't use pine, however. You won't like the taste its pitch imparts to whatever you're preparing. A gridiron supported by andiron legs will be the only other essential material. Good ventilation is also necessary when you use charcoal indoors since its fumes are just as toxic as those of carbon monoxide.

Much added life can be given to grills if you line them with aluminum foil, which not only radiates heat from coals but also helps prevent the bottom from rusting. Another good idea it to grease the rack before each use so that meat won't stick to it.

When lighting charcoal, do it right. In general, women don't understand this process at all. They usually spread out a flat mass of charcoal, drench it with starter fluid, and light it. The coals burn for about a minute and then go out. These steps are then repeated until about five gallons of fluid have been wasted. If by some unlikely chance a fire is finally started, the fluid will have impregnated the coals to such an extent that your meal will taste like it was basted with STP. This is a great way to wreck what looked like a romantic evening.

So start the coals correctly, by piling them in the shape of an inverted cone. Use a *little* starter fluid, giving it a few seconds to seep into the charcoal. Then light the cone—and relax. Electric starters are handy, too, but don't use them too far away from an outlet since a series of extension cords can lead to strain or even total collapse of their elements as they attempt to pull current.

It takes about 30 minutes for charcoal to reach the stage where each coal has a fine coating of pale gray ash with a bright red-orange glow underneath. Since it also takes about that much time to get Becky half boiled on gin and tonic, don't rush the fire or your little friend. She'll be into her second blast by the time you've fixed the salad. This is also a good time to think about serving a hot or cold soup, hot rolls or bread, or some other elementary accompaniment. But keep things simple since the main course is going to be filling. Get your equipment together, too, if you haven't done so already by this time. This should include:

> Long-handled tongs (these are vital)
> Long-handled fork and spoon
> Very sharp knife for carving
> Paint brush for applying sauce to meat
> Work gloves or an asbestos kitchen mitten
> Skewers for bits of meat or seafood
> Water pistol to slow down a fast fire

Incidentally, all meat should be removed from the refrigerator at least one hour before cooking. Where marinades are concerned, you'll need a lead time of up to 48 hours, with 24 hours the bare minimum if you expect good results. These oil-and-vinegar or wine concoctions need time to tenderize meat and add flavor to it. You can't expect this to happen just in the half hour you've got left while the fire is cranking up.

Keep an eye on your grill. A few more briquettes may have to be added after you knock down the cone and spread the coals out evenly. The heat held by charcoal is intense, and a fire you start at 7 o'clock will still be hot enough for cooking at 11. But by that time you should be lighting Becky's fire instead.

When buying meat, stick with either prime or choice cuts. Anything lower on the U. S. Department of Agriculture scale is scarcely worth eating. What it saves you in money will only cost you in prestige. Institutional-grade meat may be okay for thistle diggers on their first trip to Times Square, but most of it is pretty hard to choke down.

Good beef is evenly marbled with fat, and this is more likely to be found at a butcher shop than at a supermarket. Sure, you'll pay more, but you'll get more for your money, too. The same holds true for lamb, pork, and poultry. Your butcher knows all the signs of good quality. That's one of the things you're paying him for. If he's going to spend all of February in the Bahamas on your money, make certain he gives you the best he's got, and tell him if it ever fails to measure up.

Becky's a big chow hound. She got into the habit during her days on the farm in Kansas and has the topography to prove it. This means a 2-to 2½-pound steak is in order, and this should be an even cut, about one inch think. You don't want anything too thin that will burn.

The object is to sear the surfaces to lock in the juices in the middle. Use tongs to turn meat on a grill. Forks simply puncture the surface and allow juices to escape. To check "doneness," use a sharp knife to make a small cut in the center. Baste the meat frequently with barbecue sauce or the remains of your marinade.

If you're outdoors and the sun has gone down, you'll need some illumination to see what you're doing. Floodlights are acceptable, but their harsh glare will let the whole neighborhood see what you're up to, and Mrs. Feeny has already accused you twice of being nothing but a "common seducer." You didn't mind the last part, but the "common" really hurt. Coleman lanterns operated on white gas also throw brilliant light but manage to attract every mosquito from three counties. You might try a few "tiki" torches which are simply reservoirs of kerosene from which wide wicks protrude. Equipped with wooden stakes, they can be driven into the ground anywhere. Besides providing a pleasant light, they also attract—and immolate—insects.

In a pinch, a flashlight will do, but it can be dangerous. The last time Marty used one to check a steak, he couldn't tell if it was done since the batteries were weak. Marty, of course, was done before he ever got started.

Now that you know the basics of outdoor cooking, get on with some of the meals you can prepare—complete with vegetables! They're all easy to fix, really, and Becky looks so hungry. Poor dear. She doesn't know that the tiki torches will run dry about 10 minutes after she finishes her salad.

Before considering the recipes in this chapter, take a brief look at the following words of wisdom concerning cookouts and cookout fixings.

Hamburgers: Hamburger, sadly enough, is one of the least suitable meats for cooking over an open fire. Because of its very nature, the fat drips out of it very quickly, leaving you with dry crumbs which then fall through the grill and become cremated on the coals. If you like it *extra* rare, you can get away with it. But if you are cooking for others who like it simply rare, follow the recipe given in this chapter. It means fooling around with ice, but it does guarantee you juicy hamburgers.

Frankfurters: A frankfurter is basically a very inert object. Encased as it is in its skin, it neither lends flavor to its neighbors, nor acquires flavor from them. At current prices, hotdogs are no bargain, and lately the questions about their contents make one uneasy. Wouldn't you rather eat steak or lamb or sweet and spicy Italian sausages? Well, grill franks if you must, but baste them with a lot of barbecue sauce. How about the day she brings her kid brother along?

Lamb: Young lamb, up to eight months old, is best for outdoor cookery. Watch for meat pink in color with red, moist, porous bones. The fat should be firm and white and not too much of it. As lamb gets older, the meat becomes darker red and the bones whiter. All parts of lamb are suitable for cooking over coals.

Pork: Best-quality, prime pork is lean with streaks of firm white fat, and the meat is pinkish in color. Young pork has reddish bones. Leg cutlets, chops, spare ribs, and especially the tenderloin work extremely well over hot coals.

Veal: Veal is not really suitable for cookouts. The meat is naturally lean and needs slow and careful cooking and seasoning.

Poultry: All poultry and game birds lend themselves well to charcoal broiling. Choose young chickens, 1½ to 2 pounds in weight. Larger chickens need longer cooking. A good chicken has a rich yellow color and it is plump and fat on the inside. Good turkey, however, has a very white color with a slightly blueish tinge. Duckling, too, should have creamy white skin with a fat well-rounded breast.

Menus: One dish doesn't make a cookout, so make up a menu of accompanying dishes that you can prepare ahead of time. Have long cool drinks ready; sangría is a particularly happy choice. A salad is really essential with a cookout, and you can prepare it ahead of time and keep it crisp in the refrigerator, adding the dressing at the last minute before serving.

Charcoal-broiled food makes a pretty hearty meal, so let the accompanying dishes be fairly simple. An assortment of appetizers, a cold soup or a hot soup depending on the weather, a salad, rolls or French or Italian bread with garlic butter, dessert, and coffee, and your guest (or guests) will be purring with contentment.

Picnic cookouts: Hibachis and small grills travel easily to picnic sites. You can pack your meat in its marinade in a plastic box with an airtight lid. Don't forget the charcoal or the charcoal lighter or the matches or the tongs. And don't forget to be very careful about extinguishing the coals when you have finished. If you are at a beach, pour sand over them. And do remember not to leave any garbage or litter behind you.

Mini-hibachi: You can buy a very small hibachi for indoor use and, using skewers, cook delicious bits of meat on it—a new twist to the traditional fondue bourguignon. Use it for unusual appetizers, or for a main course. Just be careful to place it on a safe surface.

Three last words: Barbecue sauce is a sauce which you spread on meat while it is cooking or serve with the meat as a condiment.

A *marinade* is a liquid, based on oil and wine or vinegar in which the meat is put to soak for up to 48 hours. It is also used to baste the meat while cooking.

A *barbecue*. You may have noticed that I have used the word only to describe the sauce, not the meat, nor the process of cooking it. Traditionally, the word refers only to meat cooked in a sealed pit in the ground over a bed of dying coals, and to the event of cooking it in this fashion.

MY OWN EXCEPTIONALLY GOOD MARINADE FOR STEAK OR BEEF SHORT RIBS

Buy:
California country red (½ gallon)

Check Cupboard for:

Pure corn oil	**A lemon**
Soy sauce	**Garlic**
Worcestershire sauce	**Thyme**

The point is to cover the meat with the marinade, but the quantity of marinade needed depends on the size of the container you are using as well as the amount of meat you have. Ideally, you want a tight fit of meat in the bottom of a bowl with fairly straight sides to avoid waste. Cover the meat with ½ oil and ½ wine, and then add the other ingredients in the following proportions: 2 tablespoons Soy sauce, 2 teaspoons Worcestershire sauce, juice of 1 lemon, 1 crushed garlic clove, ½ teaspoon of thyme, salt and pepper to taste. Stir all these ingredients into the marinade, spooning it over the meat. Use tongs to turn the meat over from time to time. The longer the meat marinates the better. Thirty-six hours is not too long, but 4 to 6 hours will do.

Grill the meat over charcoal, and every time you pick it up with the tongs to turn it, dip it back in the marinade.

BARBECUE SAUCE I

Check Cupboard for:

Catsup	**Dry mustard**
Tabasco sauce	**Molasses**
Vinegar	**Thyme**
Worcestershire sauce	**Oregano**

Mix together all the ingredients as follows (use a blender if you have one): ¼ cup catsup; 1 teaspoon Tabasco; 2 tablespoons Worcestershire sauce; ¼ cup wine vinegar; 2 teaspoons dry mustard; ¼ cup molasses; generous pinches of thyme and oregano; salt and pepper to taste. Makes about 1 cup of sauce.

If you like the flavor of barbecue sauce and if your meat does not require the tenderizing that a marinade produces, brush it on pieces of meat before cooking, or serve it with the meat. It will improve the lowly frankfurter.

BARBECUE SAUCE II

Check Cupboard for:

Onion	**Catsup**
Coffee or red wine	**Worcestershire sauce**
Brown sugar	**Vinegar**
Dry mustard	

Mix everything in a saucepan as follows: ½ onion, finely chopped; ½ cup very strong coffee or red wine; ½ cup brown sugar; 2 teaspoons dry mustard; 4 ounces of catsup; 1 tablespoon of Worcestershire sauce; 1½ tablespoons of white or wine vinegar; salt and pepper to taste.

Simmer the mixture, stirring from time to time, over a moderate heat for about a half hour. Let it cool and store it in the refrigerator against the day you need it. Should provide about two cups of sauce.

Use as described in the recipe for Barbecue Sauce I.

Variations: Add garlic, about 1 clove, crushed.
Substitute ½ cup orange juice for the coffee for a fruity flavor that is particularly good with chicken.

SIMPLE CHARCOAL-BROILED STEAK

Buy:

**Sirloin, porterhouse, or T-
bone steak. (For amount,
consult p. 106.)**

Check Cupboard for:

Garlic   **Butter**

Trim excess fat from the edge of the steak, and cut gashes around the edges so that it won't curl up. Cut a clove of garlic and rub the meat on both sides with the cut side of garlic.

Broil close to white-hot coals for about three minutes (let it flame), then turn the steak over and repeat the process. Then raise the grill to about 6 inches from the coals, and continue to cook until it suits your preference—rare, medium, or done. To test, cut a very small slice into the meat near the bone.

When done, remove steak to a carving board, put two tablespoons of butter under it, season with salt and pepper, and carve and serve.

Variation: BRANDY STEAK: Omit garlic. Place steak in a flat pan and pour over it four or five tablespoons of brandy. Let it soak in the brandy for ten minutes, then turn it over and repeat for the other side.

Note: Steak 1 inch thick should cook about 10 minutes for rare, 13 for medium. Steak two inches thick requires about 30 minutes cooking for rare, 40 for medium. This, however, is only a rough guide, because cooking time varies with the heat of the charcoal, the type of grill, the temperature of the meat when you start.

CHARCOAL-BROILED STEAK,
SPICY MARINADE

Buy:

**Steak, boneless, top round,
club, or flank, (1½ pounds)**

Check Cupboard for:

Onion	**Soy sauce**
Garlic	**Mustard, dry**
Bourbon	**Brown sugar**

Make the marinade as follows: ½ cup Soy sauce, ¼ cup bourbon, 1 clove garlic finely chopped, ½ onion finely chopped, ½ teaspoon brown sugar, ½ teaspoon mustard powder, ½ teaspoon salt, fresh black pepper.

Marinate the steak for several hours, and grill over charcoal.

JAPANESE BROILED BEEF STEAK

Buy:

Very small steaks (4), or not quite so small (2) (ask your butcher for sirloin end or tenderloin tips, ¾ inch thick)	**Sherry, dry (1 bottle)**

Check Cupboard for:

Soy sauce	**Ginger**
Onion	**Brown sugar**
Garlic	

Mix together: ½ cup Soy sauce; ½ cup sherry; 1 very small onion grated or chopped very fine; 1 clove garlic, crushed; 1 tablespoon brown sugar; ¼ teaspoon powdered ginger; ¼ teaspoon pepper; salt to taste

Marinate the steaks in this sauce for a couple of hours. Broil steaks over coals, removing them and dipping them in the sauce *frequently*.

CHARCOAL-BROILED BEEF SHORT RIBS

Buy:

Beef short ribs (2 pounds)

Marinate the ribs in My Marinade (p. 109) or one of your own choosing, overnight in refrigerator. Remove a couple of hours before cooking. Grill over medium-hot coals for about 25 minutes, turning frequently with tongs.

JUICY HAMBURGERS

Buy:

Ground round steak (1 pound)

Red wine, dry (1 bottle)

Make:

One of the barbecue sauces

Lots of extra ice cubes in your refrigerator

Put half of the ice you can spare into a deep bowl, put the pound of ground steak on top of it in one chunk, and cover with the rest of the ice. Let it chill for about an hour. This process keeps the ground steak juicy while cooking. Then squeeze as much water out of the steak as you can using your hands alone. Add ⅓ cup red wine to the meat and work it in thoroughly. Again with your hands, form the meat into four patties about ¾ to 1 inch thick. Butter each side with left-over bacon fat, or cover with a little cooking oil, and grill over coals until done to your taste. (Three minutes each side for rare; five for medium.)

If you want to use a barbecue sauce, dip the patties into it once or twice on each side before grilling.

CHARCOAL-BROILED LAMB CHOPS

Buy:

Lamb chops, double-loin, thick (2), or thin (4)
Limes, fresh, (3 or 4)

Bacon
Mint, fresh if possible; if not, dry leaves

Check Cupboard for:

Corn oil
Tarragon

Paprika

Wipe chops with paper towelling; trim off excess fat.

Mix together: ¼ cup lime juice, ¼ cup oil, 1 tablespoon chopped fresh mint or dry leaves, 1 teaspoon tarragon, ½ teaspoon paprika, ¼ teaspoon salt, freshly ground black pepper. Pour this mixture over the chops and let them soak for 15 minutes or until you are ready to start cooking.

Broil the chops over hot coals, turning 3 or 4 times and basting with the sauce. After about 10 minutes, arrange some slices of bacon on the grill as well, and cook for another 5 to 10 minutes or until chops are done.

SHASHLIK

Buy:
Lamb, boned (1 pound)

Check Cupboard for:

Olive oil

Wine vinegar

Garlic

Rosemary

Coriander, ground

You need a pair of skewers for this recipe.

Cut the lamb into 1½-inch cubes, and place in a bowl.

Cover with ½ cup olive oil, ½ cup wine vinegar, 1 clove garlic, crushed, ½ teaspoon rosemary (crush it between your fingers), ½ teaspoon coriander, salt and pepper to taste.

Leave in refrigerator overnight, covered.

When ready to cook, arrange the meat on the two skewers, and broil over hot coals, turning frequently and basting with the remaining sauce.

SHISH KEBAB

Buy:

Lamb, lean (1 pound)

Tomatoes, cherry or plum variety (4)

Onions, small (2)

A sweet pepper, red or green

Mushrooms, a small box or can

Sauterne, California (1 bottle)

Check Cupboard for:

Lemons   **Garlic**
Corn oil or olive oil

You will need skewers for this one.

Cut lamb into 1½-inch squares.

Mix together: ½ cup Sauterne, ¾ cup oil, 1 tablespoon lemon juice, 1 clove crushed garlic, a little salt and pepper. Pour over lamb and leave overnight in refrigerator.

Before cooking, cut onions in half, cut pepper into 1-inch squares. Arrange meat, onion, tomatoes, peppers, and mushrooms on skewers. Broil over hot coals, turning frequently and basting with the remaining sauce, for about 15 minutes.

CHARCOAL-BROILED PORK CHOPS

Buy:

**Pork chops, loin (2 to 4,
    depending on their size and
    your appetite)—have the
    butcher trim off excess fat
    and slash the edges**

Either marinate them overnight in one of the marinades given, or use one of the barbecue sauces to baste them while cooking.

Rub the fat edges with lemon juice to prevent smoking.

Grill them over medium-hot coals at a distance of about 6 inches. Cook them slowly for about 20 minutes, turning them occasionally. Then cook them for another 10 minutes, basting them frequently with barbecue sauce or marinade.

CHARCOAL-BROILED PORK SPARE RIBS

Buy:

Pork spare ribs (2 pounds)

Check Cupboard for:

Corn oil
Worcestershire sauce
Soy sauce

Lemons
Garlic powder
Thyme

Place the ribs flat in a flat pan and sprinkle first one side and then the other with the above ingredients (lemon juice, that is, not whole lemons!) plus salt and freshly ground black pepper.

Remember that pork must be thoroughly cooked for safety's sake. The meat must not be pink anywhere. The cooking time will depend partly on what kind of a grill you are using, and whether or not the grill itself can be raised and lowered over the coals.

Cook the ribs over an intense heat, turning them frequently, for about 40 minutes. If they seem to be charring rather than cooking, raise the grill.

BROILED HAM STEAKS

Buy:

Ham steak, uncooked, smoked
(1 large or 2 small)

Apple cider

Check Cupboard for:

Cloves

Brown sugar

Trim excess fat from steak and gash the edges to prevent curling. Boil it for 5 minutes.

Mix together: ½ cup cider, 1 tablespoon brown sugar, 1 teaspoon dry mustard, 3 whole cloves, crushed. Pour over the ham and let stand for half an hour.

Broil ham over medium coals, basting frequently with remaining sauce, until brown on both sides—about 25 minutes.

CHICKEN CARPINELLO

Buy:

Chicken breasts, whole (2)   **White wine, dry (1 bottle)**
Italian dressing (1 bottle)

Remove the skin from the chicken breasts and discard it. Put the chicken breasts in a bowl. Cover them with a mixture of Italian dressing and white wine in the proportion 2 parts dressing to 1 part wine. Marinate for no less than 24 hours.

Grill over charcoal. Salt to taste after cooking.

WINE AND SPICE CHARCOAL CHICKEN

Buy:

A chicken cut in pieces   **California burgundy (1**
California Sauterne (1 bottle)   **bottle)**

Check Cupboard for:

Soy sauce   **Ginger**
Olive oil   **Rosemary**
Worcestershire sauce   **Paprika**
Garlic   **Cayenne pepper**
Dry mustard   **Tarragon**

Remove the skin from the chicken.

Find a large bowl, big enough to hold the pieces of chicken and the marinade. Mix directly in the bowl as follows: 3 ounces Sauterne, 1 ounce Burgundy, 1 tablespoon Soy sauce, 2 tablespoons Worcestershire sauce, 1 crushed garlic clove, ½ teaspoon each of dry mustard, ginger, rosemary, paprika, black pepper, 1½ teaspoons salt, pinch of cayenne, 1 teaspoon tarragon.

Stir and mix thoroughly and put the chicken into the marinade overnight (or for a minimum of four hours). Cook over charcoal, turning frequently, for about ½ hour, and baste it with the remaining marinade.

CHARCOAL-BROILED SWORDFISH STEAKS

Buy:

**Swordfish steaks (1 should
serve two people)**

Check Cupboard for:

An onion, small   **Dry mustard**
Lemons   **Dill**
Butter

Mix together: 1 small onion, chopped very fine, ¼ cup lemon juice, ¼ cup of water, ¼ teaspoon dry mustard, 2 tablespoons butter, ¼ teaspoon dill. Salt and pepper to taste. Warm sufficiently to melt butter.

Brush this mixture over the steaks, and broil them over medium coals until they are golden brown on both sides, turning and basting frequently. Serve with the remains of the sauce, which you have kept hot. Cooking time for inch-thick steaks: approximately 8 minutes.

Variations: Try salmon, halibut, or pompano (1 steak per person).

CHARCOAL-BROILED LOBSTER

Buy:

**Lobsters, small (2) (ask the
man at the fish counter to
cut them in half, prepare
them, and crack the
claws)**

Check Cupboard for:

Paprika   **Lemons**
Butter

Dribble melted butter over the flesh side of each lobster half, and sprinkle with salt and pepper.

Broil them over medium coals, flesh side up, for about 15 minutes, or until flesh is tender.

Serve with more melted butter, to which a little lemon juice has been added.

BAKED POTATOES IN FOIL

Buy:

Potatoes, large Idahos for
baking (1 per person)

Choice of garnishes

Check Cupboard for:

Aluminum foil

Wash and butter the potatoes. Wrap them individually in foil and lay them directly on the hot coals. Roast them for 20 to 30 minutes on each side, depending on size of potato. Test them with a fork without removing the foil.

When ready, remove them from the foil and cut a long slice along the top, or two slices criss-cross. Using gloves, push the ends together gently to fluff up the potato. Add butter, salt and pepper, and your choice of the following: sour cream, chopped chives, bits of bacon, grated cheese, parsley, paprika.

POTATOES AND ONIONS
WITH BARBECUE SAUCE

Buy:

Potatoes, medium-sized (2)

Onions, medium-sized (1)

Make:

A barbecue sauce

Check Cupboard for:
Aluminum foil

Wash the potatoes and cut them in four quarters. Peel the onion and cut it in quarters. Cut two pieces of foil and oil one side. Put 4 potato quarters and 2 onion quarters on each piece of foil and top them with a tablespoon of barbecue sauce. Fold up the foil tightly, with a double fold at each end. Cook directly on hot coals for 15 minutes a side, or until done.

ROASTED CORN ON A HIBACHI

Buy:
**Corn, fresh and sweet (at
   least two ears per person)**

Check Cupboard for:
Extra butter   **Aluminum foil**

Husk the corn. Spread each ear with butter (or garlic butter), wrap each ear in aluminum foil (double thickness), and twist each end to seal it completely.

Roast the corn over the coals of your hibachi (or other charcoal grill) for about 20 to 25 minutes, turning several times so that the ears cook evenly. They should be quite close to the coals.

ROASTED SWEET PEPPERS

Buy:
**Peppers, sweet red and/or
   green (2)**

Wash the peppers and cut them in half, removing the seeds and white material. Contrive to flatten them as much as possible, cutting them in quarters if necessary. Lay them on the grill a few inches from the hot coals. Broil them on both sides until the skin side is brown and the other side tender. Remove them to a plate (peel off the skin if you wish) and sprinkle them with a little salt, oil, and vinegar.

A delicious accompaniment to steaks and chops.

PROVENÇALE TOMATOES IN FOIL

Buy:

Tomatoes, medium-sized (3 or more)

Bread crumbs (1 box)

Check Cupboard for:

Parsley
Garlic
Olive oil

Basil
Aluminum foil
Wine vinegar

Wash the tomatoes and cut them in half horizontally. Sprinkle a good layer of bread crumbs on top, and then drip olive oil and wine vinegar onto them. Add a little crushed garlic, chopped parsley, basil, pepper, and salt to each. Wrap them in oiled foil, 2 halves per parcel, sealing the foil carefully. Place directly on the coals for 5 minutes on each side.

Other vegetables in foil:

Zucchini, peas, mushrooms, broccoli, and other vegetables can also be cooked in foil directly on the coals. They usually require no more than 20 minutes to cook, 10 minutes to a side. Make up individual packages, always including oil or butter and seasonings. Try different combinations of garlic, herbs, parsley, lemon juice. Cook peas and mushrooms together, if you like. If you cook zucchini, trim off the ends and slice it. Trim broccoli into individual servings—always discarding 2–3 inches from the bottom of the stalks—and add a little Soy sauce and ginger to the other seasonings for a Chinese effect.

Sweet potatoes and yams are slow to cook. Boil them in water with the skins on for half an hour, and then wrap them in foil with butter and brown sugar and finish them on the coals. Poke them with a fork to see if they are done.

Chapter 7
Light Suppers for Those Heavy Dates

JUST FOR THE hell of it, let's assume that you've spent a couple of weeks enticing Maureen into coming over to your house to see your collection of Aztec artifacts. You both know this is nonsense. You know it because you don't have any Aztec artifacts, and she knows it because of that look you keep slipping her. However, women are funny. Like cats, they're consumed by curiosity.

It's obvious that Maureen is not only curious but also is attracted to you—even if you do insist on wearing that patch on your jean jacket that says: "Hire the morally handicapped." You realize she likes you by the way she studies you when she thinks you're not studying her. And anyway, she's agreed to drop by at seven on Tuesday for a quick look at your layout.

"I won't be able to stay long," she explains in that husky voice that turns you on. "A cup of soup or a sandwich will be fine. Don't go to any trouble," she adds, "and take your hand off my knee."

How lucky can one guy get? Here's a quail who's already mapped out a modest menu that any moron can fulfill. And in the process, you won't have to be a prisoner to your kitchen appliances. So the decks can be cleared for action long before she even arrives.

Don't blow the whole thing by being a cheapskate. Any derelict can pry open a can of Campbell's or slap a slice of provolone between two pieces of rye bread. On the other hand, you don't want to spend a day's pay and an evening of preparation on an elaborate bouillabaisse, only to learn that Maureen is allergic to seafood. Compromise. Begin with a canned or dried preparation and embellish it in some of the ways outlined in this chapter.

Soups for Supper

One of the best ways to warm up a woman is with soup—good soup. You can transform canned soup into good soup by using milk or bouillon where the instructions call for water. Or if you're feeling creative, try mixing two soups to create a new one. A few of these hybrids are suggested on page 43, but don't let these limit you. If you enjoy two soups separately, it's safe to assume that they'll taste good in combination. A little experimentation will soon determine this, and anything that bombs can be deep-sixed.

Prepackaged soups are fine, especially if you're in a hurry, but if you really want to make an impression on Maureen, try your hand at a little homemade soup. Don't cringe—you don't have to start with beef bones and cold water.

Suppose, for instance, that you have a lot of leftover vegetables. Buy a package of fresh spinach, cook it, and eat most of it, but save some of it plus the water you cooked it in for soup. Add a chicken bouillon cube and the appropriate amount of water. Add your leftover vegetables. Heat it all up and let it simmer a little. Add a few teaspoons of instant mashed potato for thickening, and lo and behold, you have a genuine French vegetable potage. Basically, that's how you make soup—use any leftovers, gravy and vegetable water, thin it or thicken it, and season it to taste. Delicious—and what a great way to clean out the refrigerator!

Of course, if you'd rather not try your own thing with soups, then by all means try one of mine. The next few recipes will show you how to make soups that are simple, satisfying, and maybe even seductive.

STONEY'S OYSTER STEW

Buy:

Oysters, fresh (1 pint)   **Butter**
Milk (1½ quarts)

Check Cupboard for:
Paprika

Melt 3 tablespoons of butter in a saucepan, but do not let it brown. Pour the oysters and their juice into the melted butter and watch them very closely. Let them cook until the oysters appear to curl a little around the edges—but no more (who wants a tough oyster?). Then pour in 4 or 5 cups of milk, adding a little salt and pepper to taste and a dash of paprika. Let the stew heat thoroughly, but not quite to a boil. When bubbles appear around the edge, your oysters are stewed.

LEEK AND POTATO SOUP
and
VICHYSSOISE

Buy:

Leeks, large (2) (hard to find—try a fruit and vegetable market)	**An onion, medium-sized** **Potatoes, medium-sized (2)**

Check Cupboard for:

Chicken bouillon cubes	**Butter**

Leeks pick up a lot of sand and mud as they grow, so they have to be cleaned and washed. So trim off half the green end and the roots, slit the whole leeks lengthwise twice, and take them apart under cold running water, removing the silt as you go. Then cut them in cubes. Cook them in a large saucepan with 3 tablespoons of butter for about five minutes, stirring them frequently. Do not let them burn or get brown. Meanwhile, peel and cut the potatoes into cubes, and boil 3 cups of water. Add the potatoes, 3 chicken bouillon cubes, and three cups of water to the leeks. Cook very gently, just under the boiling point, for about 15 minutes until the potatoes are cooked, but not falling apart. Season to taste with salt and pepper.

This is a delicious hot soup, and can be transformed into an even more delicious cold soup. *If* a) you have a blender or b) are patient enough to do it the old-fashioned way and force it all through a sieve with the back of a wooden spoon.

Vichyssoise:

Let us say that you have managed to purée the soup. If you have eaten half of it as hot leek and potato soup, add half a cup of heavy cream to the puréed remains; if not, add a whole cup. Stir well. Add a drop or two of Tabasco and/or Worcestershire sauce. Stir well again. Set it in the refrigerator to chill thoroughly. Serve with chopped *chives* on top. Some restaurants set the bowl of chilled vichyssoise on a larger bowl of crushed ice—marvellous. Add a bottle of good-quality Rhine wine on the side.

SPLIT PEA SOUP

Buy:

Split peas, yellow, dried (1 box)
An onion, large

Croutons (1 package)
Carrots

Check Cupboard for:

Chicken bouillon cubes
Bay leaf

Fresh garlic
Cloves

Soak 1 cup of peas overnight in a bowl of unsalted water. Make 6 cups of chicken bouillon (with cubes and boiling water). It's best to add a little extra water, because some will boil away as you make the soup. Wash the peas and add them to the bouillon (now officially called stock). Grate or chop finely 1 large carrot and add it to the stock. Peel the onion and stick 2 cloves into it and put it whole into the stock (now officially called soup). Add 1 bay leaf, and 2 cloves of crushed garlic. Bring the soup to a boil, skim off any scum with a spoon (here is where a large slotted kitchen spoon is useful), and allow the soup to simmer until the peas are well cooked. Remove bay leaf and onion. Serve with croutons on top.

Variations:

If you had a nice meaty ham bone, you could use that plus the 6 cups of water, and forget the chicken bouillon. It would taste much better. Any leftover bits of ham will add flavor to it; so will pieces of hot knackwurst or frankfurter.

CORN CHOWDER

Buy:

**Corn kernels, canned, OR
  canned cream-style corn
  OR fresh corn, enough for
  1½ cups
Potatoes, medium-sized (2)**

**Bacon, or ¼ pound salt pork
An onion, medium-sized
Cream, light (1 pint), OR
  evaporated milk (1 full
  tin)**

Check Cupboard for:

Thyme

Paprika

Here's a hearty soup that's quick and easy to put together.

Peel and dice the potatoes and heat them in boiling salted water until just cooked but still firm. Use just enough water to cover the potatoes. When they are cooked, drain them, but save the water and let it cook down a little, i.e., reduce the quantity by letting it boil gently.

Meanwhile, cut three or four slices of bacon or half the salt pork into small pieces and fry them until they turn light golden. Fry the chopped onion with them.

Now you should have a bowl with cooked potatoes in it, a saucepan with the potato water in it, and a frying pan with onion and bacon.

Put all of it into the potato water. Bring it all to a boil, and then turn the heat down and simmer the soup for about 5 minutes. Then slowly add 2 cups of light cream or evaporated milk and the corn with whatever juice it has in its can. Do not let the soup boil again. Add the thyme (a pinch) just before serving, and then add a dash of paprika to each bowl.

This recipe will give you each two helpings, or some leftover chowder for the next day.

Sing the Praises of Sandwiches!

Yes, Maureen, it was a *man* who invented this remarkable gimmick, and if you think *I'm* a male chauvinist you should have caught this act. John Montague by name, he combined an aptitude for political chicanery with an addiction to gambling. As the 4th Earl of Sandwich, he gave his name to something he could eat without leaving the gaming table. It turned out to be one of his few good deeds.

Sandwich fillings can range from those peanut butter and jelly concoctions you used to chomp on as a child to almost anything, and the only limitations on what you can produce will be imposed by your own imagination.

The same may be said for bread. Where once we were limited to cakey whites, whole wheats, ryes, and pumpernickels, recent years have seen the development of a regular rash of additional loaves, such as oatmeal, sprouted-grain and multi-grain plus flat, round, Greek, and Arab breads that you can partially split open and fill like pockets. Even the white breads have blossomed forth with Italian and French forms among the favorites to be found almost everywhere. Although supermarkets stock a number of different breads, your best bet is always a local bakery where freshness is a feature that simply can't be matched by mass production followed by wide distribution.

I couldn't begin to list here the hundreds and thousands of different sandwiches you can make. However, I will recommend a couple I've found particularly good, and tell you to try as many combinations of bread and meat and vegetables, cooked and raw, and cheeses and spreads and patés and jams and jellies and marmalades and fruits as you can.

SANDWICH SUGGESTIONS

Meat and Fowl:

Chicken, turkey, duck, or goose, chopped fine and mixed with mayonnaise, celery, or bits of bacon, or both

Chicken or turkey, with leftovers, i.e. stuffing and cranberry jelly

Duck with grated orange peel

Goose with red currant jelly

Roast beef, mustard, and/or hot horseradish, pickle, and/or mustard

Salami, relish, and mustard on rye

Lamb, lettuce, and mint jelly

Liverwurst, tomato, lettuce, pickle, and/or mustard

Ham and chutney

Ham, chicken, tomato, sliced hard-cooked egg, lettuce

Ham (Prosciutto), sliced black olives, tomato

Ham (Polish), Swiss cheese, French mustard

Fish & Seafood:

Smoked clams, cucumber, and mayonnaise

Tuna, mixed with mayonnaise, chopped green pepper and green onion, thyme, dash of Worcestershire, squeeze of lemon, salt and pepper

Crab, mayonnaise, minced onion, paprika

Lobster chopped fine, mixed with mashed yolk of hard-cooked eggs, a little heavy cream, seasoned with salt, pepper, and a dash of cayenne

Sardines, cucumber, tomato, sliced hard-cooked egg, lettuce

Vegetables:

Sliced tomato, mayonnaise, basil, salt and pepper, on brown bread

Sliced cucumber, mayonnaise, salt and pepper, on Dutch Dill bread (or use real dill on light rye)

Hearts of palm, sliced; sliced tomato, water cress or lettuce, and green onion

Sliced raw mushroom, sliced raw zucchini or cucumber, tomato, green onion

Avocado, mashed, with crumbled bacon, lemon juice, salt and pepper

Cheese:

Cream cheese and—chopped chicken and/or ham; chopped olives; chopped green peppers; water cress; shrimp, whole or mashed; anchovy paste

Cheddar cheese, sliced tomato, and bacon

Cheddar cheese and chutney

Cheddar cheese and fresh green onions

Feta cheese, black olives, sliced tomatoes, lettuce

Swiss cheese, many slices sliced very thin, French mustard, lettuce

Eggs:

Chopped egg: chopped hard-cooked eggs, mixed with mayonnaise, minced onion, capers, dash lemon juice and Worcestershire sauce, basil, paprika

Fruit:

Sliced fresh strawberries, lightly sugared, and a little sour cream on crusty French bread

And for truly creative, original, and imaginative sandwiches, remember the leftovers in your refrigerator

Note: Remember to season and garnish with salt, freshly ground black pepper, and various combinations of: paprika, mayonnaise, chopped parsley, dill, basil, thyme, marjoram, fresh lemon juice, sliced pickles (sweet, sour or dill), mustard, relishes, piccalilli, Worcestershire, Soy sauce, garlic, and others that will occur to you.

OPEN-FACE GRILLED CHEDDAR SANDWICH

Buy:

Cheddar cheese, sharp, white (a chunk of best Canadian from a good cheese shop will delight you both)

Rye bread (your choice, but I suggest an unsliced loaf of the real thing from a baker)

For this sandwich you need to use the grill and not the toaster. Put, say, 4 slices of rye bread under the grill and let them toast nicely on one side. Then take them out and butter the *other, untoasted* side. On top of the butter put slices of cheese (but not right to the edge because it will overflow when it melts), and a little freshly ground black pepper. A little chopped green onion is good, too. Then put the sandwich back under the grill until the cheese melts and is bubbling. Cold beer goes nicely with this.

PAPA'S PEANUT BUTTER SANDWICH

Buy:

Light rye bread or best whole wheat (large slices preferable)
Peanut butter

An onion (a big, sweet, purple, Bermuda)
Lettuce

Butter your bread, and lay a good thick layer of peanut butter on it. Then a great round of splendid Bermuda onion, thick or thin as you please. Lay some lettuce on top, and then close it up with the top slice—then pour the beer (this one is worth an imported beer).

Papa, by the way, is Ernest Hemingway.

Omelets

Properly prepared, an omelet is guaranteed to impress anyone—particularly those chicks who think that only a woman has what it takes to create one. Needless to say, this is absurd but it explains why this subject has been shrouded with such a heavy mystique.

You will need an omelet pan, a frying pan of cast iron or heavy aluminum which you use *only* for omelets. If you like omelets, I suggest you buy a pan with a bottom diameter of about 7 inches and with sloping sides and a long handle.

The pan must be treated before you use it. There *is* a reason. One of the secrets to omelet-making is that the bottom of the pan must be absolutely smooth and stick-free, so that the eggs can slip about smoothly and easily. So first scour your new pan with steel wool and cleaning powder. Rinse and dry it. Then pour a little cooking oil into it and see that it covers all surfaces. Let it stand overnight. Just before you are ready to use it, wipe the excess oil off carefully with paper towels. Then sprinkle a teaspoon of salt into the pan, heat it, rub it firmly with another paper towel, and shake any remaining salt out. Now your pan is ready to use. If, after using it for awhile, you find that the eggs are beginning to stick, treat it with salt again as just described. Never wash the pan, just clean it out with paper towels. If you should have some sort of disaster and *have* to wash it, start all over again at the beginning of the treatment with scouring powder and steel wool.

Omelets take seconds to make, so you have to know what you are going to do before you begin. You can't stop and look at the directions halfway through. An omelet consists of a few eggs with a little salt and pepper, slightly beaten and cooked very quickly in melted butter. That's all. Just eggs and butter, really.

You can fill an omelet with all sorts of things, but you must have the filling prepared and ready to slip into the omelet at just the right moment. You can make as many different omelets as there are fillings, but the fundamental technique is the same for all of them.

BASIC OMELET

Buy:

Eggs (2 or 3 for each omelet)

Check Cupboard for:

Butter

Omelets are best made individually, one omelet per person, rather than in larger sizes.

Break two eggs into a bowl, add a little salt and pepper, and beat them with a fork (not an egg beater) until they are just mixed. Put one generous tablespoon of butter into your omelet pan and heat it over a high heat, tilting the pan in all directions so that the butter covers the sides as well. As the butter melts, it will foam, and the foam will disappear. *At this precise moment,* just before the butter starts to change color, you must slip the slightly beaten eggs into the pan. They will spread out and sizzle. Give the pan a brisk shake, away from you and then back, to loosen the eggs from the pan bottom. Continue shaking the pan, holding it at an angle of about 25° from the heat, so that the eggs slip over each other and curl into the far side of the pan.

As the eggs begin to thicken, add the filling if you are using one. If not, let the eggs thicken as you continue to shake, and increase the angle of the pan to 45° so that the omelet takes its shape in the far side of the pan and folds over. Then take a plate in your left hand and make a "V" shape of plate and pan. Turn and fold the omelet onto the plate by inverting the pan over it. Butter the top of the omelet and serve immediately. Total cooking time should not be more than a minute.

Fillings:

You can fill your omelet with any of the following: grated cheese; ham, chopped in small pieces; fresh tomato, chopped or sauteed; tomato sauce, as for spaghetti; asparagus tips; bits of bacon; cooked spinach with butter; seafood in a white or Béchamel sauce, prepared beforehand; chopped parsley and chopped fresh green onion plus another green herb such as basil or chervil; combinations such as cheese and onion, cheese and ham, these two with tomatoes or with green herbs.

If Maureen has a sweet tooth, vary the recipe by omitting the pepper and adding a tablespoon of sugar. Cook as above, and fill with one of these: jam, jelly, or marmalade; sliced strawberries and a little sour cream; bananas, sliced and sautéd in butter and brown sugar; stewed apples, spiced with brown sugar and butter (When this one's cooked, you can flame it with a little Calvados.)

SPANISH OMELET

Check Cupboard for:

Tomato purée, (1 small can)	**Garlic**
Oil, olive if possible	**Oregano or basil**
An onion, small	**Bay leaf**
Tomatoes, fresh, (1 medium, 2 small, or several cherry tomatoes)	**Sugar**
	Salt and pepper

This is one of the most popular of all omelets. To make it, just whip up this simple sauce, and then either add the sauce just before folding or pour it over the completely cooked omelet.

Mince the onion and cook it gently in a couple of tablespoons of olive oil. Chop up the tomatoes and add them to the oil and onions. Add a tablespoon of tomato purée. Add a crushed garlic clove, a bay leaf, a pinch of oregano or basil, ¼ teaspoon of sugar, and salt and pepper to taste. Stir and mix over a low heat until the onions are cooked. Cease cooking, but keep the sauce warm until ready to add it to the omelet.

HOT EGGS

Buy:

Eggs (4)	**Bacon**
Bottle of chili sauce (if it is mild instead of hot, buy a bottle of Tabasco too)	

Find an oven-proof dish that will accommodate 4 eggs in a neighborly fashion, i.e., not spread thin over acres of glass. Break the eggs into it. On top of each egg put 1 tablespoon of chili sauce (doctored with a drop or two of Tabasco if necessary) and also half a strip of bacon. Bake in the oven at 400° until the eggs are set (not hard) and the bacon is crisp.

GERMAN EGGS

Buy:

Bacon
Eggs

An onion, small
Milk

Fry 3 slices of bacon slowly in a cold frying pan.

Drain the bacon on folds of paper towel, and set aside. Dice half of the onion (unless you are both very fond of onion) and fry it slowly with just a little of the bacon fat until it is tender but not dark brown or scorched. Drain the onion on the paper towel too. If there is excess fat in the pan, get rid of it. Then add 4 eggs which you have beaten up as for scrambling, with a couple of tablespoons of milk and some salt and pepper. Add the onion to the eggs and the bacon, crumbled up. Cook as you would scrambled eggs.

Miscellaneous

So, you're out of eggs and sick of soup and sandwiches. In that case, consider the following random recipes for your hungry (and thirsty) honey.

WHOLE TOMATO STUFFED WITH CRAB, LOBSTER, OR CHICKEN

Buy:

Beefsteak tomatoes (2)
Crab or lobster, canned (two
  6½- or 7-ounce cans) or
Crab or lobster or chicken,
  fresh, cooked (1 cup)

Celery, pascal (1 small
  bunch)
Lettuce

Check Cupboard for:

Mayonnaise

You've heard of sweets for the sweet—how about tomatoes for the tomato? Here's the perfect light supper for a warm summer evening.

Wash the tomatoes and cut a hole in the stem end big enough to hold the amount of crabmeat salad you want to stuff it with. If the crabmeat is tinned, run it quickly under the cold water tap to freshen it. Crumble 1 cup of it into small pieces in a bowl and add enough mayonnaise to give it the right consistency. Wash and trim the celery and chop finely enough to fill ½ cup. Mix it with the crab and mayonnaise, adding more mayonnaise if necessary. Season with salt and pepper. Then add for further seasoning your choice of: paprika, chopped green onion, dill, tarragon, lemon juice, curry powder.

Stuff the tomatoes with the mixture, and serve on a bed of lettuce leaves.

WELSH RAREBIT

Buy:

Cheddar cheese (½ pound)　　　　　**Eggs**
Beer or ale

Check Cupboard for:

Colman's dry mustard　　　　　**Butter**
Cayenne pepper

Welsh rarebit takes only a few minutes to prepare, but you cannot walk away and leave it. You have to stand over it and stir it constantly; I promise you, however, that it really is quick.

Cut the cheese into small pieces and put it in a saucepan with 1 tablespoon of butter, ½ teaspoon of dry mustard, ¼ teaspoon salt. Have ⅓ of a cup of beer or ale ready beside the stove. Have 1 egg slightly beaten with a fork in a little bowl ready beside the stove. Then turn on the burner to a low fire and put the saucepan over it, stirring until the cheese melts. Pour the beer in slowly, stirring all the while. When the melted cheese and beer are nicely mixed, remove the pan from the stove and, still stirring constantly, mix in the beaten egg.

Serve immediately, poured over hot toast or broiled tomato slices—and drink the rest of the beer.

HOT BUTTERED RUM

Buy:

Dark rum (the really dark Jamaican kind), 80 proof

Butter
Honey

Check the Cupboard for:

Cinnamon sticks
Cloves

Nutmeg

A speciality of mine, this is, and a marvelous, heart-warming drink on a cold winter's night!

Put the kettle on to boil, and let's discuss it. I specified 80 proof because what we are trying to achieve is joy and not a state of blotto. This drink goes down so easily and smoothly and happily that you are apt to forget the rum content. Put 2 ounces of good Jamaica rum into a *large* pottery or pewter mug. Add ½ a cinnamon stick, a ¼ teaspoon mixed together of nutmeg and ground clove. Add a couple of teaspoons of honey. Add a generous nugget of butter. Fill up the mug with boiling water and stir. Enjoy. Shall we have another? On the second round you can adjust the spices and honey to your own and her own taste.

MULLED WINE

Buy:

Red wine, respectable (1 bottle)

An orange
A lemon

Check Cupboard for:

Cinnamon sticks
Cloves

Sugar or honey

Into a saucepan put one cup of water, 1 stick of cinnamon, 6 cloves, the grated rind of 1 orange (avoiding the white part) and of ⅔ a lemon, and 2 level teaspoons of sugar or honey. Bring this to the boil, add immediately 2 cups of red wine. Bring just to the boil once more, remove from fire, and serve. Add a slice of orange or lemon for garnish.

IRISH COFFEE

Buy:

Irish whisky   **Heavy cream (½ pint)**

Check Cupboard for:

Coffee

Whip the cream and put it in the refrigerator to chill.

Make a pot of fresh coffee, but stronger than usual. Warm a couple of 7-ounce glasses (if you have no 7-ounce *goblets*) by running the hot tap into them.

Pour 2 ounces of whisky and 1 teaspoon of sugar (more if you prefer) into the warm glasses and stir. Add the coffee and float the whipped cream on top.

Chapter 8

A Dozen Dinners for Deserving Demoiselles

REMEMBER THAT TALE about the British political agent in the wilds of Borneo who donned a dinner jacket every evening? Why did he bother? Simple. This gesture was his one remaining link with civilization. If he had chosen not to observe this rite, he would have run the risk of being consumed by the savagery around him and might easily have turned into someone you'd expect to find in the backwaters of a Joseph Conrad novel.

Okay. You live in San Francisco. Or Chicago. Or Washington, D. C. So this doesn't apply to you. You're smack dab in the lap of civilization—complete with your brand new Pontiac, a fancy pad, and enough women to start your own roller derby team.

But take a look at yourself. How often do you "dress" for dinner? I mean in a tuxedo, pal. Sure, when you get home from the office, you want to relax. So you crawl out of your suit and climb into mocassins and an old pair of jeans. Once you've cracked that first beer, there's still time to turn on the TV. And while you scratch your belly like an awakening sloth, you can get a reading on all the day's muggings, robberies, and ball scores.

This life style is perfectly acceptable to you. Unfortunately, it just won't fly with the opposite sex unless the love of your life is a den mother for Hell's Angels.

Barbara isn't this sort of a girl at all. Perfectly turned out and completely tuned in, she oozes elegance. And remember, you met her at that wedding reception in the Hamptons, the one that looked like a fashion show for Bonwit's and Brooks Brothers. Even you had a suit on and you looked great in it, too, because she said so. To you. And that's how the story of Barbara began.

The story of Barbara could easily end on matters sartorial. If you expect her to come to dinner while you're dressed for a Dixie greased pig catch, you might as well make hot dogs for one.

The same goes for the evening's atmosphere. Everything must be perfect, right down to the two dozen red roses on your coffee table where the ashtray proclaims its first scrubbing since the Flyers took the Stanley Cup. The Chinese laundryman's index finger is blue from dialing you to protest that the napkins and tablecloth from your last dinner have been ready for six months., Bail them out now. You're going to need them.

Get with it where your menu is concerned. What is the bill of fare going to be? You're going to have to lay the raw materials into your larder now so that they'll be there when you need them. It just won't do to discover at 8:30 p.m. that you'll have to make do with bologna because you forgot to purchase prosciutto.

The twelve full-course meals that follow can all be classics of the culinary art—guaranteed to whet the appetite (for food or whatever) of the most delicate and discerning doll. Consider these menus your ultimate weapons, and wield them carefully and effectively.

Among other things, you'd do well to discover some of her likes and dislikes in the world of fine food. There's no sense in busting your hump over grilled mackerel if it's aroma reminds her of simmering overshoes. So get her to commit herself to something she really likes. Then prepare it with a vengeance!

While the food is cooking, slip into a role that reflects the menu. It will amuse her when you announce that a forthcoming Italian dish was made famous by The Flying Linguinis of circus fame. If Chicken Paprika's on deck instead, explain that it was named after a Hungarian general who lost his nerve during the Turkish invasion of Transylvania. You want to penetrate her reserve in order to see what lies behind it. The meal—and the mood you bring to it—can combine to conquier her without a struggle.

A DOZEN DINNERS

Menu #1

Plate of Sliced Salami, Prosciutto, and Mortadella
My Old Man's Spaghetti
Garlic Bread
Verona Salad
Zabaglione

Menu #2

Shad Roe
Roast Beef
Baked Acorn Squash
Broccoli Hollandaise
Baked Apples with Honey and Walnuts

Menu #3

Oyster Salad
R.E.'s Foolproof Pork Chops
Baked Stuffed Tomatoes
Greens and Radish Salad
Lemon Cream

Menu #4

Broiled Half Grapefruit
Curried Chicken and Rice
Yogapple Cream

Menu #5

Avocado Stuffed with Crabmeat
Spanish Rice and Shrimp
Catalan Salad
Superb Strawberries I

Menu #6

Melon and Prosciutto
Baked Striped Bass
Parsley Potatoes
French-Style Spinach
Tossed French Green Salad
Sherbet

Menu #7

Baby Scallops Provençale
Grilled King Mackerel
New Potatoes with Lemon
Peas with Little Grapes
Superb Strawberries II

Menu #8

Fresh Cream of Mushroom Soup with Sherry
Mixed Grill
Minted Peas
Endive and Watercress Salad
Stewed Rhubarb and Grandma's Custard

Menu #9

Mushrooms in Herbs and Lime
Veal Scallopini alla Marsala alla Zelda
Tino's Noodles
Torino Salad
Ice Cream Cremona

Menu #10

Russian Eggs
Escalope of Veal Viennoise
Eggplant Tedesco
Austrian Salad
Chocolate Mousse

Menu #11

Consommé with Eggs
Chicken Paprika
Stuffed Peppers
Grapes with Sour Cream

Menu #12

Chilled Tomato Soup
The Total Salad
Bowl of Fresh Fruit

Menu #1
Plate of Sliced Salami, Prosciutto and Mortadella
My Old Man's Spaghetti
Garlic Bread
Verona Salad
Zabaglione

The Day Before:

Make the spaghetti sauce.

Before Barbara Arrives:

Arrange the platter of cold meats and store in the refrigerator.
Wash the lettuce, dry it, and store in the refrigerator.
Prepare the bread to go into the oven.
Make the salad dressing.
Put the largest pot of water on the stove and salt it.
Remember that it will take some time to come to the boil.

Just Before Barbara Arrives:

Make sure the water is nearly boiling for the spaghetti.
Put the lettuce in the salad bowl.
Make sure the spaghetti sauce is hot.

After Eating the Spaghetti and Salad:

Make the zabaglione.

PLATE OF SLICED SALAMI, PROSCIUTTO, AND MORTADELLA

Buy:

From a good Italian deli, ¼
   pound each of: Genoa
   salami, prosciutto ham,
   and mortadella sausage
   (sliced)

Italian pepper pickles (1 jar)
   or fresh (⅛ pound)
Pimientos (1 small jar)
Lettuce (1 small head)

Lay the meats out on a platter covered with a bed of lettuce. They will look particularly attractive if you roll them into cylinders. Garnish the platter with pepper pickles and strips of pimiento.

You will have marvelous leftovers for tomorrow's sandwiches.

MY OLD MAN'S SPAGHETTI

Buy:

Ground round steak (½ pound)
Ground lean pork (½ pound)
Salt pork slice (⅛ pound)
Tomatoes, whole, Italian plum (2 2-cup-sized cans)
Tomato paste, Italian (2 small cans)

Onions, medium (2)
Garlic
Parsley (1 good-sized bunch)
Celery
Sweet peppers, green or red (2)
Mushrooms (¼ pound)
Chili peppers, dried (1 jar)
Spaghetti (1 1-pound box)

Check Cupboard for:

Olive oil
Sugar
Oregano

Basil
Bay leaf

The Sauce:

Get out your next-to-largest pot (you need the very largest for the spaghetti itself). Peel and chop roughly the two onions and 3 cloves of garlic. Put a large puddle of olive oil in the pot and add the onions and garlic. Let them fry very slowly. Put the ground round steak, the ground pork, and the salt pork (diced) into a frying pan, mix it with a wooden spoon to break it up, and let it fry until nearly cooked and well separated.

Open the cans of tomatoes and tomato paste, and put them and the fried meat into the pot with the onions. Add a large bay leaf, 1 teaspoon of oregano, and ½ teaspoon of basil. Stir well and allow to cook over a low to moderate heat.

Chop enough parsley to fill ½ cup. Chop enough celery to fill ½ cup. Chop enough sweet pepper to fill ½ cup. Add them to the pot. Add a couple of pinches of dried chili peppers and 1 teaspoon of sugar. Salt and pepper to taste. If the sauce tastes too sour or acid, add a little more sugar.

Let the sauce cook, stirring occasionally, for a couple of hours over a *low* fire, and with a lid on. It should thicken slightly. It will be much better the day after it is cooked.

This sauce recipe makes more than enough for two people and you will have quite a bit left over. It keeps very well and improves with a few days' aging. You can even freeze some of it. Use it with another batch of spaghetti, or else on rice, on an omelet, on a minute steak, on noodles—you could even make a lasagna.

The Pasta:

Boil salted water in the biggest pot you have, or buy an especially big one just for spaghetti! If the pot is too small, the pasta will stick to itself; it needs to move about freely as it cooks.

Half a pound of spaghetti will serve two people. Break it in half, or stand it on end and it will slip down into the pot as it cooks. Stir it with a fork to make sure it doesn't stick. Ten minutes is about long enough to cook it, but test it by fishing out a strand and biting it. Just before it is ready it will have a white dot in the center of the strand. As soon as the white dot disappears, the spaghetti is perfectly done "al dente," meaning judged by your teeth. Drain immediately. Serve onto big plates and put a lump of butter in the middle of each serving before you pour on the sauce.

GARLIC BREAD

Buy:

A fresh loaf of Italian bread   **Garlic**
Butter

Leave about ⅛ pound of butter out of the refrigerator to soften. Mash 2 cloves of garlic with the flat side of a knife, or use a garlic press. Mix the garlic thoroughly into the butter.

Take a bread knife and cut the loaf of bread into partial slices, not cutting through the bottom crust. Spread the garlic butter between the slices.

Just before dinner, put the loaf into the oven at 300° for about 15 to 20 minutes.

Now you *know* that she can't spend the rest of the evening with any-one else but you.

VERONA SALAD

Buy:

Escarole lettuce (1 head)   **Lemons**
Ripe olives, pitted,
   preferably from a deli and
   not canned (¼ pound)

Check Cupboard for:
Oregano

Wash the lettuce, separating the leaves and choosing the best. Dry them, and store them in a plastic bag in the refrigerator until dinner time.

Make a French dressing (see p. 12) with lemon juice instead of vinegar and add to it ¼ teaspoon of oregano and 1 clove of crushed garlic.

Assemble the salad at the last minute, putting the crisped lettuce into the bowl with a handful of ripe olives. Pour the dressing over it, and toss well.

ZABAGLIONE

Buy:

Marsala wine (1 bottle)   **Italian almond cookies (1**
Eggs (4)   **package)**
Sugar, powdered (1 pound)

Beat together 4 egg yolks and 2 tablespoons powdered sugar until they become thick and lemon-colored. Put them in a heavy bowl with a round bottom, and set the bowl in hot but not boiling water. With the beater (use an electric hand beater if you have one), beat the mixture constantly while adding (little by little) 2 tablespoons of Marsala. Keep beating until the zabaglione begins to hold its shape but is still smooth. Put it immediately into *heated* cups or tall glasses.

Serve warm, with almond cookies on the side.

Menu #2

Shad Roe
Roast Beef
Baked Acorn Squash
Broccoli Hollandaise
Baked Apples with Honey and Walnuts

The Day Before:

Cook the baked apples.

Before Barbara Arrives:

Soak the broccoli and trim it.
Make sure you get the roast and later the squash into the oven on time.
   Take the first steps at breakfast time.
Parboil the roe; you can sauté it at the last minute.

Just before Barbara Arrives:

Have the roe ready to sauté, with all seasonings at hand.
Make the Hollandaise sauce, and keep it warm in the double boiler or in
   a saucepan at the back of the stove over the lowest possible heat.
Make gravy for the roast if you want to.

While You Eat the Roe:

Cook the broccoli.

SHAD ROE

Buy:

Shad roe or lemon sole roe
  (roe from 1 shad is enough
  for 2 servings—lemon sole
  roe is a little smaller)

Lemons
Butter

Check Cupboard for:
Dill

Parsley

Boil a kettle of water.

Put the roe in a saucepan and cover with boiling water continuing ½ tablespoon of salt and 1 tablespoon of vinegar. Simmer for about 7 minutes. Drain. Cover with cold water and let stand for 5 minutes. Drain again.

Cut the parboiled roe in pieces. Melt 3 tablespoons of butter in a frying pan, and add a little lemon juice and ¼ teaspoon of dill. Sauté the roe in this mixture for about 10 minutes. Serve garnished with lemon wedges and parsley.

ROAST BEEF

Buy:

Beef roast, chuck, lean (4
  pounds)

Chuck is not a tender cut of meat, but this method of cooking it will make it very tender. Furthermore, the meat will not shrink in cooking, and it will be very juicy.

Preheat the oven to 300°, while you have your breakfast.

Oil the meat all over with corn oil or other cooking oil. Use your hands. Place the meat on a rack in a roasting pan, and put it in the oven. Leave it in the oven at 300° for exactly thirty minutes, and then turn the oven down to 185°. Do not look inside the oven, do not touch the meat, above all do not baste it. Go away to your office or out shopping or what you will. The roast will be perfectly done at dinner time. It doesn't matter whether you have breakfast at 10:00 a.m. or at noon. The meat can cook for 6, 7, or 8 hours, or more. Have faith.

You can make a gravy well before dinner and warm it up when you need it. Transfer the roast into another roasting pan. Pour off most of the excess fat in the old roast pan, saving a little of it (a tablespoon or two) for the gravy. Put the pan over a low fire on top of the stove and add to it 1 tablespoon of flour. Stir and blend with a wooden spoon. When the flour is well mixed and bubbling, add *slowly* a cup of liquid (water; ½ water & ½ milk; ½ water & ½ red wine; take your choice). Stir the gravy well and allow it to cook slowly for at least 10 minutes, adding more liquid if necessary. Season with salt and pepper and with any herbs you like. Thyme is good with beef. When it is cooked, pour the gravy into a small saucepan for the sake of convenience when you come to reheat it.

BAKED ACORN SQUASH

Buy:
An acorn squash

Check Cupboard for:
Butter   **Maple syrup**

This squash is going to have to share the oven with a roast being cooked by the slow method, so it will have to go in a lot sooner than it would under other circumstances. Put the squash in the 185° oven, whole, on a small dish, 3½ hours before dinner. It will be ready when dinner is ready. Then simply cut it in half, scrape out the seeds with a spoon, and put a generous lump of butter together with salt and pepper into the middle of each half. For a particularly delicious flavor, add a teaspoon of maple syrup to each half.

Some people cut acorn squash in two before baking them. I've discovered, however, that they dry out this way; whereas if you leave them whole they are juicier and have a better flavor.

For cooking them under normal circumstances, leave them whole and bake them for two hours at 350°.

BROCCOLI HOLLANDAISE

Buy:

Broccoli, fresh in season (1
    pound)—choose broccoli
    whose buds are dark green
    and tightly closed; the stems
    should be short and crisp or
    frozen broccoli if you have
    no choice

Eggs
Lemons

Check Cupboard for:

Butter

Cayenne

Soak the broccoli in cold salted water (covered) for half an hour. Then cut off the tough outer portions of the stalks and the tough outer leaves. The stalks take more peeling than you might think, but close inspection will show you how much to remove. If the individual stalks are inconveniently large, split them into smaller pieces. Boil them for about 15 minutes in a pan with a very tight lid and in about 1 inch of water.

Hollandaise Sauce:

Use either a double boiler or a very heavy but small saucepan. In it put 3 egg yolks and beat them until they are smooth but not fluffy. Then add 2 tablespoons of lemon juice, 2 tablespoons of hot water, ½ cup of melted butter, ¼ teaspoon of salt, and a pinch of cayenne. If you are using a double boiler, have the water in the lower half simmering, and beat the sauce with a wire whisk until it begins to thicken (about 5 minutes). If you are using a saucepan, make sure that it is over a very low heat. Pour over the hot broccoli.

If the sauce curdles, add slowly 1 tablespoon boiling water, beating constantly.

BAKED APPLES STUFFED WITH HONEY AND WALNUTS

Buy:

Apples, firm and juicy (at
    least 4)

Walnuts, shelled (1 small
    package)

Check Cupboard for:

Honey
Butter

Heavy cream, optional (½ pint)

Preheat oven to 400°.

Core the apples, being careful not to make holes in the bottoms. Into the holes, pour some honey and add a bit of butter. Then stuff in pieces of walnut.

Put them in a baking pan into which you have poured a little boiling water. The water will prevent the apples from burning or sticking.

Bake them for 30 minutes, or until they are soft.

Cool, and serve with cream if you like.

Menu #3
Oyster Salad
R.E.'s Foolproof Pork Chops
Baked Stuffed Tomatoes
Greens and Radish Salad
Lemon Cream

The Day Before:

Make the lemon cream.

Before Barbara Arrives:

Make the oyster salad and store it in the refrigerator.
Get the tomatoes ready to put into the oven.
Wash and store the lettuce in the refrigerator.

Just Before Barbara Arrives:

Put the pork chops on to cook.
Assemble the salad.
Turn on the oven.

When Barbara Arrives:

Put the tomatoes in the oven.

OYSTER SALAD

Buy:

Oysters, fresh (½ pint) or
   canned whole (1 8-ounce can)
Lettuce, a crisp variety such
   as iceberg (1 head)

Mayonnaise
Lemons
Parsley
Wine vinegar, white

Check Cupboard for:

Dill (dried)

If you have fresh oysters, cook them in one cup of simmering water for 5 minutes.

If you have canned oysters, drain them.

Mix together ¼ cup mayonnaise and 1 tablespoon wine vinegar and ¼ teaspoon of dill. Arrange lettuce on each plate and divide the oysters between them. Pour the mayonnaise and wine vinegar mixture over the oysters, and put the plates into the refrigerator to chill. When you are ready to serve, garnish each plate with a lemon wedge and some parsley.

R.E.'S FOOLPROOF PORK CHOPS

Buy:

Pork chops, ½ inch thick (2
   large, or 4 small)
Mushroom soup, condensed
   (1 can)

Mushrooms (¼ pound)
Onions
Red wine

Check Cupboard for:

Bay leaf

Get out your big iron frying pan. Fry the pork chops, adding just a little oil if necessary. When the chops are beginning to brown, add the onion you have chopped up. When the onion has fried and begun to brown, put the mushroom soup undiluted into the pan and stir everything well. Add a bay leaf. Add about ½ cup red wine. Turn the heat down and cover the pan. Let it simmer and bubble for about 30 minutes. Inspect it from time to time and turn the chops over. If the sauce seems to be getting too thick, add a little more wine. Just before serving add the ¼ pound of mushrooms, sliced. Add salt and pepper to taste.

BAKED STUFFED TOMATOES

Buy:

**Tomatoes, smooth, medium-
   sized (2)**
**Cheese, grated Parmesan (2-
   3 ounces or a small box)**

Bread crumbs (1 box)

Check Cupboard for:

An onion (small)

Parsley

Preheat the oven to 400°.

Cut a thin slice off the tops of the tomatoes and scoop out the seeds and pulp. Throw away the seeds, but keep the pulp. Salt the tomatoes lightly, and turn them upside down to drain for half an hour.

Mix the tomato pulp with an equal amount of bread crumbs. Chop some or all of the small onion, depending on size, and add it to the mixture. Chop some parsley and add it. Salt and pepper to taste. Mix everything well, and stuff the mixture into the tomatoes, topping them with a lump of butter and some grated cheese.

Bake at 400° for 20 minutes.

GREENS AND RADISH SALAD

Buy:

Iceberg lettuce (1 head)
Radishes (1 bunch)

Chives

Make:

A French dressing (see p. 12)

Wash, dry, and tear up the lettuce and put it away in the refrigerator. Trim the radishes. Chop the chives.

To assemble salad, slice the radishes into thin slices. Add the chives. Add the dressing just before serving.

LEMON CREAM

Buy:

Lemons   Heavy cream (½ pint)

Check Cupboard for:

Sugar

Put 1 cup of sugar and 1 cup of water in a saucepan over a low heat just long enough to dissolve the sugar. Set it aside to cool.

Squeeze enough lemons to provide ½ cup of lemon juice.

When the sugar-water mixture is cool, whip 1 cup of heavy cream (the aerosol variety will *not* do). Mix together the cream, the lemon juice, and the sugar and water. Freeze it in a tray in the refrigerator, stirring at *least* twice during the freezing. The more you stir, the creamier it will be.

Menu #4
Broiled Half Grapefruit
Curried Chicken and Rice
Yogapple Cream

The Day Before:

Roast the chicken.

Before Barbara Arrives:

Assemble the various ingredients for the curry, mix the dry ones, chop
the apple and onion, and so forth.

Just Before Barbara Arrives:

Make the Yogapple cream, and put it in the refrigerator.
Turn on the broiler for the grapefruit.
Start the curry cooking. You can keep it hot by covering it tightly if it is
ready a little too soon.

BROILED HALF GRAPEFRUIT

Buy:

A grapefruit

Check Cupboard for:

Honey   **Sherry**

Preheat the oven to 450° or cook in broiler.

Cut the grapefruit in half. With your grapefruit knife, cut the fruit free
from the rind, cut out the core at the center, and cut the fruit away from
the membranes in each section. If you have the patience, you can even
remove the membranes between the sections.

Put the grapefruit halves in a baking dish. Into each half drip a little
honey and a little sherry.

Bake them in the oven or under the broiler until the surface is slightly
browned, about 15 minutes under the broiler, a little longer in the oven.

CURRIED CHICKEN AND RICE

Buy:

A chicken, quartered (3 pounds)
An apple
An onion (small)
Raisins, dark (1 box)
Limes (1 or 2—substitute lemons if limes not available)

Curry powder (1 small jar)
Turmeric powder (1 small jar)
Rice, long grain (1-pound package
Mango chutney (1 jar)
Yogurt, natural (1 pint)

Check Cupboard for:

Cooking oil
Garlic
Cinnamon powder

Ground cloves
Thyme
Chicken bouillon cubes

Preheat the oven to 350°.

Put the pieces of skinned chicken in a pan, drizzle a little oil and lemon juice over them, and roast them in the oven for about 30 to 35 minutes. Remove them.

Boil about 4 cups of water. Core, peel, and chop the apple. Chop the onion. Squeeze a lime and have the juice handy. Mix together the following dry ingredients: 2 teaspoons curry powder, ½ teaspoon powdered cinnamon, ¼ teaspoon ground cloves, ½ teaspoon thyme, ½ teaspoon turmeric powder, and ½ teaspoon freshly ground pepper.

Put 2½ tablespoons of oil in the bottom of a large saucepan with two mashed garlic cloves. Heat the oil, allowing the garlic to fry gently, but not brown. Add 1 cup of long grain rice and stir it well with a wooden spoon. Let it heat well, but not too long or it will turn into Rice Crispies. Stir in the dry ingredients, remove the saucepan briefly from the stove, and mix well. Add 3 cups of boiling water and a chicken bouillon cube. Return the pan to the stove. Add some of the pieces of chicken—the 2 breasts, thighs, drumsticks. You won't need it all—reserve the rest for a snack some other time. Add the chopped apple and onion and ¼ cup of raisins. Add the lime juice. Bring everything to the boil, and then turn the heat down so that the curry simmers gently.

Cook with a tight lid until *almost* all of the liquid has been consumed. You can discover this by tipping the saucepan slightly to one side. To be sure, taste a few grains of the rice to see if they are cooked. If you want a more liquid curry, you can always add a little more chicken bouillon before serving.

Serve with side dishes of mango chutney and fresh natural yogurt. Just be sure you save at least ½ pint of yogurt for the dessert.

YOGAPPLE CREAM

Buy:

Yogurt (1 pint is already on the shopping list for the curry, but you will need a little over ½ pint here)

Applesauce, canned, unsweetened (1 jar)
Almonds, shelled, blanched (1 small package)

Check Cupboard for:

Cinnamon powder

Honey

Put a little oil in a frying pan and toast the almonds in it until they brown slightly. Turn them constantly. Tip them out onto paper towels to absorb the oil. Let them cool.

Mix in a bowl equal amounts of yogurt and applesauce. Add cinnamon to taste, and a little honey if the mixture is not sweet enough. Add the almonds, mix well, and chill in the refrigerator.

Menu #5
Avocado Stuffed with Crabmeat
Spanish Rice and Shrimp
Catalan Salad
Superb Strawberries I

Before Barbara Arrives:

Sort out the ingredients of the Spanish Rice, chop the pepper and onion, and have the rest ready to go.
Prepare the strawberries, except for the whipped cream, and store them in the refrigerator.
Wash the lettuce and dry it, and store it in the refrigerator.
Prepare the crabmeat mixture. Stuff the avocado just before serving.

Just Before Barbara Arrives:

Assemble the rice and start it cooking.
Assemble the salad in a bowl. Add dressing just before serving.

AVOCADO STUFFED WITH CRABMEAT

Buy:

**An avocado—make sure it is
    ripe**
**Crabmeat, fresh—canned
    crabmeat tends to be 75%
    bits of shell**

A sweet pepper, red
Parsley

Check Cupboard for:

Mayonnaise
Dill

Lemon

Slice open the avocado and remove the seed.
Chop about ½ of the pepper finely.
Mix the crabmeat and pepper with enough mayonnaise to bind.
Add ¼ teaspoon of dill, a little chopped parsley, and a squirt of fresh lemon juice.
Fill the avocado halves with this mixture, and add a little parsley as a garnish.
Chill before serving.

SPANISH RICE AND SHRIMP

Buy:

**Shrimp, fresh, unshelled (½
    pound)**
**Peas, frozen (smallest
    package available)**

**Saffron (1 small jar or
    package; if unavailable,
    use turmeric)**
Rice, long-grain (a 1-pound box)

A sweet pepper, green
Olive bits, if available, or stuffed
   green olives (1 small jar)

An onion, medium-small

Check Cupboard for:

Olive oil
Garlic
Chicken bouillon cubes

Lemons
Oregano

Chop about ½ of the green pepper. Chop roughly the onion. If you have not found olive bits, cut whole olives in halves or quarters, depending on size. Chop 2 garlic cloves.

Boil a kettle of water and make 3 cups of chicken bouillon with cubes. Put 2½ tablespoons of olive oil in the bottom of a large saucepan with the chopped garlic. Heat the oil and let the garlic cook in it, but not brown. Add 1 cup of long-grain rice, and stir well. Allow the rice to heat thoroughly, and then add 2½ cups boiling chicken bouillon. Bring to the boil, and then turn the heat down so that the rice simmers. Now add the green pepper, the olives, and the onion, and ¼ teaspoon of oregano. Add saffron according to the instructions on the package—I can't be more precise because different varieties of saffron vary in strength. Add ½ teaspoon of freshly ground black pepper, a scant ½ cup of frozen peas, a teaspoon of fresh lemon juice, and the unshelled shrimp. Mix thoroughly and allow to cook with a tight lid until the liquid is consumed. Judge this by tipping the pot slightly to one side. Watch carefully, or the rice will burn on the bottom. If you find it a bit dry when it is cooked, stir in a little more chicken bouillon to moisten it.

Serve, and peel the shrimp with your fingers while you eat. Sangría is the perfect accompaniment (see p. 100).

CATALAN SALAD

Buy:

Boston, Bibb, or garden
   lettuce (1 or 2 heads,
   depending on size)
Olives, black, preferably
   from a deli (¼ pound of
   small ones)

A sweet pepper, red
Anchovies, flat (1 can)

Check Cupboard for:

Olive oil   **Garlic**
Wine vinegar, red **Basil**

Make a French dressing (see p. 12), and add ¼ teaspoon of basil to it.

Wash the lettuce and separate the leaves. Dry them, and put them in the refrigerator to crisp. Cut the sweet pepper into julienne strips.

Just before dinner, assemble the salad. Tear the lettuce into a salad bowl, add the strips of sweet red pepper and a good handful of black olives. Cut about half the anchovies into smaller pieces. Add the dressing at the last minute and toss well.

SUPERB STRAWBERRIES I

Buy:

Strawberries in a small box (about 1 pint)

Orange juice (the smallest carton or frozen can, or better still, a fresh orange or two for squeezing)

Heavy cream (½ pint, for whipping)

Curaçao (the smallest bottle the liquor store will sell you)

Check Cupboard for:

Sugar

Wash the strawberries under a cold faucet. As you do so, pull off the stalk and leaves and as much as possible of the little white core that may, or may not, come out easily with the stalk. Mix ¼ cup orange juice, ¼ cup sugar, and 1 tablespoon of Curaçao. Pour over the strawberries. Serve with freshly whipped cream.

Menu #6
Melon and Prosciutto
Baked Striped Bass
Parsley Potatoes
French-Style Spinach
Tossed French Green Salad
Sherbet

The Day Before:

Make the Béchamel sauce and store it in the refrigerator.

Before Barbara Arrives:

Boil the spinach and put it aside.
Wash the lettuce and a little spinach and put them into refrigerator to
   crisp.
Assemble the melon and prosciutto and store in the refrigerator.
Preheat the oven for the fish.
Prepare the fish to go into the oven.
Chop the parsley for the potatoes.

Just Before Barbara Arrives:

Assemble the salad, except for the dressing.
Put the fish in the oven.
Cook the potatoes.
Begin to fry the spinach—you can always turn it off for a little while.

After Eating the Melon and Prosciutto:

Finish the fish sauce, the potatoes, and the spinach.

MELON AND PROSCIUTTO

This dish depends not on cooking skill but on the quality of the ingredients used. If you can't find good-quality ingredients, try another first course.

Buy:

**Italian prosciutto—find a
real Italian delicatessen or
butcher shop, and have the
prosciutto sliced as thin as
possible—accept no
substitutes (½ pound)**

**Melon, preferably canteloupe,
but any sweet melon except
watermelon will do.**
Lemons

Peel the melon and remove the seeds. Cut it into ½ x 2″ pieces.

Trim any excess fat from the slices of prosciutto and cut them into
pieces large enough to go 1½ times round the pieces of melon. Wrap the
melon in the prosciutto and nail it with a toothpick. Serve with lemon
wedges and a turn of freshly ground black pepper.

BAKED STRIPED BASS

Buy:

**Striped bass, fresh, cleaned,
whole (3–4 pounds)**
**White wine, dry (you only
need a little, so plan on
drinking the rest with
dinner, and get a nice one)**

Butter
Eggs
Parsley
Lemons
Milk

Check Cupboard for:

Flour

Dill

Make a Béchamel Sauce (see p. 11).

Preheat the oven to 400°.

Wash the fish, including the belly cavity, under cold running water.
Dry it with paper towels, and put it on a rack in a large baking dish or
oven-proof platter. Dot it with butter, and sprinkle it with fresh lemon
juice. Salt and pepper lightly. Bake it at 400° for 30 to 45 minutes depending on how thick it is. To judge whether it is done, carefully flake one
place with a fork. The skin should be crisp and the meat should be tender
and juicy.

To Finish the Sauce: Add to it the juice from the fish pan, and warm it up. Just before serving, remove it from the heat, and let it drop below the boiling point. Add 2 egg yolks, which you have stirred with a fork so that they are not whole, and stir the sauce vigorously. Add 3 tablespoons of butter, one at a time, and stir thoroughly. Add slowly, stirring constantly, 1 tablespoon of lemon juice. Add ¼ cup dry white wine, a little dill, chopped parsley, and salt and pepper to taste.

PARSLEY POTATOES

Buy:

New potatoes, if available; if not, the smallest potatoes you can find (1 pound)	**Parsley** **Butter**

Little new potatoes cook very quickly. Start them in cold salted water and boil them for about 12 minutes. Peel them after they are cooked; the skin comes off very easily. If they are too hot to handle, hold them under cold water for a minute. Put them back into the pot, and add ½ cup of butter (1 stick) and let it melt. Add 1 tablespoon of lemon juice, a lot of chopped parsley, and salt and pepper to taste. Turn the potatoes in the melted butter until they just begin to brown a little here and there. Serve, and pour the melted butter over them.

Dill or mint is very good with little potatoes.

FRENCH-STYLE SPINACH

Buy:

Whole spinach, fresh (1 bag)

Check Cupboard for:

Garlic	**Lemons**
Olive oil	

Put the whole spinach (pick it over for spoiled leaves first) into a large pot with a tablespoon or two of water. It will make its own water as it cooks, but keep an eye on it nevertheless. Cover it with a tight lid. It will cook in a matter of 3 to 5 minutes. When it has shrunk to a fraction of its volume and is dark green in color, it is done.

Turn it out into a colander or sieve, and press the excess water out of it with the back of wooden spoon.

Put a little olive oil and a mashed clove of garlic into a frying pan. Let the garlic cook gently for a minute or two, but don't let it brown. Add the spinach, spread it out, and fry it slowly, turning it over constantly. The excess water will steam off. Let the spinach fry slowly for 10 or 15 minutes. Add a little fresh lemon juice and salt and pepper to taste.

TOSSED FRENCH GREEN SALAD

Buy:

Lettuce, any kind (1 head)
A cucumber
Green onions and/or fresh
   chives

Spinach, fresh (several
   leaves)

Check Cupboard for:

Olive oil
Wine vinegar

Thyme
Garlic

Make a French dressing (see p. 12) and add to it a little garlic and ¼ teaspoon thyme.

Wash and dry the lettuce and the spinach, separating the leaves. Put it in the refrigerator to crisp.

Remove the roots, outer skin, and about half of the green tops of the onions. Chop them. Chop the chives.

When you are ready to assemble the salad, slice the cucumber, peeling it or not as you prefer. (Some people find the green skin indigestible.)

Put all the ingredients into the salad bowl, and add the dressing at the last minute. Toss thoroughly.

SHERBET

This one's easy. Just scoop a little lemon or lime sherbet into two bowls. Serve.

Menu #7

Baby Scallops Provençale
Grilled King Mackerel
New Potatoes with Lemon
Peas with Little Grapes
Superb Strawberries II

Well Before Barbara Arrives:

Cook the peas and put them aside until needed.
Chop tomato, parsley, garlic, and onion for the scallops.
Wash the potatoes and put them in the pot ready to cook later.
Make the strawberry dessert and put it in the refrigerator.
Grate the lemon peel.

When Barbara Arrives:

Be ready to assemble and cook the scallops, fish, potatoes and peas.
Remember that the scallops cook in 5 minutes,
        the fish cooks in 15 minutes,
        the potatoes cook in 13 minutes, and
        the peas and grapes just have to heat.

BABY SCALLOPS PROVENÇALE

Buy:

Scallops, small, fresh (½)
A tomato (small)
Parsley

Garlic
An onion (small)

Check Cupboard for:
Olive oil

Slice the tomato in half, removing the core. Squeeze the halves over the sink to get rid of excess seeds and liquid. Chop the tomato into very small pieces. Chop about ½ a small onion into very small pieces. Chop the parsley. Mash 2 cloves of garlic and chop them.

Drain the scallops. Pour a little olive oil into a frying pan and heat it over a low to moderate heat. Add the chopped tomatoes, onion, parsley, and garlic. Mix and fry them very gently for a few minutes. Then add the scallops and fry them, turning them often, for about 5 minutes. They will be white through when they are done. Salt and pepper to taste.

Serve immediately.

GRILLED KING MACKEREL

Buy:

King mackerel (2 1-inch-thick   **Lemon**
slices, or about 1 pound)   **Dill**
Parsley

Check Cupboard for:

Butter
French Dijon mustard with
white wine (no substitutes)

Preheat the broiler to 500° for 10 minutes.

If the slices of fish are moist, dry them with a paper towel. Butter them on both sides. On one side, spread a fairly generous layer of Dijon mustard. On top of it sprinkle parsley, dill, and a little pepper. Add a couple of squirts of lemon juice.

Put the mackerel slices on a sheet of aluminum foil (no pan to wash afterwards) and slip them under the broiler for about 15 minutes, perhaps a little more. Check for doneness by flaking off a little piece with a fork. Salt to taste at the table.

NEW POTATOES WITH LEMON

Buy:

**New potatoes; if
unavailable, buy very
small potatoes (1 pound)**

**Lemons
Butter
Chives**

Grate enough lemon rind to fill about ½ teaspoon.

Chop the chives.

Wash the potatoes. You will use 6 to 8, depending on size.

Start the potatoes in cold salted water. When they boil, let them boil for about 12 minutes, or until tender when pierced with a fork. Drain them.

Peel the potatoes (or leave them in their skins. Some people prefer them unskinned.)

Combine in a saucepan 2 tablespoons butter, ½ teaspoon grated lemon peel, 1 teaspoon lemon juice, and 1 teaspoon chopped chives. Warm it all over a low heat.

Add the potatoes and turn them and reheat them in this mixture until they are well coated. Season with salt and pepper to taste. Serve, and pour the extra sauce over them.

PEAS WITH LITTLE GRAPES

Buy:

**Peas, frozen (1 package)
Grapes, white, seedless
(small bunch)**

Check Cupboard for:

Tarragon

Butter

Cook the peas according to the instructions on the package.

Melt 1 tablespoon of butter in a saucepan and add 1 cup of peas and ½ cup of the grapes. Add salt and pepper to taste, and a pinch of tarragon. Heat the peas and grapes, stirring them, just until they are hot through.

Serve immediately.

SUPERB STRAWBERRIES II

Buy:

**Strawberries in a small box
    (about 1 pint)
Claret wine (a small bottle—
    unless you have plans for
    it during the main course
    or later in the evening)**

Check Cupboard for:

Sugar

Wash the strawberries. Pour ¼ cup (or less) claret over them. Sprinkle with sugar. This dessert tastes better if it's prepared ahead of time. Serve with a flourish.

Menu #8

Fresh Cream of Mushroom Soup with Sherry
Mixed Grill
Minted Peas
Endive and Watercress Salad
Stewed Rhubarb and Grandma's Custard

The Day Before:

Make the custard and cook the rhubarb.

Before Barbara Arrives:

Make the soup. Leave it on the back of the stove ready to be warmed up.
Deal with the watercress and store it in the refrigerator with the endive.
Take the meat out of the refrigerator so that it reaches room temperature
    before you cook it.
Boil the potato. Parboil the sausages.
Prepare the other vegetables for the mixed grill, and generally line up
    everything needed to cook it.

Mince and prepare the mint for the peas.
Put the peas in a pot ready to cook.
Make the salad dressing.

Just Before Barbara Arrives:

Assemble the salad, except the dressing.
Warm the soup.
Turn on the broiler.

Just Before Dinner:

Start the mixed grill so that it cooks while you eat the soup.

FRESH CREAM OF MUSHROOM SOUP WITH SHERRY

Buy:

Mushrooms, fresh (¼ pound)   **Milk**
Sherry, dry   **Eggs**

Check Cupboard for:

Flour

Remove the stems from the mushrooms, trimming off the bottoms if they look woody. Slice the tops and chop the stems. In a saucepan put a tablespoon of butter and melt it. Add the mushrooms and cook them for 5 minutes over a moderate heat, stirring them frequently. Then sprinkle 1 tablespoon of flour over the mushrooms and add 1½ cups of milk. Stir well, and cook until the soup begins to thicken slightly. Mix together 1 egg yolk and 2 tablespoons of sherry, beating them slightly. Remove soup from fire, and stir in the sherry and egg mixture.

Season to taste with salt and pepper.

Garnish with parsley or paprika.

MIXED GRILL

Buy:

Lamb chops, 1 inch thick (2)
Lamb kidney, split (1)
Pork sausages (2)
Bacon
A tomato, small

Mushrooms (smallest
quantity possible)
Artichoke hearts (1 small can)
A potato
Parsley

Check Cupboard for:

Corn oil

Preheat the broiler to 500°.

Everything cooks at once and very quickly, so have it all ready and lined up.

Parboil the sausages for 5 minutes, drain, and set them aside. Boil the potato, peeled, until it is tender. Then slice it. Halve the tomato, removing the core.

Choose the largest mushrooms, and remove the stems.

Line the broiler rack with aluminum foil.

Put onto it: the 2 lamb chops, the split kidney, and the pork sausages. Broil for 7 minutes.

Turn the chops over and the sausages and the kidney. Put onto the broiler with them—the tomato halves, the mushroom caps, 2 or 4 artichoke hearts, slices of the potato. Put a little cooking oil on all of these vegetables, and a little salt and pepper. Add 2 or 4 bacon strips. Broil for another 7 minutes, turning the bacon once.

Serve immediately onto dinner plates, and garnish with a little parsley.

MINTED PEAS

Buy:

Peas, small, frozen (1
   package)

Mint, fresh if possible; if
   not, dried (small jar)

Check Cupboard for:

Butter

Vinegar or lemon

Chop and then mince the mint as finely as possible. Make a paste by adding small quantities of a half-and-half mixture of vinegar and water to the minced mint, and add a little sugar to taste. You may use lemon juice instead of vinegar.

Cook the peas according to the directions on the package. Drain them, and add a tablespoon of butter and the mint. Turn the peas in the butter and mint until well mixed, and serve.

ENDIVE AND WATERCRESS SALAD

Buy:

Endive, Belgian (2 heads)   **Watercress (1 bunch)**

Check Cupboard for:

Olive oil   **An egg**
Vinegar   **French Dijon mustard**

Make:

French mustard dressing
(see p. 13)

Hard-cook 1 egg. Cool and chop it.

Wash the watercress and remove the tough stems so that you are left mostly with the leaves and a few of the smaller, more tender stems. Shake out the excess water and dry the cress. Store in the refrigerator until needed. It is not usually necessary to wash endive; merely remove any wilted outer leaves.

Just before dinner, assemble the salad. Tear the leaves of endive into the salad bowl, and add the watercress. Add the chopped egg, and at the last minute the dressing. Toss well.

STEWED RHUBARB AND GRANDMA'S CUSTARD

Buy:

Rhubarb (1 pound) Note: rhubarb is grown out of doors and in hot houses. Hot house rhubarb is pale pink with light green leaves. The out-of-door variety is much darker in color and requires longer cooking. You may also need to peel it a little.

Eggs (3)
Oranges or lemons (1 or 2)

Check Cupboard for:

Sugar
Milk

Vanilla extract or sherry

THE RHUBARB: First trim the leaves and stems. The leaves are not to be eaten under any circumstances; they can be dangerous. Wash the stalks. If they seem young and tender, do not peel them, just cut them into 1-inch chunks. Put them into a saucepan with ½ cup of sugar and a little grated orange or lemon peel, and just enough water to keep them from burning. They make their own juice while cooking. Cover them and cook them over a low heat until they are just tender. This takes not more than 7 minutes for young rhubarb, and perhaps 15 for tougher stalks. Put aside to cool and then into the refrigerator in a bowl.

THE CUSTARD: Beat three eggs well. Put into a saucepan 2 cups of milk and scald them. This means heat the milk just until a little rim of small bubbles forms around the edge next to the sides of the saucepan. To the scalded milk, add ¼ cup white or brown sugar, ⅛ teaspoon of salt. Then, stirring quickly, pour in the 3 slightly beaten eggs. Cook the custard over a very, very low heat until it coats a spoon. If you have a thermometer (and you should), use it. The custard is cooked when it reaches exactly 175°. Remove from stove, cool, and store in the refrigerator. Flavor it with ½ teaspoon of vanilla essence or sherry to taste.

Serve the rhubarb in dessert dishes with the custard poured over it.

Menu #9

Mushrooms in Herbs and Lime
Veal Scallopine alla Marsala alla Zelda
Tino's Noodles
Torino Salad
Ice Cream Cremona

Note: you need *two* large frying pans for this menu. You might make do with a roasting pan on top of the stove of the noodles, but a frying pan is best. You need its thick bottom.

The Day Before:

Make the Ice Cream Cremona. (Taste it, too.)
Prepare the mushrooms and let them marinate overnight.
Wash the lettuce and store it in the refrigerator.

Before Barbara Arrives:

Take the meat out of the refrigerator so that it reaches room temperature before you cook it.
Chop an awful lot of parsley. You might as well put some into the salad too. And the veal.
Slice the lemon and set it aside.

Just Before Barbara Arrives:

Assemble the mushrooms onto plates on the lettuce. Store in the refrigerator.
Have the veal ready to go, with all ingredients close at hand.
Boil the water for the noodles, and have it ready to sling them in.
Assemble the salad.

MUSHROOMS IN HERBS AND LIME

Buy:

Mushrooms, fresh (¼ pound)
Lettuce, any kind (1 head)
A lime

Chives, fresh, if available (1 bunch)

Check Cupboard for:

Olive oil   **Tarragon**

Wash the mushrooms, but only if necessary, and dry them carefully, discarding some of the stems if they seem old or woody. Slice them and put them in a bowl. Combine in a measuring cup 3 tablespoons of olive oil, the juice of 1 lime, 2 tablespoons chopped chives, ¼ teaspoon crushed tarragon, and salt and pepper to taste. Mix well and pour over the mushrooms. Put them away to chill (covered) in the refrigerator. Toss slightly before serving, and serve them on a bed of crisp lettuce leaves.

Don't forget to wash, dry, and store the lettuce as well.

VEAL SCALLOPINI ALLA MARSALA ALLA ZELDA

Buy:

Veal, very thin slices—have   **Marsala wine (1 bottle)**
the butcher pound it (1   **Lemons**
pound)   **Butter**

Check Cupboard for:

Flour   **Rosemary**

Get out your big iron frying pan.

Put some flour on a large plate, and lay the veal slices in it so that each side is slightly coated.

Melt ⅛ pound of butter in the frying pan. Add the veal and brown each side quickly. Pour in ½ cup of Marsala, and allow meat to simmer for 5 minutes, turning down the heat a little. Season with salt and pepper, and with ⅛ teaspoon rosemary, crushed between your fingers.

Slice a lemon.

Serve the veal piping hot garnished with the lemon slices. Pour the remaining butter and Marsala over the veal.

TINO'S NOODLES

Buy:

Egg noodles (1 pound)
**Parmesan cheese, grated (2
 or 3 ounces)**

Butter
Parsley

Boil ½ pound of noodles according to the instructions on the box. Drain them in a colander and then dry them on a clean dish towel. In a frying pan, melt 4 tablespoons of butter. Add the noodles and stir and toss them in the butter over a moderate heat. Add about ¼ cup of chopped parsley, a good handful of grated cheese, and salt and pepper to taste. Continue to stir and toss the noodles until they begin to brown a little.

Serve them with the veal.

TORINO SALAD

Buy:

Romaine lettuce (1 head)
**Olives, ripe or green, from a
 deli (3 or 4 ounces)**
**Tomatoes (1 or 2, depending
 on size)**

**Italian pickled peppers,
 from the deli (1 small jar)**

Check Cupboard for:

Olive oil
Wine vinegar

Garlic
Oregano

Make a French dressing (see p. 12). Add 1 clove of crushed, minced garlic and ¼ teaspoon of oregano.

Wash the lettuce, separating the leaves and discarding outer, tough, or wilted ones. Dry and store in the refrigerator.

When ready to assemble the salad, tear the lettuce into the salad bowl, add tomatoes chopped or quartered, a generous amount of olives, and five or six pickled peppers. Pour on the dressing at the last minute, and toss well. Salt and pepper to taste.

ICE CREAM CREMONA

Buy:

**Vanilla ice cream, best
  quality (1 pint)**
Raisins (1 box)
**Slivered almonds (1 small
  package)**

**Peaches, fresh (1 or 2) or
  canned (1 can)**
**Brandy (1 bottle or a
  miniature)**

Make sure that among your collection of plastic storage jars etc., you have one bigger than 1-pint size with a tight lid. If not, buy one.

Let the pint of ice cream stand on the kitchen table until it is soft but not liquid.

Plunge the peaches in boiling water for 30 seconds or so to facilitate peeling. Peel them, remove the stone, and mash them, either with a food mill or a blender or just brute force with a sieve and wooden spoon.

Put ¼ cup raisins in a very small saucepan and cover them with water. Boil them for about 15 minutes. This will make them soft, plump, and juicy.

Toast the slivered almonds in some oil in the frying pan until they begin to turn brown. Drain them on paper towels.

When the ice cream is soft, dump it into a bowl and add the mashed peaches, the raisins, the almonds, and a couple of jiggers of brandy. Mix very well. Cram it all into a larger container with a tight lid, and stick in the freezer to refreeze.

Menu #10

Russian Eggs
Escalope of Veal Viennoise
Eggplant Tedesco
Austrian Salad
Chocolate Mousse

The Day Before:

Make the Chocolate Mousse.
Hard-cook 4 eggs, peel and store in the refrigerator.

Before Barbara Arrives:

Make the sauce for the eggs.
Put the eggplant, salted, in a bowl to soak as described.
Wash and dry the lettuce and store it in the refrigerator.

Just Before Barbara Arrives:

Assemble the eggs and sauce on two plates and keep in the refrigerator.
Assemble all the ingredients for the veal and have them handy.
Assemble the salad, except for the dressing. Keep it cool in the refrigerator.
Remember, the eggplant cooks in about 20 minutes, the veal in about 10.

RUSSIAN EGGS

Buy:

Eggs (4)
**Lettuce, any kind (1 small
    head)**
Mayonnaise

Parsley
Chili sauce (1 small jar)
Lemons

Check Cupboard for:

**White pepper (in your other
    pepper mill)**

Hard-cook 4 eggs. Plunge in cold water. Peel. Set aside to cool and then chill.

Wash the lettuce, separate the leaves, dry, and store in the refrigerator.

Mix together in a measuring cup (because it is convenient) 4 tablespoons mayonnaise, 1 tablespoon chili sauce, 2 teaspoons chopped parsley, ½ teaspoon salt, ¼ teaspoon freshly ground white pepper, and 1 teaspoon lemon juice. Mix well.

When ready to serve, slice the eggs, and arrange 2 eggs on each plate on a bed of lettuce leaves. Pour the sauce evenly over the eggs and serve.

ESCALOPE OF VEAL VIENNOISE

Buy:

**Veal, cut into very thin
slices and pounded (4 slices)**
**Anchovy fillets, the rolled
variety (1 small can)**

Lemons
Bread crumbs (1 box)
Eggs (2)

Check Cupboard for:

Flour

Butter

Prepare 3 plates: 1 with some flour on it; 1 with 2 slightly beaten eggs; 1 with bread crumbs.

Take each veal slice and dip it first into the flour on both sides so that it is lightly coated. Then dip it into the beaten egg on both sides so that it is well coated. Then dip it into the bread crumbs so that it is well-coated on both sides. Then lay each piece on a large piece of wax paper.

Melt 5 or 6 tablespoons of butter in a frying pan. When it is hot and bubbling, add the veal. Cook it for 4 or 5 minutes until it is golden brown on one side and then turn it over and cook for 4 or 5 minutes on the other side until that is golden brown too.

Add salt and pepper to taste.

Garnish each slice with a slice of lemon topped with a rolled anchovy filled with a caper in the middle.

EGGPLANT TEDESCO

Buy:

An eggplant, small

Lemons

Check Cupboard for:

Olive oil
Garlic

Oregano

Peel the eggplant and cut it into ¼-inch thick slices.

Arrange it in layers in a large bowl, sprinkling each layer generously with salt. Cover the slices with ice-water and put a dish on top with a weight on it to keep the slices submerged. Let it sit for at least an hour at room temperature—this will remove the bitter juices from the eggplant.

Meanwhile, mix together ½ clove of mashed garlic, ½ teaspoon of salt, ¼ teaspoon of oregano, 4 tablespoons of olive oil, and 1 tablespoon of fresh lemon juice. And some freshly ground black pepper.

Preheat the oven to 450°

Drain and rinse the eggplant and lay the slices on a baking sheet or a sheet of aluminum foil and brush onto them all of the sauce. (Eggplant is very absorbent.) Bake them in the oven for 20 minutes, brushing the rest of the sauce onto them at least twice. Serve piping hot.

AUSTRIAN SALAD

Buy:

Red cabbage (1 small head)
**Romaine lettuce (1 small
    head)**
Green onions

Check Cupboard for:

French Dijon mustard
Olive oil
Wine vinegar
Caraway seeds

Make a French mustard dressing (see p. 12), and add to it ¼ teaspoon caraway seeds.

Wash the Romaine lettuce, separate the leaves, discarding outer, tough, or wilted ones. Dry and store in the refrigerator.

Chop the green onions, having removed the roots, outer skin, and about half the green tops.

When ready to assembly the salad, shred some of the red cabbage and put into the bowl with torn pieces of Romaine lettuce. Add the chopped green onions. Pour on the dressing just before serving and toss well.

CHOCOLATE MOUSSE

Buy:

Unsweetened baker's chocolate (1 small package)

Plain gelatin (1 small box)
Milk
Heavy cream (1 pint)

Check Cupboard for:

Sugar

Vanilla essence

Cook in a heavy saucepan over very low heat 1 cup of milk, 2 ounces of unsweetened chocolate, ¼ cup of sugar, 1 teaspoon of gelatin (or follow instructions on the package). Let the chocolate melt, stirring frequently. Take an egg beater and beat the liquid until it is well blended and smooth. It must not boil, so keep the heat low. Put it aside to chill—it will thicken slightly.

Add 1 teaspoon of vanilla to the mixture and beat again until it becomes light. Then fold in the whipped heavy cream. Put the whole bowl into the freezer of your refrigerator and let it set and chill. Don't quite freeze it.

Menu #11

Consommé with Eggs
Chicken Paprika
Stuffed Peppers
Grapes with Sour Cream.

Before Barbara Arrives:

Parboil the peppers and make their stuffing. Have them ready to go into the oven.
Assemble the grape dessert.
Make the sauce for the chicken.
Put the consommé in a saucepan ready to heat.

When Barbara Arrives:

Get the chicken and then the peppers into the oven.
At the last minute, prepare the consommé.

CONSOMMÉ WITH EGGS

Buy:

Consommé (1 can)   **Eggs**

Dilute the consommé according to the instructions on the can. Let it come to the boiling point and serve immediately into two warmed bowls. Immediately break an egg into each bowl and put a saucer over each so that the heat will be retained and the eggs will poach slightly. Serve immediately, and let each person stir the egg into her soup.

CHICKEN PAPRIKA

Buy:

Chicken, small, cut into   **Red onions (2 small)**
   pieces (3–4 pounds)
Sour cream (small
   container)

Check Cupboard for:

Paprika   **Sugar**
Butter   **Flour**
Wine vinegar   **Cooking oil**

Preheat oven to 350°.
Oil the pieces of chicken, put them in a roasting pan, and roast them for about half an hour.

Chop the red onions finely.

In a heavy saucepan, melt 2 tablespoons of butter and cook the red onions in it very gently for about 10 minutes, but do not allow them to brown or burn. Keep the heat low. Then add 1 tablespoon of paprika and mix it well. Then add 2 tablespoons of flour. Stir well and when the flour begins to bubble and thicken, add slowly one cup of chicken bouillon (hot) made with a cube. Stir until this sauce thickens. Add 1 teaspoon of vinegar and ¼ teaspoon sugar. Stir well. Salt and pepper to taste.

After 30 minutes, take the chicken from the oven, remove the skin, put the pieces back in the roasting pan, pour the sauce over them, and get it back in the oven as quickly as you can. Don't leave the oven door open—it will cool off and waste time.

Let it all cook for another 15 to 20 minutes. Remove from the oven, stir in ½ cup sour cream, and serve immediately.

STUFFED PEPPERS

Buy:

Peppers, sweet, green (2, medium-sized)
Cheddar cheese, sharp, aged (¼ pound)

Bread crumbs (small box)
An onion

Check Cupboard for:

Cooking oil

Any green herb

Cut a slice off the peppers at the stem end and scoop out the seeds and tough white membranes. Boil some water in a saucepan big enough to hold the peppers, and when it boils drop the peppers in and parboil them for 5 minutes. Remove and cool them while you make the filling.

Preheat the oven to 350°.

Mince the onion. Make about ½ cup of chicken bouillon with a cube. Grate some cheese. Make a mixture of equal amounts of bread crumbs and cheese, and mix in the onion. Add a green herb (marjoram or rosemary—you choose) and salt and pepper to taste. Stuff the peppers with as much as you can cram into them, and then. pour just a little chicken bouillon and about ½ teaspoon of oil into each to moisten the stuffing. Put the peppers in a small roasting pan in the oven, and bake for 20 to 25 minutes or until the peppers are tender when pierced with a fork.

Serve with the chicken paprika.

GRAPES WITH SOUR CREAM

Buy:

**Grapes, green, seedless (a
medium-sized bunch)**

**Sour cream (1 small carton)
Sugar, brown or maple**

Remove grapes from their stems and wash them in cold water. Dry them. Arrange them in two dessert dishes. Sprinkle the sugar lavishly over them, and top with lots of sour cream. Put them away in the refrigerator to chill for at least two hours before dinner.

Menu #12

Chilled Tomato Soup
Total Salad
Bowl of Fresh Fruit

The Day Before:

Make the soup and store it, saving the sour cream to add just before
    serving.
Make the salad dressings.
Cook any vegetables that need it and store them in the refrigerator.
Wash, dry, and store the lettuce.

Before Barbara Arrives:

You will have a lot of washing and slicing and chopping to do, so start
    early.

CHILLED TOMATO SOUP

Buy:

Tomato soup, condensed (1 can)   **An onion (small)**
Sour cream (1 small carton)

Check Cupboard for:

Basil   **An egg**

Hard-cook the egg, plunge it in cold water, peel it, and chill it.

Mix together the tomato soup, all the sour cream, the small onion finely chopped, ½ teaspoon dried basil, ½ teaspoon salt, freshly ground black pepper. Store in the refrigerator to chill thoroughly. Serve garnished with finely chopped egg.

If you should need to prepare this soup in a great rush, mix it up as described, put it in a cocktail shaker with a lot of ice cubes, and shake the hell out of it.

THE TOTAL SALAD

Buy:

Many of the following:

Lettuce (choose two or three): Romaine, escarole, endive, Bibb, Boston, Bronze, chicory, oak leaf, iceberg, field, dandelion

Cabbage, green or red

Spinach, raw

Watercress

Cucumber

Onions, red, Bermuda or sweet, yellow

Garlic

Green onions, also known as scallions

Tomatoes, ordinary, beefsteak, cherry

Beets (cooked but not pickled) sliced, or whole baby beets

Celery (Pascal variety)

Peppers, sweet, green, or red

Pimientos (in a jar)

Peas (cooked)

Green beans (cooked)

Carrots, raw, julienne, sliced, or grated

Radishes

Parsley

Any fresh herbs you can find

Mushrooms (raw)

Zucchini (raw, sliced like cucumber)

Artichoke hearts
(marinated, cooked)
Lima beans (cooked)
Corn (cooked)
Kidney beans (cooked)
Asparagus (cooked)
Cauliflower (raw)
Fennel
Palm hearts
Potatoes (cooked)
Olives, green or ripe
Eggs (hard-boiled)
Cheese, Swiss strips,
Cheddar grated, Parmesan
Ham, strips or rolls

Chicken, portions or chunks
Tongue, strips
Turkey, portions or chunks
Roast beef, slices or rolls or
strips
Bacon, crumbled
Salami
Anchovies
Shrimp
Lobster
Crab
Tuna
Salmon
Pickles
Croutons

The principle of The Total Salad is that you put everything into it that has ever occurred to anyone to put into a salad.

Obviously you can't put in everything. The thing to do is to roam the supermarket choosing things in the following categories: traditional salad fixings; raw vegetables (or cooked) less frequently used, cheese, meat and/or fish; odds and ends. This way you can choose whatever looks most fresh and appetizing.

Build your salad, having spent a great deal of time washing and drying lettuce and chopping and slicing and washing and mincing and cooking everything else, in the biggest bowl you can find or borrow or buy. If desperate, use a dish-washing bowl.

Line it with different kinds of lettuce (it is not going to be tossed!) and arrange all the ingredients in piles and layers, so that people can serve themselves and pick out what they want.

Have several different kinds of salad dressing available, and again, let people serve themselves. Serve with lots of garlic bread (see p. 143).

BOWL OF FRESH FRUIT

The Total Salad is pretty filling, but there's always room for a nice piece of fruit. Buy the best you can find, a selection or 3 or 4 different kinds, and keep them cold until serving. Some may need washing, and don't forget to polish the apples and make them shiny.

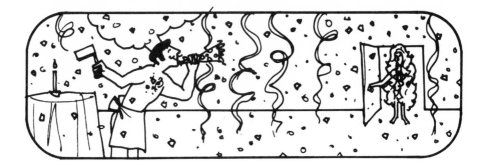

Chapter 9

But Damn It All, Doris, It's Groundhog Day

IF DORIS HAILS from Portland, Oregon, and works in your office in Portland, Maine, the odds are good that on Christmas, Easter or other national holidays she'll be amenable to a festive romp *chez vous*. The airfare home and back would wipe her out for a month. Furthermore, you've been spouting off about your skills with skillet, pot, and platter, so she's anxious to see how you measure up—in more ways than one. She may even bring the wine.

If it turns out she's booked solid for all foreseeable holidays, there's no need for you to come unglued. "Why wouldn't she be?" you've probably already asked your soap-smothered visage in the bathroom mirror. "In a sweater, she looks like a dead heat in a zeppelin race."

If she can't make it for Christmas or the celebration of her birthday (or yours), ask her over for Groundhog Day. Or better yet, dream up your own special event and the chow to go with it. The fact that no one has ever heard of Louisiana Purchase Remembrance Day or the 465th anniversary of the Uzbek Invasion of Khorasan doesn't mean that you can't lay on a meal and chase Doris over the sofas and tables with the same lip-smacking glee you would use on the 4th of July or Memorial Day.

Another good angle is to find something in Doris' past that is worth perpetuating. There's certainly going to be something in her future if things work out at all, and it's always nice to give a balance to the proceedings. This doesn't have to be anything momentous, but if you can invent a theme for the evening, it will serve as a viable beginning for practically anything up to and including arraignment on the following morning. How about the 17th anniversary of her graduation from kindergarten?

As for the better known events, certain dishes have long been associated with several of them. Thanksgiving and Christmas commonly call for turkey, although goose is sometimes served for Yule. In New England, cold salmon is a tradition on the 4th of July. New Year's Day, on the other hand, is not as closely identified with any fixed fare (unless you count Bromo Seltzer), and anyway, who says you have to roast a turkey or goose for Christmas when any number of possibilities present themselves—such as veal, duck, lamb, chicken and other thoughts suggested here. What does Doris like to eat? Make this your departure point in mapping out a menu.

Once she commits herself to an event at your place, lay on the atmosphere with all four feet. When that special evening arrives, you'll want everything to be perfect. Your martini glasses will have been frosted in the freezer for an entire day. The tablecloth is *not* the one you stuffed into your suitcase the last time you left The Hilton. The candles are new, not those uneven stubs you have leaning out of old Chianti bottles. The silverware gleams and includes nothing from the collections of United Air Lines or the Penn Central Railroad. The lights are low, the music is soft. The TV is officially "broken," in case she asks, and if you feel she won't believe this, you can clip off the plug with a pair of wire cutters and easily replace it the next day. Assuming she's not hip to electricity, this ploy should suffice to preserve the evening for absorbing conversation. If you've got to compete with "Kojak" or "The Mary Tyler Moore Show," you'll lose, since you're only an amateur entertainer. True, you have talent, but don't test it against the pros. Besides, you can't speak to her of love in the midst of a commercial message of importance to denture wearers—no matter how delicious the dinner was or what the occasion or nonoccasion happens to be.

NINE MEALS PERFECT FOR ANY OCCASION

Menu #1

Fresh Hors d'Oeuvre
Veal Normandy Style with Shallots, Mushrooms,
   and Cream
Purée of Spinach Béchamel
Omelette Normande Flamed with Calvados
Cheese

Menu #2

Sliced Cucumber with Swedish Herring in Dill
Vichyssoise
Cold Poached Salmon with Herb Mayonnaise
Asparagus with Drawn Butter and Lemon
Fresh Strawberries and Cream

Menu #3

Smoked Scottish Salmon
Roast Duck with Orange Sauce
Wild Rice
Festive Green Beans
Belgian Endive and Tomato Salad
Syllabub

Menu #4

Pâté Maison
Roast Stuffed Chicken Leonard
Roasted Paprika Potatoes
Little Peas Cooked in Lettuce
Green Salad
Summer Pudding

Menu #5

Caviar on Toast
Beef Stroganoff
Noodles with Poppy Seeds
Cucumber and Yogurt Salad
Fresh Fruit Salad Father William

Menu #6

Shrimp Cocktail
Roast Leg of Lamb
Baked Potatoes with Sour Cream and Chives
Mint Sauce
Baked Zucchini Parmesan
Crème Renversée

Menu #7

Artichoke Hearts Vinaigrette
Beef Bourguignon
Seasoned Rice
Green Bean and Onion Salad
Ann's Peaches

Menu #8

Fresh Oysters or Cherrystone Clams
Roast Pork with Potato and Apple
Tomatoes Provençale
Red Cabbage and Romaine Salad
Cheese and Fruit

Menu #9

Pâté de Foie Gras
Jellied Consommé with Sherry
Roast Turkey
Traditional Stuffing
Mashed Potatoes
Cranberry Sauce & Jelly
Celery and Olives and Sliced Tomatoes
Cranberries Jubilee or Christmas Pudding
    with Brandy Butter

Menu #1

Fresh Hors d'Oeuvre
Veal Normandy Style with Shallots, Mushrooms,
    and Cream
Purée of Spinach Béchamel
Omelette Normande Flamed with Calvados
Cheese

The Day Before:

Make the Béchamel sauce.

In the Morning:

Prepare the various elements of the hors d'oeuvre and put them in the
  refrigerator.

Before Doris Arrives:

Assemble the hors d'oeuvre, still keeping it cool.
Chop the shallots and slice the mushrooms.
Cook and purée the spinach.
Take the cheese out of the refrigerator four hours before dinner.
Peel, core, and slice the apples. Put a little lemon juice on them to pre-
  vent them from turning brown.

Twenty Minutes Before Dinner:

Start preparing the veal.
Heat the spinach and the Béchamel sauce together.

Note: the Omelette Normande has to be prepared just before eating.

FRESH HORS D'OEUVRE

Buy:

A tomato, medium
A cucumber, small
Beets, baby if possible (1
  bunch)
Carrots (a few)

Radishes (small bunch)
Sardines, Norwegian
  brisling (1 can)—optional
Salami, small dry variety (¼
  pound)—optional

Make a French dressing (see p. 12)
Wash the beets and trim off all but an inch of their tops. Do not cut off
the roots. Boil small beets whole for about 30 minutes in a saucepan,
without salt. Larger ones may take up to an hour to cook. Test them with
a fork, and when they are tender, drop them into cold water and the skins
will slip off in your fingers. Let them cool and slice them.

Core and slice the tomato. Peel and slice very thinly about half the cucumber. Trim the radishes. Pare and grate 1 or perhaps 2 carrots, depending upon size. Put the tomato, carrot, cucumber, and beet in separate small bowls, and pour a little French dressing over each. Now select 3 or 4 different green herbs, crumble between thumb and forefinger, and sprinkle a different one over each of the four vegetables. For example, basil on the tomato, dill on the cucumber, tarragon on the carrot, and marjoram on the beets. Don't overdo the herbs; use just a little of each. Mix them gently into the vegetables. Put everything away in the refrigerator to cool until you are ready to assemble the hors d'oeuvre and put it on the table.

Then, distribute a little of everything on each plate, adding a few lettuce leaves if you like. Try to make the vegetables look attractive on the plate, garnish them with parsley, and add a dash of paprika.

Note: A small serving of lentil salad (see p. 94) is an excellent addition to a plate of fresh hors d'oeuvre.

VEAL NORMANDY STYLE WITH SHALLOTS, MUSHROOMS, AND CREAM

Buy:

Veal, cut for escalope (¾ pound)

Mushrooms, fresh (¼ pound)

Shallots (a few)

Heavy cream (½ pint)

Parsley

Check Cupboard for:

Pepper, whole white peppercorns

Butter

Veal prepared in this manner cooks very quickly, so it's a good idea to assemble everything you need beforehand. Have the parsley chopped. Get out two frying pans, a large one and a small one. Fill your pepper mill with white peppercorns. Peel and chop finely two shallots. Slice the mushrooms.

Put a little butter in the small frying pan and gently fry the shallots until they just begin to brown slightly. Remove them from the pan and keep them warm in the oven (200°). Fry the sliced mushrooms gently, and then add them to the shallots.

Melt a tablespoon of butter in the large frying pan, and when it is bubbling add the slices of veal. Cook them for a few minutes and then turn them over. Continue cooking until the meat has partially browned on each side. Then add the mushrooms and shallots, some parsley, and some freshly ground white pepper. Turn the heat down, and add ½ cup of heavy cream. Stir the cream, blending it with the mushrooms and shallots and with the meat juice that will be released from the bottom of the pan. Add more cream if necessary. Place each serving of veal on a dinner plate, and pour the cream and mushroom sauce over it.

PURÉE OF SPINACH BÉCHAMEL

Buy:
Spinach, fresh (1 bag) or
   frozen chopped (1 package)

Check Cupboard for:
Butter   **Milk**
Flour

Make a Béchamel sauce (see p. 11), but *halve* the recipe—be sure to make it well ahead of time—even the night before—and store it in the refrigerator or a cool place until you need it.

Spinach requires very little time to cook and very little water to cook in. If you are using fresh spinach, rinse it in a colander and remove any wilted or spoiled leaves. Use a whole bag, because it reduces dramatically in volume when it is cooked. Put just a little water—say half a cup—in a saucepan large enough to contain the spinach, and cook it over a medium heat. The spinach will reduce itself to less than a quarter of its original size and turn dark green. It is then done.

If you have a blender, purée the spinach, add it to the ½ cup of Béchamel sauce, and heat. Season with salt and pepper and with a little lemon juice and/or nutmeg if you wish.

If you have no blender, use a foodmill, or mash the spinach in a sieve and then add to the sauce.

OMELETTE NORMANDE FLAMED WITH CALVADOS

Buy:

**Calvados (French apple
 brandy—1 bottle)**

Apples, hard juicy (2 or 3)
Eggs (4)

Check Cupboard for:

Brown sugar

Butter

The cooking of the omelet has to be done at the last minute, but you can prepare the apples ahead of time.

Peel, core, and slice 2 or 3 apples. Fry them in butter in a frying pan, stirring them gently and trying to preserve the slices whole. (This will depend more on the kind of apple than on your skill.) Give them a squirt of lemon juice, and add 2 tablespoons of brown sugar. Don't let the apples cook dry, and don't let them burn. When they are *almost* cooked, turn off the heat and put them away until you are ready to make the omelet.

Assemble the apples, 4 eggs, the omelet pan, a very small saucepan for heating the Calvados, a large spoon, matches. Reheat the apples.

Make a 4-egg omelet (see p. 131). Before folding it, put half the cooked apples inside of it. Then fold and put the rest of the apples over it. While the omelet is cooking, heat 3 ounces (or more) of Calvados in a small saucepan. When the omelet is ready, take a spoonful of hot Calvados and hold a lighted match underneath it. When the Calvados flames up, pour it over the omelet and apples, then add the rest of the Calvados, letting it catch and being careful not to put out the flames.

Serve immediately.

CHEESE

For advice on choosing and buying cheese, see p. 37. One or two varieties of cheese is enough to offer after a large meal. Serve the cheese with very simple biscuits, such as one of the Scandinavian flatbreads. A bunch of cool, freshly washed grapes makes a good accompaniment to the cheese.

Menu #2

Sliced Cucumber with Swedish Herring in Dill
Vichyssoise
Cold Poached Salmon with Herb Mayonnaise
Asparagus with Drawn Butter and Lemon
Fresh Strawberries and Cream

The Day Before:

Make the vichyssoise.
Make the mayonnaise.
Make the court bouillon.

In the Morning:

Cook the salmon.
Hard-cook 2 eggs.
Hull and slice the strawberries.

Before Doris Arrives:

Trim the asparagus and put it in cold water in its saucepan.
Put the salmon on a platter and garnish it.
Put the mayonnaise in a serving bowl.
Make the hors d'oeuvre.
Put the strawberries into individual dishes.

Just Before You Sit Down to Eat the Vichyssoise:

Start cooking the asparagus. It takes 15 to 20 minutes.
Melt the butter after you have finished eating the salmon.
Serve the asparagus on fresh plates as a separate course.

SLICED CUCUMBER WITH SWEDISH
HERRING IN DILL

For recipe, see p. 29.

VICHYSSOISE

For recipe see p. 124.

COLD POACHED SALMON WITH HERB MAYONNAISE

Buy:

Fresh salmon (1-pound
   slice)
Cheesecloth (1 or 2 yards,
   but it often comes in a
   package)
Parsley
A carrot

An onion
Celery (1 stalk)
Wine, dry white (1 bottle)
Tomatoes (2 or 3)
Cucumber
Lettuce

Check Cupboard for:

Butter
Black peppercorns
Cloves
Bay leaf

Eggs
Parsley
Green mayonnaise (see page
   89)

To poach fish, you need a large long pan with a cover and a rack inside it. You can contrive a reasonably good arrangement if you have two aluminum roasting pans 13 x 9½ inches, and a rack which fits, but it is best to buy a fish kettle.

Make a court bouillon for fish as follows: Melt 1 tablespoon of butter in a pan and add to it 1 sprig of parsley and 1 tablespoon each of chopped carrot, onion, and celery. Cook these things together for about 3 minutes. Add 3 peppercorns, 1 whole clove, 1 bay leaf, 1 teaspoon of salt, 2 cups dry white wine, and 1 quart water. Bring the mixture to the boiling point and simmer it for fifteen minutes. Strain it.

Wrap the piece of salmon in cheesecloth. This is so that you will be able to remove it from the pan when it is cooked without having it fall into pieces. Lay the salmon on the rack in the kettle or pan, and pour in the court bouillon to a depth of 2″. Heat the kettle (on the top of the stove) with its cover on until the bouillon comes to the boil, and then turn it down and let it simmer gently, allowing 8 to 12 minutes cooking time per pound of fish. Remove the fish carefully and lay it on a platter to cool. Peel the cheesecloth off while the fish is still hot, or it will stick. Put it away in the refrigerator until dinner time and let it chill.

Just before you expect Doris to ring the bell, take the salmon out of the refrigerator and place it on a serving platter. Garnish the edges of the platter with some slices of tomato, cucumber, hard-cooked egg, and lettuce. Sprinkle with chopped parsley.

Put the mayonnaise into your best-looking small serving bowl, and maybe sprinkle a little paprika on top. If the weather is very hot, it might be wise to put the fish back in the refrigerator until you serve it. Otherwise, you can lay a moist tea-towel over it.

ASPARAGUS WITH DRAWN BUTTER AND LEMON

Buy:
Asparagus (1 pound)

Check Cupboard for:
Butter   **Lemon**

The best way to cook asparagus is in a saucepan designed specifically for the purpose. The asparagus stands upright (with an elastic band or bit of string around it). The bottoms of the stalks, which are tougher than the rest, then cook in boiling water, and the tenderer tops cook in steam. If you have a double boiler, you can make do by standing the stalks in the bottom pan and inverting the top pan over them. You need a fairly tight fit, or the steam will all escape and the asparagus tips won't cook. You may have to fall back on a large saucepan and immerse the asparagus in water, which is a pity.

Wash the asparagus in fresh water, and remove lower scales which often contain sand. Cut off the lower tough part of the stalks. Keep the asparagus standing in cool water two inches deep until you are ready to cook them.

Stand them up in an asparagus pan with enough boiling salted water to cover the lower halves. Cover tightly, and cook for 15 to 20 minutes. You will have to turn the heat down when the steam starts to build up, or the pot will boil over.

Meanwhile, melt ⅛ pound of butter in a small saucepan. Add to it the juice of ½ lemon (or more, according to taste), salt and pepper, a little chopped parsley, and/or the herb of your choice.

Serve the asparagus onto two plates and pour the lemon-butter sauce over them.

FRESH STRAWBERRIES AND CREAM

Buy:

Strawberries, best available (1 or 2 little baskets)
Heavy cream or sour cream (½ pint)

Fruit (super fine) sugar (1 pound)

Wash the berries in fresh running water, but gently. If the strawberries are perfectly shaped and have an excellent flavor, just remove the stems and sprinkle the berries with fruit sugar. Put them away in the refrigerator until you wish to serve them.

If the flavor is not all that might be desired, remove the stems and then slice the strawberries into a bowl and sprinkle them with fruit sugar. They will make a nice juice, and their flavor will be improved.

Before serving, place the berries in individual dishes, add more sugar if needed, and top with heavy or sour cream.

You may like to pour a little kirsch or brandy over the berries.

Menu #3

Smoked Scottish Salmon
Roast Duck with Orange Sauce
Wild Rice
Festive Green Beans
Belgian Endive and Tomato Salad
Syllabub

The Day Before:

Make the basic orange sauce.

Before Doris Arrives:

Prepare the duck to go into the oven. Calculate its cooking time, and heat the oven beforehand.

Brown the almonds.

Put the beans, water, and bouillon cube into a saucepan, ready to cook.

Wash the rice, and judge its cooking time.

Take the butter out of the refrigerator so that it will soften and spread easily on the brown bread.

Prepare the salad and put it in the refrigerator with a damp cloth over it, but no dressing.

Make the syllabub and put it in the refrigerator to chill.

Prepare the salmon and brown bread.

Just Before Dinner:

Add the duck's pan juices to the sauce.

Start to cook the beans.

Put the syllabub into individual dishes.

After the Main Course:

Pour the dressing over the salad and serve it.

SMOKED SCOTTISH SALMON

For recipe, see p. 25.

This time, make sure you get Scottish salmon, and make sure that it is sliced off the fish itself, not imported in little plastic packs.

Buy a very thinly sliced brown bread. There is one on the market now called a Melba Thin Dietslice. It is not a *diet* bread; it is merely cut in very thin slices.

ROAST DUCK WITH ORANGE SAUCE

Buy:

**Duck (small, but at least 3
    pounds)**
White wine, dry (1 bottle)

**Orange juice, frozen,
    unsweetened (1 can)**
Oranges, fresh (2 or 3)

Check Cupboard for:

Butter
Flour

Basil
Parsley

A word about ducks: Duck is a fat bird and therefore it does not require basting while it cooks. On the contrary, you have to remove some of the fat that drips off it while it is cooking. Consequently, you really must use an oven rack or the duck will be sitting in a puddle of fat while it cooks. To help get rid of excess fat, examine the bird before you put it in the oven and locate areas of fat under the skin. Prick these with the tines of a fork from time to time while the duck is cooking and the melted fat will run out. You do not have to truss a duck, because its wings and legs are short.

Preheat the oven to 300°.

If your duck is frozen, leave plenty of time for it to thaw. Then remove the parcel of giblets, and inspect the inside for lumps of fat that you can remove easily. Then slice an orange into rounds and put it, rind and all, into the duck.

Put the duck on a rack, and insert a meat thermometer into the thigh muscle next to the body. The oven should be at 300°. Allow 25 to 30 minutes cooking time per pound. When the meat thermometer reads 185°, the duck is done, and its skin should be crisp and brown. During cooking, drain off the fat from time to time, and prick the skin to allow more to drain out.

The sauce: Dilute the orange juice according to the instructions on the can. In a sauce pan, put 1½ tablespoons of butter, and two of flour, and proceed to follow the basic instructions for sauces on p. 10. Instead of milk or water, make a mixture of about half and half white wine and orange juice.

Allow the sauce to cook slowly, and have it ready by the time the duck is cooked. Then you will have to juggle things around a little. Take the duck out of the oven, rack and all, put it into another roasting pan or onto an oven-proof serving platter, and put it back in the oven to keep warm. (Turn the oven down to low.) Pour as much fat as you can out of the duck pan, preserving carefully the dark-colored meat juices. Put the pan over a hot heat on top of the stove, and add a little orange juice and wine mixture (*not* the sauce) to it and stir with a wooden spoon. All the bits of meat and juices will mix with the liquid, and you can then pour this mixture into the sauce. Season the sauce with salt and pepper to taste, and add a little basil—particularly good with duck. If the sauce is too thin, follow instructions on p. 11, for thickening it.

If the duck is very small—3 pounds—just cut it in half to serve it, and arrange slices of orange from the inside of the duck around it. Put the sauce in a gravy boat and allow people to serve themselves. Garnish with chopped parsley.

WILD RICE

Buy:
Wild rice (smallest package available)

Wild rice costs a small fortune, but do try it at least once. Its flavor is incomparable. As a compromise, you can buy packages of mixed wild and domestic rice. The cooking time for wild rice is somewhat unpredictable, simply because it is a wild natural product and varies according to the growing season and the harvest. It may cook in 30 minutes, it may need an hour. So allow plenty of time, and if it is not done after 30 minutes, just add a little more water and continue to cook until it is tender.

Wash ⅓ cup of wild rice well under cold running water, and drain it. Put it into a saucepan with 1 cup of cold water and ¼ teaspoon salt. Cover and bring to a boil.Remove cover and continue boiling without stirring until the rice is tender. If necessary, add more water. When it is cooked, drain away any excess water, and add a knob of butter. Season to taste.

FESTIVE GREEN BEANS

Buy:

**Green beans, French cut,
frozen (1 package)**

**Almonds, slivered (1 small
package)**

Check Cupboard for:

Lemons
Chicken bouillon cubes

Parsley
Oil

Put some oil in a frying pan and heat it and then add 2 or 3 tablespoons of slivered almonds. Turn down the heat so that they will not burn, and turn them over and over until they begin to brown. Remove them immediately and let them drain on several layers of paper towel.

Prepare the green beans according to the directions on the box, but add a chicken bouillon cube to the cooking water. Undercook the beans so that they are just slightly crisp, *al dente*. Drain. Add a squirt of lemon juice, the almonds, some chopped parsley, and salt and pepper to taste.

BELGIAN ENDIVE AND TOMATO SALAD

Buy:

**Belgian endives, white and
fresh (2 or 3)**
Tomatoes (1 large or 2 small)

An onion, very small

Make a French mustard dressing (see p. 13).

Trim the root ends of the endives, disassemble them, and tear the leaves into a salad bowl.

Wash the tomatoes, remove the cores, and slice them into the bowl.

Peel the onion, and put a few very, very thin slices into the bowl. Add the dressing just before serving.

SYLLABUB

Buy:

Heavy cream for whipping
   (½ pint)

Lemons

Sherry, medium dry (1 bottle)

Check Cupboard for:

Sugar

Into a large bowl, put ¼ cup sugar, the juice of 2 lemons, the grated rind of 1 lemon, and 2 tablespoons sherry. Let it stand for about 30 minutes.

Whip the cream. Then whip in the lemon and sherry and sugar. Put the bowl in the refrigerator to chill for several hours.

Menu #4

Pâté Maison
Roast Stuffed Chicken Leonard
Roasted Paprika Potatoes
Little Peas Cooked in Lettuce
Green Salad
Summer Pudding

The Day Before:

Make the pudding.
Make the pâté.

Well Before Doris Arrives:

Calculate the cooking time of the chicken and plan accordingly what
    time it must go into the oven.
Peel and parboil the potatoes.
Assemble all of the ingredients for the peas and put them all in the sauce-
    pan ready for cooking.
Wash and dry the lettuce and put it in the refrigerator wrapped in a
    towel.

Arrange the pâté on a plate with its garnish and put it back in the refrigerator.

Put the chicken in the oven.

Put the potatoes in the oven 1¼ hours before dinner time.

If you are using whipped cream on the pudding, whip it and store it in the refrigerator.

Just After Doris Arrives:

Put the peas on to cook 20 minutes to half an hour before dinner is ready.

After you have finished the main course and the peas, dress the salad.

Take the pudding out of the refrigerator just before serving.

PÂTÉ MAISON

If you happen to live near a really first-class deli, buy a slice of really first-class pâté. It is quite rich, so ¼ pound is ample.

If not, make your own (see p. 33).

If you buy a slice, lay it on a bed of lettuce leaves, and decorate it with parsley.

If you make your own, pack it into an attractive bowl, and decorate the top with parsley, or bits of hard-cooked egg, and/or slices of olive.

Serve with slices of crusty bread and sweet butter.

ROAST STUFFED CHICKEN LEONARD

Buy:

Chicken, preferably not frozen (3 or 4 pounds)

Pine nuts and/or almonds, whole

Cheese, 2 or 3 kinds—a sharp aged cheddar, a mild orange cheddar, perhaps one other similar cheese—(¼ pound or less of each)

Check Cupboard for:

Dried chopped green onions   **Bacon**
Lemons

Preheat the oven to 300°.

Remove the giblets from inside the chicken. Remove any accessible lumps of fat. Rub inside of chicken with lemon wedges.

Toast the almonds in oil in a frying pan, turning them constantly until they begin to brown. Drain them on several layers of paper towel.

Cut up the cheese into small lumps and stuff the chicken with a mixture of nuts, cheese, and a little dried green onion. Turn the flap of skin at the neck end over the back. Tie the legs together with the pope's nose tucked up between them. Continue the same bit of string and lash the wings to the sides of the body. Lay a couple of bacon strips across the breast. Oil the chicken lightly all over and place it breast-up, on a rack in your roasting pan. Stick a meat thermometer into the thigh muscle next to the body. Place it in the 300° oven and cook for 35 to 40 minutes per pound of chicken or until the meat thermometer reads 185°. Do not baste.

If you want to make a chicken gravy, the principle is the same as for making a basic sauce, except that you can do it right in the roasting pan. When the chicken is done, put it in another pan, turn the oven down low, and put the chicken back in to keep warm. If there is a lot of fat in the roasting pan, pour some of it off. Put the pan over a moderate heat on top of the stove. Add a tablespoon of flour to the fat and juice and stir it with a wooden spoon. As the flour begins to thicken and turn a little brown, slowly add about a cup of water (or of milk or half each or even a little wine) and keep stirring. Scrape all the matter off the bottom of the pan with the wooden spoon, and adjust the heat down if necessary. Add more liquid until you get the right consistency. Taste the gravy before seasoning it.

You can use the same method to make gravy for any roast.

Serve it in a gravy boat with a little chopped parsley on top.

ROASTED PAPRIKA POTATOES

Buy:

Potatoes, medium-sized for
 roasting (3 or 4)

Check Cupboard for:

Paprika

Boil water in a saucepan big enough to hold the potatoes.

Peel and wash the potatoes. If they are quite big, cut them in half. Put them into boiling salted water for 10 minutes.

Put them in a baking pan with some fat from the chicken or some corn oil. Sprinkle them with paprika, and bake them in the same oven as the chicken for about 1 hour or until they are soft. Turn and baste them occasionally.

Any leftovers will be very good sliced and fried for breakfast.

LITTLE PEAS COOKED IN LETTUCE

Buy:

Little peas (petit pois), frozen (1 package)
Green onions (1 or 2 bunches)
Lettuce, preferably Boston or leaf (1 head)

Chervil (fresh probably not available, so buy a jar of dried)
Parsley

Check Cupboard for:

Butter   **Sugar**

Wash the lettuce and shake it as dry as possible. Then put it on your wooden chopping board and shred the whole head with a sharp knife. Put the shredded lettuce into a saucepan. Open the package of peas and dump them on top of the lettuce. Trim the roots off the green onions, and discard all but the white part at the bottom. Put about 12 little onions in with the peas. Chop parsley and add about a tablespoonful. Add a teaspoon of dried chervil. Add a teaspoon of sugar. Salt and pepper to taste.

Put about 2 tablespoons of water into the pot, and place it over a low to medium heat. As the water begins to boil and cook the lettuce, the lettuce itself will provide more water. Stir everything together at this point, and let the peas and lettuce simmer for about 20 minutes with a tight lid. When they are ready, there should not be much water left and the peas and lettuce will have a moderately thick consistency.

Serve as a separate course after the chicken.

GREEN SALAD

Buy:

**Lettuce, 2 kinds such as
 Romaine and bronze or
 Boston (2 heads)**

Check Cupboard for:

Olive oil   **Wine vinegar**

This recipe is for the classic and consequently very simple green salad of French cooking. The details of preparation are important.

Wash the lettuce, separating the leaves and selecting those you will use to make a salad for two people. Shake these leaves dry and tear (never cut with a knife) them into bite-size pieces. Then *dry* the lettuce with a clean tea towel—that's right, dry it—and put the lettuce and the towel into the refrigerator to crisp. Don't take it out until you are ready to serve the salad. Then put it into a bowl.

Immediately before serving add 1 tablespoon of olive oil to the salad. Toss the lettuce with a fork and a spoon about 30 times to ensure that the oil coats every piece of lettuce. In tossing, lift the pieces of lettuce gently about 4 to 6 inches above the bowl and drop them with a slight whirling motion. When all the lettuce is well coated with oil, add a scant tablespoon of wine vinegar (or fresh lemon juice), and a little salt and pepper to taste. Toss again to mix these last ingredients.

Serve immediately.

SUMMER PUDDING

Buy:

**Bread, white, crusty if
 possible (1 loaf)**
**Red fruit, a choice of the
 following fresh, frozen, or
 canned: plums, cherries,
 strawberries, raspberries,
 blackberries, black
 raspberries, loganberries,**
**blueberries. Some of the
 fruit should be canned,
 because you will need the
 juice. Try canned dark red
 cherries and frozen
 raspberries, plus whatever
 else you like.**
Cream, heavy (½ pint)

Wash the fresh fruit and remove stones, stems, and so forth. Defrost the raspberries. Drain the canned cherries and have the juice ready to use in a separate cup.

Line a good-sized deep bowl with thickish slices of bread, not overlooking the bottom. Then pack your fruit, mixing the varieties well, on top of the bread and fill the hollow completely. Add some of the juice from the different kinds of fruit—enough to soak the bread but not more.

Put the bowl into the refrigerator to chill *thoroughly.*

To serve, invert the bowl over a serving dish, and if you have not put too much juice in, the pudding will not collapse.

Serve with heavy cream or whipped cream.

Of course, there's nothing to stop you from putting a little kirsch or Cointreau or brandy into the pudding.

Menu #5

Caviar on Toast
Beef Stroganoff
Noodles with Poppy Seeds
Cucumber and Yogurt Salad
Fresh Fruit Salad Father William

The Day Before:

Make the fruit salad and put it in the refrigerator.
Make the melba toast.
Make the beef stroganoff and store it in the refrigerator.

Before Doris Arrives:

Make the cucumber and yogurt salad.
Prepare the garnish (egg, onion, etc.) for the caviar.
Take the beef stroganoff out of the refrigerator.
Calculate the cooking time of the noodles, and put a large saucepan of salted water on the stove.

Just Before Doris Arrives:

Arrange the caviar for serving, but keep it in the refrigerator until needed.
Put the beef over a very low heat.
Boil the water for the noodles.

While You Eat the Caviar:

Put the noodles on to cook.
Make sure the beef will be hot on time.

At the Table:

Serve the cucumber and yogurt salad with the main course.
Flame the fruit salad at the table for special effect.

CAVIAR ON TOAST

Buy:

Caviar, black, imported
Russian or Iranian (1 or 2
  ounces)

Lemons
Onions, small (1 or 2)
Melba toast

Check Cupboard for:

Eggs

Hard-cook 1 or 2 eggs.
Mince a small onion as finely as possible.
Peel the egg, chop the white finely, and crumble the yolk.
Cut a lemon into wedges.
Put the caviar into a bowl surrounded by crushed ice.
On side dishes, arrange the lemon wedges, minced onions, chopped egg white, crumbled egg yolk, and the pieces of melba toast (unbuttered).
Eat the caviar on pieces of toast, garnishing with onions and egg and a drop or two of lemon juice.

BEEF STROGANOFF

Buy:

Beef, sirloin, cut in narrow
  strips 2 to 2½-inches long
  (1 pound)
An onion

Sour cream (1 small
  container)
Tomato purée (1 can)
Beef bouillon (2 cans)

Check Cupboard for:

Butter   **Flour**

Mince enough onion to produce 2 tablespoons of finely minced onion.

Melt 2 tablespoons of butter in the bottom of a large saucepan, and add 1 tablespoon of flour to make a *roux*. When it bubbles nicely and just begins to brown, add 2 undiluted cans of beef bouillon. Allow this mixture to simmer gently for about 10 minutes. Then stir in 1 tablespoon of tomato purée and mix thoroughly and allow to cook for a couple of minutes. Add a tablespoon of sour cream, stir that in thoroughly, and allow to cook for a couple of minutes. Continue in this fashion until you have added 2 tablespoons of tomato and 3 of sour cream. Keep the heat down to low, and continue cooking very slowly.

Put 2 tablespoons of butter into a frying pan, let the butter melt, and add the 2 tablespoons of minced onion. Sauté the onion until it is transparent and just beginning to turn golden. Then add the beef strips, and fry them, turning constantly until they are cooked on the outside and just beginning to brown here and there. Finally, add the entire contents of the frying pan to the mixture in the saucepan and cook slowly with a cover until the beef strips are done.

Season to taste with salt and pepper.

This dish improves with age and is best prepared the day before.

NOODLES WITH POPPY SEEDS

Buy:

Poppy seeds (1 small   **Egg noodles (1 package)**
  package)

Check Cupboard for:

Butter

Cook the noodles according to the instructions on the box. About half a box should be sufficient for two people.

When they are done, drain them and add a generous lump of butter. Sprinkle them with poppy seeds, and serve them on a heated platter.

Allow people to help themselves to noodles and then to the beef stroganoff on top of the noodles.

CUCUMBER AND YOGURT SALAD

Buy:

A cucumber
Yogurt, natural (1 pot)

Dill or mint, fresh if
available (1 bunch)

Peel and slice thinly about half of the cucumber. Put it in a bowl with several tablespoons of yogurt. Season with chopped fresh mint or dill, and salt and pepper. Put in the refrigerator to cool until needed.

Remember: You need a greater quantity of a fresh herb than of the same herb dried for the same effect.

FRESH FRUIT SALAD FATHER WILLIAM

Buy:

A selection of whatever
fresh fruits are available. Do
not buy canned fruit. Do,
however, buy 1 package of
frozen raspberries.

Pear liqueur, preferably
Swiss and made from
William pears (1 bottle, or
a miniature if available)

Wash, remove stones, peel and otherwise prepare and slice the fruit and put it in a bowl. Add at least part of the package of frozen raspberries and *all* of the juice it produces as it thaws. Put the fruit salad away in the refrigerator to cool and mature.

Just before serving, heat a couple of ounces of pear liqueur, take up some of it in a tablespoon and hold a match under it until it catches fire, light the rest of the liqueur with it, and pour it all over the fruit salad.

Menu #6

Shrimp Cocktail
Roast Leg of Lamb
Baked Potatoes with Sour Cream and Chives
Mint Sauce
Baked Zucchini Parmesan
Crème Renversée

The Day Before:

Make the crème renversée.
Make the mint sauce.
Make the cocktail sauce for the shrimp.

Next Morning:

Put the leg of lamb in the oven, with the potatoes.

Before Doris Arrives:

Prepare the zucchini and get them into the oven on time.
Deal with the shrimp.

Just Before Doris Arrives:

Assemble the shrimp cocktail.

SHRIMP COCKTAIL

Buy:

**Shrimp, raw or cooked,
    fresh or frozen unshelled
    (½ pound) or shelled (¼
    pound)**

**Lemons
Horseradish (1 small bottle)
Lettuce**

Check Cupboard for:

**Tabasco
Worcestershire sauce**

**Celery salt
Ketchup or chili sauce**

The sauce: Mix together lightly the following: ½ cup ketchup or chili sauce, 1 tablespoon lemon juice, 1 teaspoon celery salt, 2 teaspoons Worcestershire sauce, 6 drops Tabasco, 1 teaspoon grated horseradish, a little freshly ground black pepper, and salt to taste. Put the sauce in the refrigerator to chill.

The shrimp: If your shrimp are fresh and unshelled, cook them in the shell in boiling water or court bouillon (see p. 193) until they turn pink (about 12 to 15 minutes). Allow them to cool in the water in which they were cooked. When they are cool, remove the shells with your fingers and remove also the black line along the back.

If your shrimp are frozen and shelled, but cooked, drop them into boiling water and let them stand for a minute before draining.

If your shrimp are frozen raw in the shell, cook them like fresh shrimp in the shell, but only for 8 to 10 minutes.

Cool the shrimp, and serve them in individual dishes on a few lettuce leaves and with a little of the cocktail sauce. Do not drown them in it, or you will lose their delicate flavor.

ROAST LEG OF LAMB

Buy:
Leg of lamb, small

Check the Cupboard for:
Corn oil

As soon as you get up in the morning, turn on the oven to 300°. It is wiser to measure the internal temperature of the oven with an oven thermometer other than the one installed in the oven door. These are usually inaccurate up to 50°.

Get out the leg of lamb and oil it all over with corn oil. The easiest way is to use your hands.

Put it on a rack in a roasting pan, and when the oven hits 300°, put the lamb in and leave it for exactly 30 minutes—no longer. At the end of 30 minutes, turn the oven down to about 185°. Now go about your day's business and forget about the lamb. Do not touch it. Do not salt it or pepper it or interfere with it in any way. Do not even open the oven door. Leave it strictly alone. It will be done to perfection when dinner is ready in the evening. It can cook for 7 hours, 8 hours, 9 hours—it makes no difference. Just make sure the heat in the oven is about 185°, no higher.

This sounds an unorthodox way of cooking meat. Nevertheless, it produces a juicier, more flavorful, and tenderer roast than any other method. It works equally well with beef, pork, chicken, or turkey.

How to carve the lamb: Easy. Grasp it firmly by the protruding shank bone and hold it with the large end down resting on the platter or carving board. Cut slices down parallel to the bone.

BAKED POTATOES WITH SOUR CREAM AND CHIVES

Buy:

**Potatoes, large, the long,
   slender variety (2 or 3)**
**Sour cream (small
   container)**

**Chives, fresh (1 bunch) or
   frozen (1 pot)**

Check Cupboard for:

Butter

Scrub the potatoes and oil the outsides.

Since the oven is occupied by the lamb which is cooking at a very low temperature, the baked potatoes will have to fit into this schedule.

If you are going to be home during the day, put the potatoes into the oven in a small roasting pan with the lamb about 3½ hours before dinner.

If you are going to be out, put them in the oven in the morning as soon as you light it, and take them out after the 30-minute roasting at 300° which the lamb gets. Put them in again the minute you get home in the evening after work.

When they are done and you are ready to serve dinner, cut them crosswise on top, pinch them to open the cuts, and push into them a good lump of butter. Put a bowl of sour cream with chopped chives mixed into it on the table, and let people help themselves. Pass the salt and pepper, too.

MINT SAUCE

Buy:

**Mint, fresh (1 bunch) or
   dried mint, or a jar of mint
   jelly**

Check Cupboard for:

Wine vinegar   **Sugar**

If you have fresh mint, remove the leaves from the stems and wash them and shake them dry. Then chop the mint leaves as fine as you can with a sharp vegetable knife.

Make a half-water, half-vinegar mixture in a measuring cup, and add it slowly to the chopped mint until you have a thick mixture. I cannot give you an exact measurement because it depends on the size of the bunch of mint. Add about a teaspoon of sugar or less, depending on quantities, and taste it. Adjust until you like the flavor. It tastes better after it has been standing for a couple of hours.

BAKED ZUCCHINI PARMESAN

Buy:

Zucchini (2 or 3)
Garlic, fresh (usually sold in
**   packages of 2 or 3 bulbs)**

Parmesan cheese, grated (¼
**   pound freshly grated, or a**
**   little box)**

Check Cupboard for:

Butter

Boil a saucepan full of water, and when it is boiling hard, put the whole zucchini into it for about 5 minutes.

Remove them, trim off the stem end, and slice them in half lengthwise.

Lay them, cut side up, in a baking pan. Sprinkle a thin layer of grated Parmesan cheese onto each one. Dot each with little bits of butter. Crush a few garlic cloves with a broad knife on your chopping board (or use a garlic press), and put a few little bits on each piece of zucchini. Add a little salt and pepper. Pour about half a cup of water into the pan to prevent the zucchini from sticking or burning.

Put them into the oven with the lamb for about 40 minutes, and then serve. If you are not slow-roasting meat, bake them at 325° for about 20 minutes.

CRÈME RENVERSÉE

Buy:

Eggs (6)   **Sugar**
Milk   **Vanilla essence**

A traditional and favorite dessert in France which is much easier to prepare than it sounds.

For this dish, you need a metal oven pan roughly 4″ x 6″, and about 3″ deep. Don't use glass—the caramel won't stick to it.

Get out your heavy iron frying pan and put 1 cup of white sugar into it. Put it over a moderate heat and stir with a wooden spoon. The sugar will begin to melt and then liquify and turn a caramel color. Keep stirring and let it come to a full rolling boil. Then add ½ cup of water, stir, and let the caramel come to the boil again. This time let it boil for several minutes. Pour this mixture into the metal oven pan and let it set. (You will find that the caramel sticking to the pan washes off very easily with a little hot water.) Pick up the oven pan and tip it from side to side so that the caramel coats the sides. Do this several times as the caramel cools. Let it set for several hours in the refrigerator, preferably overnight.

Preheat the oven to 325°.

Put 3 whole eggs and 3 egg yolks into a mixing bowl and beat them with an egg beater until they are well mixed.

Put 1 pint of milk, ¼ cup of sugar, and ½ teaspoon of vanilla essence into a saucepan over moderate heat. Stir until the sugar melts, and continue cooking until the milk forms a ring of bubbles around the edge of the saucepan. Remove the saucepan from the stove, and slowly add the beaten eggs, stirring constantly. Now pour this custard mixture into the oven pan.

Set the oven pan into a larger pan which contains a little water, and put the whole business into the oven. The outer pan with water in it prevents the custard from becoming tough and the caramel from melting too much. Bake for about 45 minutes at 325°, or until the custard is cooked—i.e. when a straw slipped into the middle of it comes out clean.

Allow to cool and then chill in the refrigerator before serving.

Menu #7

Artichoke Hearts Vinaigrette
Beef Bourguignon
Seasoned Rice
Green Bean and Onion Salad
Ann's Peaches

The Day Before:

Prepare the artichoke hearts and put them in the refrigerator.
Prepare the peaches and store in the refrigerator.

Before Doris Arrives:

Prepare the beef in the morning so that it can cook for four hours.
Cook the green beans and put them away to chill.
Assemble the seasoning and bits for the rice.
Mince the onion for the salad.

Just Before Doris Arrives:

Put the rice on to cook.
Assemble the salad.
Whip the cream for the peaches, unless you plan to use it liquid or to use
    sour cream.
Get out the artichokes and put them on a bed of lettuce.

ARTICHOKE HEARTS VINAIGRETTE

Buy:

**Artichoke hearts (1 full-
   sized can)**
Parsley
Capers
An onion (small)

**Cucumber pickles, sour (1
   small jar)**
An egg
Lettuce

Make a French dressing (see p. 12).
Hard-cook 1 egg.
Chop enough parsley to fill ½ cup. Drain and chop 1 tablespoon capers.

Chop finely enough onion to fill 1 teaspoon. Chop enough sour pickle to fill 1 teaspoon. Chop the hard-cooked egg.

Combine these ingredients with the French dressing and beat them with a fork until they are well mixed.

Drain the can of artichokes. Put the artichokes in a bowl and cover them with the dressing (now called a sauce vinaigrette) and let them marinate for several hours. Chill them.

Serve the artichoke hearts on a bed of lettuce, and, if you like, garnish the plates with pieces of tomato, green and/or black olives, strips of sweet pepper, or anything suitable you have on hand.

Sauce vinaigrette can be served with whole, cold, cooked artichokes, with cold cooked asparagus, with cold shrimp or crabmeat, with tomatoes and cucumbers and beets and other salad vegetables.

BEEF BOURGUIGNON

Buy:

Round steak, cut in 2-inch cubes (1 pound)
Salt pork (⅛ pound)
Onions, very small, about 1-inch in diameter (6)

Red wine (1 bottle)
Potatoes, very small (6)
Mushrooms (¼ pound)

Check Cupboard for:

Beef bouillon cubes
Marjoram

Thyme
Flour

Preheat the oven to 250°.

Use a deep, covered metal pan that can be used on top of the stove and in the oven.

Dice the salt pork and put it in the bottom of the pan. Put it over a moderate heat and add the onions. Let them fry in the fat from the pork until they brown. Take out the onions and put them away for later use. Now add the cubes of steak to the salt pork, and let them brown well, turning them with a wooden spoon to ensure even cooking. Sprinkle 1 tablespoon of flour over the steak. Add about ½ teaspoon of salt, and ¼ teaspoon each of marjoram and thyme. Add some freshly ground black pepper. Stir the meat and seasonings well and add ½ cup of red wine and ½ cup of beef bouillon made from a cube. Cover the pan and put it in the oven for 4 hours. Inspect it from time to time, and if it shows signs of cooking dry, turn down the heat a little and/or add a little more red wine or beef bouillon.

Peel the potatoes and wash and slice the mushrooms. Add these and the onions to the dish after the four hours are up and about 45 minutes before dinner, 45 minutes being the cooking time necessary for these vegetables at a low oven heat. When the dish is done, taste and adjust seasoning if necessary.

SEASONED RICE

Buy:

Rice, long-grain (1 package)
A sweet pepper, red or
   green, very small

An onion, small
Parsley

Check Cupboard for:

Chicken bouillon cubes

Rosemary

Chop the parsley.

Dice about ½ the pepper. Cut the onion into small pieces.

Prepare the rice according to the recipe for Basic Infallible Rice, p. 14, but add a chicken bouillon cube to the water before you pour it over the rice, and let it dissolve. After adding the water to the rice, add the pepper, the parsley, and the onion, ¼ teaspoon of rosemary, and salt and pepper to taste. Cook as usual.

GREEN BEAN AND ONION SALAD

Buy:

Green beans, fresh (½
   pound) or frozen (1
   package)—do not buy
   French-cut beans

An onion, medium
A sweet pepper, red, very
   small

Check Cupboard for:

Marjoram
Olive oil

Wine vinegar

Make a basic French dressing (see p. 12) and add a ¼ teaspoon of marjoram to it.

If you have fresh green beans, wash them, and trim off the ends, but otherwise leave them whole. Cook them in boiling salted water about ½ inch deep for 15 to 20 minutes with a lid on. Check to make sure they don't boil dry. Drain them, and put them away in the refrigerator to chill in a bowl, covering them with the French dressing.

If you have frozen green beans, follow the instructions on the package and after cooking put them in the refrigerator to chill, as described above.

Mince or chop the onion as finely as you can. Cut the red pepper into strips.

To serve, arrange the beans lengthwise on a narrow dish, garnish them with the minced onion and pepper strips, and pour over them some of the dressing. Season to taste with salt and pepper, if necessary.

ANN'S PEACHES

Buy:

Peach halves (1 12-ounce can)

Cream, heavy (½ pint)

Check Cupboard for:

Lemons
Brandy

Brown sugar
Nutmeg

You can use fresh peaches for this dish, but canned seem to be a little juicier.

Preheat the oven to 350°.

Place the peaches, cut side up, in a shallow baking dish. Into the cavities left by the stones, put 1 teaspoon brown sugar, ½ teaspoon butter, a few drops of lemon juice, and a sprinkling of nutmeg. Splash a little brandy over them, and bake for 20 minutes in a 350° oven. Chill them and serve with whipped cream (or sour cream).

What to do with the leftover peach juice? Well, there is a recipe for a funny sort of drink, and some dames go for it. Mix equal quantities of peach juice, plain yogurt, and medium sherry, and chill it. You can do it with canned peach or apricot nectar as well.

Menu #8

Fresh Oysters or Cherrystone Clams
Roast Pork with Potato and Apple
Tomatoes Provençale
Red Cabbage and Romaine Salad
Cheese and Fruit

The Day Before:

Order the oysters and clams from your fish shop, and arrange to collect them (or have them delivered as late in the day as possible tomorrow).
Make the cocktail sauce for the oysters and/or clams.

Before Doris Arrives:

Chill the fruit in the refrigerator.
Wash the lettuce and store it in the refrigerator.
Make the French mustard dressing.
Peel the potatoes and apples to go with the pork.
Have the pork ready to go into the oven so that it will be ready to go into the oven at the right time.
Prepare the tomatoes and have them ready to go into the oven half an hour before the pork is ready.
Remove the cheese from the refrigerator (4 hours before dinner).

Just Before Doris Arrives:

Assemble the salad in a bowl, without the dressing, and store it in the refrigerator.
Collect the oysters and/or clams, arrange them for serving, and store them in the refrigerator.

FRESH OYSTERS OR CHERRYSTONE CLAMS

Buy:

Oysters, fresh, or
   cherrystone clams, fresh
   (6 to 12 per person)
Horseradish, hot, grated (1
   bottle)

Lemons
Oyster crackers, or thinly
   sliced brown bread
Parsley

Check Cupboard for:

Worcestershire sauce
Tabasco

Butter

If you want to serve fresh shellfish, you really do have to live near a good fish shop or else near the sea. If you don't, you can always fall back on smoked oysters and clams, which are pretty good too.

If you do have fresh shellfish, ask the man in the fish shop to open them for you IF it is very close to dinner time. If not, do it yourself.

Oysters and clams reveal their delicate flavors best when not weighed down with violent sauces, but some people like them that way, and you aim to please, not to preach. If you want to serve a tomato cocktail sauce with them, see the recipe on p. 209.

If you are opening the shellfish yourself, leave the oyster or clam in the deep half of each shell. Arrange them on a layer of crushed ice and decorate the platter with a few sprigs of parsley. Serve a plate of lemon wedges and little dishes of horseradish and cocktail sauce if you wish. Offer either oyster crackers or a plate of thin slices of buttered brown bread.

Note: Most fish shops also sell oyster crackers, horseradish, and whatever else you need to accompany fish and shellfish.

ROAST PORK WITH POTATO AND APPLE

Buy:

Pork, fresh—(a 3-pound slice
   of fresh pork leg cut through
   the top of the leg so that it is
   a flat piece of meat with a
   piece of bone in the center)

Potatoes, medium (4 or 5)
Apples (3 or 4)—try
   Greenings, Granny Smiths,
   or McIntoshes
Lemons

Check Cupboard for:

Butter   **Rosemary**

Preheat the oven to 350°.

Dot the bottom of a good-sized roasting pan with butter. Peel and slice enough spuds to cover the bottom to a depth of an inch or a little more. Peel and slice the apples and spread them on top of the spuds. Sprinkle about a teaspoon of sugar over the apples. Add a pinch of salt and a squeeze of lemon juice, distributing them over the apples. Then lay your slice of pork on top and salt and pepper it lightly. Take about ½ teaspoon of rosemary in the palm of your hand and crush it with your fingers. Sprinkle it over the pork and the apples. Bake without a cover for ½ hour per pound of pork.

RED CABBAGE AND ROMAINE SALAD

Buy:

Romaine lettuce (1 small   **Red cabbage (1 small head)**
  head)

Check Cupboard for:

Dijon mustard

Make:

French mustard dressing
  (see p. 13)

Wash the romaine lettuce thoroughly under cold running water, separating the leaves. Dry as many leaves as you are going to need, and put the rest away moist in a plastic bag in the refrigerator. They keep very well. Remove the outer leaves from the red cabbage. Put in the refrigerator to chill.

When you are ready to make the salad, shred part of the red cabbage into the salad bowl and tear the leaves of romaine. Add the dressing just before serving.

If you have any other fresh salad fixings in the refrigerator, such as green onions or bits of sweet pepper, by all means add them.

TOMATOES PROVENÇALE

Buy:

Tomatoes, medium-sized (2 or 3)
Parsley
Garlic

Bread crumbs
Parmesan cheese, grated (1
or 2 ounces or a small box)

Check Cupboard for:

Olive oil

Basil

Preheat the oven to 350°.

Wash the tomatoes and slice them in half through the thickest dimension.

Chop the parsley.

On top of each tomato half, arrange in the following order: a layer of bread crumbs, a little olive oil, a very little garlic (mashed with a knife or crushed with a garlic press), some Parmesan cheese, chopped parsley, a little basil, salt and pepper to taste.

Place the tomatoes on a shallow baking dish. Put a little oil in the bottom of the pan to prevent the tomatoes from sticking or burning on the bottom. Put them in the oven with the roast pork and bake for about half an hour, or until they are done and slightly browned.

CHEESE AND FRUIT

Offer a selection of about 3 carefully chosen and contrasting cheeses, tastefully arranged on a cheese board garnished with sprigs of parsley and perhaps a few black olives and tomato wedges. (For general advice on choosing cheese, see p. 37.) Remove from the refrigerator 4 hours before serving (unless it is 95° in the shade! in which case use your judgment).

Choose a selection of the most perfect fruit available, and chill it. Particularly good choices are: a perfect bunch of grapes, well-ripened pears, peaches, nectarines, apples (with ripe cheddar), fresh figs.

If you have managed to find some really splendid cheese (a first-quality Camembert or Brie), treat yourself to a good-quality French Bordeaux.

Menu #9
Pâté de Foie Gras
Jellied Consommé with Sherry
Roast Turkey
Traditional Stuffing
Mashed Potatoes
Cranberry Sauce & Jelly
Celery and Olives and Sliced Tomatoes
Cranberries Jubilee or Christmas Pudding
 with Brandy Butter

Note: Even the smallest turkey will be way too much for you and Doris. Accordingly, all the recipes on this menu except for the potatoes will accommodate more than two people.

A Couple of Days Before:
Make the cranberry sauce and/or jelly.

The Day Before:
Make the jellied consommé.
Make the stuffing and store it in the refrigerator.
Make the cranberries jubilee, omitting the brandy, and store it, tightly covered, in the refrigerator.
If you are serving Christmas pudding, make the brandy butter.
If you plan to eat at midday, put the turkey, stuffed, into the oven a little after midnight.

Before Doris Arrives:
Open the *pâté de foie gras* and arrange it on its plate, keeping it cool, not cold, until dinner time.
Make the turkey gravy.
Slice the tomatoes and pour French dressing over them.
Arrange the celery and olives.

Just Before Doris Arrives:
Cook the potatoes and keep them hot.
Set out the *pâté de foie gras*.

During Drinks and Pâté:

Put the jellied consommé on the table.

After the Consommé:

Make sure the mashed potatoes are hot.
Put the sliced tomatoes, the cranberry sauce, and the celery and olives on
the table.
Carve and serve the turkey and stuffing and potatoes.

After the Turkey:

Make sure the cranberries are hot, and add the brandy and flame them.

PATÉ DE FOIE GRAS

No pâté maison for this occasion, and no recipe either. At least once you deserve the very best. Buy a can of imported French *pâté de foie gras* made in Strasbourg and truffled. It is very rich, so do not buy too much. There is a 7¼-ounce size, but since dinner will be large, a smaller can should suffice.

Open both ends of the can so that you can slip the loaf of pâté out without mutilating it. Serve it at room temperature on a bed of lettuce, accompanied by French bread or crusty rolls and sweet butter.

JELLIED CONSOMMÉ WITH SHERRY

Buy:

Consommé, beef, undiluted (1 can)

Check Cupboard for:

Lemons   **Sherry, medium dry**

Open the can of consommé and pour it into a small bowl. Add an ounce or two of sherry and set the bowl in the refrigerator to jell for 3 or 4 hours.

To serve, break up the jellied consommé slightly with a fork and put it in individual bowls with a lemon wedge.

ROAST TURKEY

Buy:

**A turkey, small (the smallest
are usually 6 or 7 pounds)**

If you are planning to eat the turkey for dinner, preheat the oven to 300° in the morning.

If you are planning to eat the turkey at midday, preheat the oven to 300° *late* the night before.

Remove the bag of giblets from inside the turkey. Oil the turkey all over with corn oil—use your hands. Tie the legs together, tucking the pope's nose between them, and lash the wings to the sides of the body. Place the bird on a rack in a roasting pan, and roast without touching again for exactly 30 minutes at 300°. Then turn the oven down to 185°, and do not interfere with the turkey again until ready to serve. Let it cook for 8 to 10 hours or more; the exact time does not matter.

If you wish to stuff the turkey, it will make no difference in the cooking method or time. A stuffing recipe follows.

Important: If you have had to buy a frozen turkey, you must allow time for it to defrost. If you defrost it in the refrigerator, allow 2 days for a 4 to 10 pound turkey. If you defrost it under cold running water, allow 4 to 6 hours for a 4-to 10-pound turkey.

Gravy: See recipe for Roast Stuffed Chicken Leonard, p. 201.

TRADITIONAL STUFFING

Buy:

Brown bread (1 loaf)   **Celery (1 bunch)**
Corn meal (1 small box)   **An onion, medium-sized**
Sausage meat (1 pound)   **An apple, medium-sized**
Parsley   **Mushrooms (¼ pound)**

Check Cupboard for:

Sage   **Thyme**

Simmer the turkey giblets (heart, gizzard) and the neck in enough lightly salted water to cover them (add more if necessary) until they are done. Save the water. Save the liver to put in the gravy. Cut up the heart and gizzard in small pieces, and trim as much meat as you can from the neck, discarding the skin.

In a huge bowl, put the brown bread torn into little pieces. Then add all of the following things before attempting to mix: ½ cup corn meal; the sausage meat (no skin); the heart, gizzard, and neck meats; ¼ cup chopped parsley; ½ cup chopped celery; 1 chopped onion; the apple, peeled, cored, and chopped; the mushrooms, sliced; some of the water in which the giblets were cooked (save the rest in case it is needed); 1 teaspoon sage; ¼ teaspoon thyme; salt and pepper to taste.

Now, wash your hands, roll up your sleeves, and mix, squeeze, and blend the stuffing. If it seems too dry, add a little more of the giblet juice. Taste it. You may prefer a stronger flavor of sage, so add some more. How about salt and pepper? When you have it nicely adjusted, again using your hands, cram as much as you can into the turkey's backside. You can also stuff the head end, and fasten the skin flap with a skewer. Tie up the turkey as described on the previous page, and cook according to instructions.

You will probably have some stuffing left over. Put it in a shallow baking pan of such a size that the stuffing is about 2 inches deep. Put it in to bake with the turkey about 3½ hours before dinner.

MASHED POTATOES

Buy:

Potatoes, medium-sized (3 or 4).
 Use instant if you must, but
 you can't beat the real thing.

Check Cupboard for:

Milk   **Butter**

Do not peel the potatoes before cooking.

Put them into enough cold salted water to cover them and a little bit more. Let them boil until they are tender when pierced with a fork. Depending on the number and size potatoes, this may take from 15 to 35 minutes. Peel immediately. Put them through a food mill into a warm saucepan, or else use a potato ricer. Add 2 tablespoons of butter, 3 table-spoons of milk (more depending on the consistency you prefer), salt and pepper to taste. Stir and mix over a very low fire with a wooden spoon to warm them up again. Be careful not to let them burn on the bottom. Turn off the heat and keep them tightly covered until serving to preserve heat.

Suggestions: Mix in some chopped parsley or a little grated Parmesan cheese.

CRANBERRY SAUCE AND CRANBERRY JELLY

Buy:

Cranberries, fresh (1 pound)

Check Cupboard for:

Sugar

You can buy excellent cranberry sauce and cranberry jelly canned, but both are very easy to make.

In a large saucepan put 2 cups of sugar and 2 cups of water. Stir. Bring to the boil and allow to boil for 5 minutes. Add the cranberries and cook them until the skins pop, about 5 minutes. Remove them from the heat and let them cool and then chill. This makes cranberry sauce.

To make cranberry jelly, cook them for about 10 minutes longer or until a drop of sauce jells when it falls on a cool plate. Pour the sauce into a bowl or mold and chill it in the refrigerator until it becomes firm.

CELERY AND OLIVES AND SLICED TOMATOES

Buy:

A selection of green and black olives from a good deli
Tomatoes, medium ripe (2 or 3)

Celery (use the rest of the bunch you bought for the turkey stuffing)

Trim the celery into convenient lengths using the tender inner stalks. Wash them carefully. Crisp them in the refrigerator in a little ice water with a squirt of lemon juice.

When dinner is ready, put the celery and olives onto a long dish to accompany the main course.

Make a French dressing for the tomatoes (see p. 12). Core and slice the tomatoes and marinate them in French dressing until ready to serve. Sprinkle with parsley.

CRANBERRIES JUBILEE

Buy:

Cranberries, fresh (½ pound)   **Vanilla ice cream (1 pint)**
Brandy

Check Cupboard for:

Sugar

Put 1 cup of sugar and 1½ cups of water in a saucepan and stir to dissolve the sugar. Bring to a boil and boil for 5 minutes. Add the cranberries and bring to the boil again. Cook for 5 minutes. (*If* you have a chafing dish, light it, and put the cranberries into the blazer pan at this point. If not, proceed with the saucepan; it will taste just as good.) Now serve the ice cream. Heat ¼ cup or more of brandy. Ignite it (by taking some into a spoon and heating it with a match until it catches) and pour it over the cranberries. Blend it in well and pour the sauce over the ice cream.

CHRISTMAS PUDDING

You can buy marvelous imported English Christmas puddings around Christmas time, and they come in a series of very convenient sizes, including one which is perfect for two people. Some of them even come in china pudding bowls. so that all you have to do is stand them in a pan of boiling water for the length of time specified on the package.

There is absolutely no point in making a Christmas pudding for two people. The process is not difficult but it is very time-consuming and simply not worth the effort for less than 8 or 10 people. In any case, they really ought to be made in September—several of them—and put away to age in brandy for two months. If, however, you really seriously want to try your hand at it, write to me and I'll send you the dope.

Christmas pudding is traditionally served flaming, with a sprig of holly on top. Heat a few ounces of brandy in a small pan. *Don't* boil it! Take up a spoonful and hold a lighted match underneath it, at the same time pouring the warm brandy over the pudding. When the spoonful lights, pour it over the pudding, and the whole thing will catch and flame. Rescue the holly.

BRANDY BUTTER

Buy:

Brandy   **Lemons**

Check Cupboard for:

Butter

                                Sugar, confectioner's (1 pound)

You need ⅓ cup butter. The easiest way to measure this quantity is to remember that a quarter-pound stick of butter equals 8 tablespoons of butter, and frequently the paper it is wrapped in is marked off in 8 parts. Cut off about 5½ parts; this equals ⅓ cup.

Let the lump of butter sit in a bowl at room temperature until it is soft but not melted. Cream it thoroughly with a wooden spoon (this means stir and mash it with a wooden spoon until it is the consistency of heavy cream). Then beat in gradually 1 cup of confectioner's sugar, and keep beating until the sauce is the texture of whipped cream. Then beat in, a drop at a time, ½ teaspoon of vanilla extract. Finally, beat in 1 tablespoon of brandy.

Chill the sauce. Serve it heaped in an attractive bowl with a sprig of holly on top.

Chapter 10

The Morning After

Now LOOK at what you've gone and done! There she is in your pajama tops, still in the sack, and fast asleep. What looked like a midnight quickie has now become something quite different. Something however, with vast possibilities of its own.

Before she returns to consciousness, take a shower, shave, and get dressed or at least put on a pair of trousers. Then check to see if she's come back to life. If she's still out-to-lunch, no matter. You've got a pantry that's loaded with restoratives, and now's the time to see what you can do with them.

Remember—at this point she'll be wondering why she did it. Your task is to tease her palate (and perhaps ease the pain in her head). With any luck at all, this will soften her heart all over again which means that almost anything can happen.

Start with the coffee. Not that bitter instant brew with the brackish taste of brake fluid. This will only tarnish your shimmering image. Make her an honest cup of "real" coffee with freshly ground beans. Prepared in a percolator or a drip pot, this won't take much more time than boiling water for the instant variety.

For a touch of elegance, float a blob of freshly whipped cream on the top of the coffee. It only takes about two minutes to beat up some chilled heavy cream—assuming you bought the eggbeater that was listed among the essentials in Chapter 1. Add a tiny bit of powdered sugar to the bowl while you're beating.

You'll know by now if this chick is a good boozer. If she can handle the sauce in style, you may want to slip a shot of Irish whiskey into her coffee. But if it's a weekday, don't plan on seconds (for yourself, at least). You won't make much of an impression at the office if your talents are limited to sharpening a few pencils or falling asleep at a conference.

Fresh coffee—in almost any form—is standard to both breakfast and brunch, but if you happen to be on a cocoa kick, you can still come up with a few creative ideas that will take it out of the ordinary. Naturally, cocoa *does* begin with an instant mix. But to this you can add a small pinch of cinnamon or half a teaspoon of instant (yech!) coffee for a curious mocha effect. Again, whipped cream on top is further proof that you're not a barbarian.

She may enjoy a glass of juice—grapefruit, orange, or tomato. For some strange reason, liquefied apricots are always referred to as "nectar," but that's rather appropriate to this occasion when you think about it. Soft-pedal the prune juice, however. A lot of ladies (and gentlemen) still haven't forgiven it for lousing up an otherwise acceptable childhood.

If you're still up to no good, you may want to consider adding a little vodka to the glass. But straight or spiked, make certain you serve the drink ice cold. It will offer little allure in a lukewarm state.

By now the need for a tray may present itself. No problem. You have a tray handy (don't you?) and it's got plenty of room on it for hot or cold cereal. The latter can be enhanced with sliced fruit.

Hot cereal is a cinch to prepare within one to 10 minutes, depending on the type you buy. Just read the directions on the package. It won't demand any more skill than is required in adding water and stirring until the mixture is thoroughly heated. You can even read the paper while you're doing this, since you don't have to look at the pot. You'll *hear* when the cereal is ready. (It makes a sort of "sloop, ploop" muffled bubbling noise when it's thickened.) Brown or white sugar and light cream (or Half-and-Half) add the finishing touches.

In summer, add strawberreies, blueberries, raspberries or sliced peaches or bananas to cold cereal. Or skip the cereal and serve the fruit by itself with sugar and cream.

Muffins? Coffee cake? Of course! But buy them at a good bakery and keep them fresh in the refrigerator. Wrapped in aluminum foil and warmed for 15 minutes or so in an oven set at 300 degrees, they'll be ready by the time your coffee is brewed.

These are just the basics for breakfast or brunch. You'll find a lot of specifics in this chapter as well. The point of all this, of course, is to get something started in the kitchen—something that will carry its inviting aroma to her pillow and serve as a soft reminder that she, too, must answer the bell that sounds in all of us with each new day.

There's more than one way to ring her bell and you may know only one of them so far. Find out what sort of a sound it makes when you appear at the bedroom door bearing an attractive tray and wearing a smile that can only assure her it was all worthwhile after all.

BERGEN'S POST-BACCHANAL BLUEBERRIES

Buy:

Blueberries (a small box, about 1 pint or 2 cups)
Sour cream (½-pint carton is the smallest sold), OR

Plain yogurt (½ pint, i.e. 8 ounces)

Check Cupboard for:

Sugar (very fine sugar is better for fruit than either the regular granulated or the powdered confectioner's sugar)

Wash blueberries, picking out the little bits of stalk and leaf that are always left in the boxes I buy. Putting them into a colander after washing helps the water to drain off thoroughly. Sprinkle them with sugar lightly (have more at hand on the table). Serve with a good half-cup dollop of sour cream or yogurt for each of you.

SPIKED MANDARIN ORANGES

Buy:

Mandarin orange segments (a smallish can)
Cointreau, Triple Sec, or Curaçao (the smallest bottle the liquor store will sell you; a miniature is just right)

Open the can of orange segments. Add about 2 tablespoons of the orange-flavored liqueur (but if you've had a shot of vodka in the fruit juice and are thinking of Irish Coffee to follow, watch out). Serve in two bowls.

STUFFED MELONS

Buy:

A small, ripe melon (cantaloupe, honeydew, whatever)

Strawberries or raspberries (fresh, or 1 frozen package of either)

Check Cupboard for:
Sugar (just in case)

Cut the melon in half, making sure it's really ripe enough to eat. Scoop out the seeds with a spoon. Fill the hole with drained strawberries or raspberries.

There's a catch to this one: it needs some advance planning. To make sure the melon is ripe, it's best to buy it several days ahead. Then on the night before you have to remember to take the package of frozen strawberries/raspberries out of the freezing compartment and put it in a dish in the main part of the refrigerator, or out on the kitchen table, so that it will have time to thaw. She wouldn't appreciate the crunch of ice slivers. If you've bought fresh berries, wash them and toss with a little sugar; chill overnight.

HEART-WARMING OATMEAL

Buy:

Oatmeal (a 1-pound box of Quick Quaker Oats, or some comparable brand, will last a long time)

Dried fruit (raisins, dates, figs, apricots)
Half-and-half or light cream (½ pint), unless you prefer milk

Check Cupboard for:
Brown sugar

Cook the oatmeal with water.in a medium-sized saucepan as instructed on the package, stirring once or twice to make sure it doesn't burn or stick to the bottom of the pan. Quick Quaker Oats will cook in 1 minute if you put the oatmeal into boiling water, as they suggest, but the cereal will be creamier (less apt to get lumpy) if you bring the oats and cold water to a boil together. Keep the heat fairly low. Add a pinch of salt. Also a pinch or two of cinnamon, which is particularly tasty with the raisins or dried fruit that you are also going to chop and toss in. Serve (and fill the saucepan with cold water as soon as you have served, or you'll regret this whole idea) with lots of brown sugar and cream or milk or Half-and-Half.

BOILED EGGS

Buy:
Eggs (2)   **English muffins, or bread**

Check Cupboard for:
Butter

Boiled eggs are not a big deal. Since you're heating water for coffee, anyway, you might as well take this extra step and show her that you're trying. Into a small saucepan of boiling water deep enough to cover the eggs, carefully slip the 2 eggs (slide them off a tablespoon). Turn the heat down as low as possible, and cook them for 2 to 3 minutes if you like them soft, 3 to 5 minutes for medium cooked. This method works best if you have the eggs at room temperature—and that means remembering to take them out of the icebox well in advance. If your eggs are cold, they will crack open as they hit the boiling water. Solve this problem by starting the eggs in *cold* water and bringing them to the boiling point slowly; then turn off the heat, slap on the saucepan lid, and time the 3 or 5 minutes (no longer) while the eggs just sit there. For very soft eggs, rescue them from the water as soon as it has boiled. Make sure that the coffee and toast will be ready on time; the eggs will continue cooking within their shells until they are cracked (unless you dunk them in cold water), so a couple of minutes' delay can be disastrous. Crack off the top of the egg, add a little salt, and drop a lump of butter right inside.

A scholarly footnote: The Fraziers, authors of *Aphrodisiac Cookery, Ancient and Modern,* state that all ancient peoples agreed that the egg is an aphrodisiac. "The Arabs, the most noted exemplars of erotic egg cookery, recommend the eating of three egg yolks daily for virility," they write.

THE CONTINENTAL BREAKFAST

Buy:

**French croissants (from a
  bakery or the frozen-food
  section of a supermarket)**
**Sweet butter (absolutely
  unsalted)**

**Imported jams (those from
  Switzerland, England and
  Germany are best)**

Check Cupboard for:
Milk

Warm the croissants in a low oven (about 325°—and wrap them in aluminum foil so they don't dry out), while you're making the coffee. Make the coffee a little stronger than usual. Heat some milk (but don't let it boil), and pour equal proportions of hot milk and coffee simultaneously into each cup or mug to make real *café au lait.* It's good with a little brown sugar.

When Breakfast Becomes Brunch

Brunch implies that either you're not planning to go anywhere or it's already too late to get there. Of course, weekends and holidays generally don't count in this respect since presumably no moral obligations are involved.

Keep in mind, too, that everyone deserves a day off from the office occasionally. Why should it just be when you're sick? This is a thoroughly unimaginative outlook on the part of management and one to be thwarted from time to time.

Experienced brunchers have been known to make a meal meander from sometime before noon until God knows when. And during this time, all sorts of folderol can creep into the scene, indicating that you needn't be limited to bloody marys and the daily newspaper. However, bloody marys are a good way to start.

BLOODY MARYS

Buy:

Vodka
Tomato juice (a can or two of the best)

Lemons (1 or 2 fresh ones, depending on how many drinks you plan to fix)

Check Cupboard for:

Worcestershire sauce
Basil

Dried green onions
Pepper (freshly ground)

You may already have your own favorite method, but try this one for a spicy change of pace. Take a *large* glass, pour in 1½ jiggers (or so) of vodka. If she's allergic to vodka, try gin. Fill up with tomato juice. Add a generous squeeze or two of fresh lemon juice, a heavy dash of Worcestershire sauce, ¼ teaspoon of dried basil (crush it in the palm of your hand slightly, before throwing it in), ¼ teaspoon of dried green onions, salt and black pepper to taste. Stir. Sip.

If she loathes bloody marys, consider tempting her anew with sparkling red wine, imported English cider, Asti Spumanti or even champagne (a good brand is essential; anything behind the Western Auto label, for instance, is out!).

POACHED EGGS

Buy:

Eggs

English muffins

If you do not have an egg poacher, use any saucepan and put about 1¼ inches of water in it. Bring the water to the boil, and then turn it down so that it just simmers. Break an egg into a cup, and then gently slip it into the simmering water from the cup. Add a second egg, or however many you wish to poach. Leave the eggs in the water for about 3 minutes, and then rescue them with a slotted spoon.

Serve them on toasted English muffins, with lots of butter, salt, and pepper.

SHIRRED EGGS IN CREAM

Buy:

Eggs   **Heavy cream (½ pint)**

Check Cupboard for:
Bread crumbs

Preheat the oven to 400°.

For this dish, you will need a pair of shallow baking dishes, each large enough to hold 2 eggs. They may be of ovenproof glass or pottery.

To prepare four eggs, mix 6 tablespoons of heavy cream with 8 tablespoons fine bread crumbs, and add salt and pepper to taste. Divide the mixture between the 2 baking dishes, and put about ¼ of it into each dish, then add 2 eggs, and then cover them with the remaining mixture.

Bake them until the egg whites are firm (4 or 5 minutes).

SWISS EGGS

Buy:

Eggs   **Sherry, medium (1 bottle or**
Cream, light (½ pint)   **miniature)**
Cheddar cheese, grated (1 or
** 2 ounces)**

Check Cupboard for:
Butter   **Bread or muffins to toast**

Melt a tablespoon of butter in a small frying pan and add ½ cup of light cream. Break the 4 eggs into a cup and slip them gently one at a time into the cream. Add salt and pepper. Let the eggs cook *slowly* over a low to moderate heat until the whites are nearly firm. Then sprinkle them with a couple of ounces of grated cheddar cheese.

Make some toast while the eggs finish cooking.

When the egg whites are firm, serve the eggs onto hot buttered toast. Add a tablespoon of sherry (or more) to the cream mixture in the pan and pour it over the eggs.

SPECIAL SCRAMBLED EGGS AND BACON

Buy:

Eggs   **Bacon**
Cottage cheese

Fry the bacon very slo-o-owly over a low heat, pouring off the fat from time to time. Fold some paper towels and have them handy for draining the bacon.

Put 4 eggs in a bowl with 4 tablespoons of cottage cheese, ¼ teaspoon of dried shredded green onions, and salt and pepper to taste. Beat them with a fork or rotary beater, and then scramble them in a frying pan with a little of the fat from the bacon. Keep the heat moderate, and move the eggs constantly. Do not let them brown.

PLAIN OLD FRIED EGGS
WITH BACON AND SAUSAGE
AND PERHAPS CHICKEN LIVERS, TOMATOES,
AND MAYBE HASH-BROWN POTATOES . . .

Buy:

Eggs   **Chicken livers (¼ pound)**
Bacon (½ pound)   **Tomatoes, small (2 or 3)**
Sausages (4 if possible, or ½   **Potatoes (1 pound)**
  pound)

Check Cupboard for:

Bread or muffins   **Milk or Half-and-Half**
Coffee

If you can manage to boil a couple of potatoes the night before, it will speed up the cooking of hash-brown potatoes no end.

For this kind of cheerful fry-up, one of those griddles that covers two burners is just the ticket because you can cook every thing on it at once. (If you haven't gotten round to buying one yet, break out all your frying pans and turn the oven on. You can cook bacon and sausages under the broiler and keep things warm in the oven.)

Better get the potatoes on first—cooked or raw, peel them and chop them up fine (about 1 cupful, diced) and season them with salt and pepper before cooking. It's a good idea to cook them in bacon fat, but they take much longer to cook than your bacon will, so unless you have saved bacon fat from another day, you'll have to use cooking oil. Put about 1½ tablespoons of oil in a heavy frying pan (even if you do have a griddle) and stir the diced potatoes in it until they are well-coated with oil. Turn the heat down and let the potatoes cook until they are tender and form a nice crisp crust on the bottom. For pre-cooked potatoes, this will take about 20 minutes; for raw, 30 minutes or more. Add a little more cooking oil if the potatoes start to stick. When you serve them, fold them over like an omelet so that you have the crust on top and bottom.

While the potatoes are cooking, get the sausages and bacon on to the griddle. Sausages need to be well-cooked and bacon profits from slow cooking, so start these first and then take a break to deal with fruit juice or table setting and coffee making. A few chicken livers will go onto the griddle next, in company with some slices of tomato or just tomato halves, depending on size. Push the bacon out to the edges, and turn the sausages, piercing them with a fork if necessary. Turn the chicken livers around in the bacon fat so that they begin to cook on all sides. The eggs will cook in the last few minutes, so don't add them until everything is just about ready. Check the potatoes, drain the bacon on paper towels, turn the tomatoes and livers and sausages, make toast and store it in the oven, and *then* fry a couple of eggs.

Timing is everything in an operation like this one, but if certain items are ready sooner than you need them, just keep them warm in the oven (about 250°). This holds for bacon, buttered toast, sausages, hash-brown potatoes, for everything, in fact, except the eggs.

The most common reason for a failure in this kind of fried or grilled breakfast is the attempt to cook everything too quickly and to turn up the heat too high. Things get scorched before they are cooked, so take it gently and let breakfast cook slowly.

MEXICAN EGGS

Buy:

Eggs
An onion (medium)
**Cheddar cheese, grated (2 or
  3 ounces)**
Green chilies (1 small can)

Tomato purée (1 small can)
**Tomato sauce with bits of
  meat in it (1 small can)**
**Corn muffins or tortillas or
  corn bread**

Check Cupboard for:

Corn oil

Garlic

Chop up the onion and a clove of garlic and fry them in 2 tablespoons of oil *slowly* until they become soft and golden. Then add the tomato sauce and about ½ the tomato purée and season the mixture to taste with salt and pepper. If the tomatoes taste too sharp or too acid, add ½ to 1 teaspoon of sugar to adjust the flavor. Then add some chilies, omitting the seeds which are pretty fiery, but use your own judgment as to how much heat you want for breakfast. Simmer this sauce for about 10 or 15 minutes, and then add the grated cheddar cheese. Allowing 2 eggs per person, put 4 eggs on top of the sauce in the pan, making a little indentation for each to fit into. Cover the pan, and let the eggs cook until the whites are firm—about 8 to 10 minutes.

SAUTÉ BANANAS

Buy:

Bananas (2 or 3)

Check Cupboard for:

Butter
Sugar, dark brown

Bacon
Flour

Peel the bananas and cut each one in half twice—first the long way and then crosswise. Dredge them with flour.

Get out two frying pans.

In one, place as many slices of bacon as you have of banana. Cook them until they are done but not crisp.

Meanwhile, put a generous lump of butter into the other frying pan, and lay the banana halves in it. Treat them gently so that they will not break—use two lifters, or a lifter and a spoon to turn them. As they begin to brown, add several spoons of brown sugar. When the bananas are lightly browned and soft, remove them from the pan, pour the butter and sugar over them, and lay the bacon strips on top.

FRENCH TOAST

Buy:

Eggs

Bread (stale—yes stale if possible; it absorbs better)

Check Cupboard for:

Butter
Milk

Maple syrup (or jam, or marmalade, or cinnamon and sugar)

For 4 slices of French toast, mix together 1 beaten egg, ½ cup milk, 1 teaspoon (or less, to taste) of sugar, a pinch of salt. Soak the bread slices in this mixture for several minutes.

Heat your two-burner griddle (or a large heavy iron frying pan) and put a little butter or bacon fat on it. Gently move the soaked bread on to the griddle with an egg lifter. Slowly spoon any leftover egg mixture over the bread surface as it cooks. After 5 to 10 minutes, gently turn and brown the other side.

Serve with butter and maple syrup (or jam, or marmalade). For a change, try it sprinkled with cinnamon sugar (combine ¼ cup sugar with 1 teaspoon of powdered cinnamon).

PANCAKES (BLUEBERRY, MAYBE)

For "Mix" Pancakes Buy:

Pancake mix (1 box)
Blueberries, wild (1 can)

Milk
Eggs

For Homemade Pancakes Buy:

Milk
Baking powder
Eggs
All-purpose flour

Butter
Blueberries, wild (1 can)
Lemons, sour cream,
     raspberry jam (all optional)

Check Cupboard for:

Sugar

Maple syrup

For Easy "Mix" Pancakes:

In a bowl mix the prepared packaged flour, egg, milk, and fat according to directions (you may want to halve the suggested quantity, for two). Use an egg beater and beat until the batter is almost smooth. If you like thick pancakes, add more flour mix; if you like thin ones, add more milk.

For Homemade Pancakes:

Mix in a bowl ½ cup milk, 2 tablespoons melted butter, and 1 egg. Beat slightly. Then add 1 cup all-purpose flour, 2 teaspoons of baking powder, 2 tablespoons sugar, ½ teaspoon salt. Add the flour all at once, and stir enough to moisten all the flour. Do not beat. Add a little more milk for thinner pancakes. Add ½ cup drained blueberries, if you like.

Preheat the oven to 300° (to keep the pancakes warm).

To cook the pancakes, use a heavy iron frying pan (or a two-burner griddle). Grease the pan with about 1½ tablespoons of cooking oil and heat it. (If you have an electric frying pan, set it at 380°.) Use a pitcher or a tablespoon to drop the pancake batter onto the pan. The first pancake is an experiment and may not work if the pan isn't hot enough, so don't worry about it. Drop enough batter into the pan to make a pancake about 3 inches in diameter. The batter will spread out and as it begins to cook, bubbles will form and cover the top. When the top is covered with bubbles, use a pancake turner and lift the edge of the pancake to see if the underside has browned. If so, flip it over to brown on the other side. The second side cooks more quickly than the first. You may have to adjust the heat a little. If the pancakes start sticking, add a little more oil, but when you do, wait for a moment to let the pan heat up again. Once you have cooked about three pancakes, you are an expert.

Keep them warm in the oven, spreading them out on a sheet of aluminum foil. Don't pile them up. Keep them in one layer to prevent them from getting soggy.

Serve with maple syrup and butter or fresh lemon juice and sugar or sour cream and raspberry jam.

BLINTZES

Buy:

Eggs
Milk
All-purpose flour
Cottage cheese (1 medium-sized pot)

Cream cheese (1 4-ounce package)
Sour cream (1 small container)

Check Cupboard for:

Butter
Sugar

Jam

You must make the batter for blintzes at least ½ hour ahead of time and let it stand. The cheese for the filling has to be at room temperature or nearly so.

The batter: put in a bowl 2 eggs, beaten; 1 cup of milk; ½ teaspoon of salt; 1 cup all-purpose flour. Stir (do not beat) until smooth. Cover and let stand for at least ½ hour.

The filling: cream in a bowl the cottage cheese, the cream cheese, 2 tablespoons of butter, and ⅓ cup sugar. Blend them until they are smooth.

Preheat oven to 300° (to keep the blintzes warm).

Cooking blintzes is similar to cooking pancakes, but the batter and the end product are much thinner, and blintzes will not form bubbles during cooking the way pancakes do.

Grease very lightly the bottom of a 6-inch heavy iron frying pan, and heat it. The batter should be quite thin—just thick enough to coat a spoon.

Pour in enough batter to spread out and form a thin layer covering the bottom of the pan. As the edges turn golden, carefully check the underside, and when it is light brown, turn the blintz, cooking the second side for not more than 30 seconds to 1 minute. Store each one in the oven. When you have used up all the batter, start filling the blintzes. Place about 1½ tablespoons of filling on the bottom third of each blintz and roll it up. Place them in a greased baking pan, turn the oven up to 375°, and brown the blintzes for about 15 minutes or until they turn golden.

Serve them with sour cream and jam.

FLAMING PANCAKES

Buy:

Oranges
Lemons
Cognac or Curaçao (a
   miniature, if possible)
Butter

Sugar, powdered or very
   fine
Eggs
Milk
All-purpose flour

Make the same batter as for blintzes (see p. 242).

While the batter is standing, prepare the sauce. Cream in a bowl ½ cup butter and ½ cup powdered sugar. Add to it the grated rind and juice of 1 orange, plus a little lemon juice and rind, and the miniature bottle (1½ ounces) of cognac or Curaçao.

When the blintzes are cooked, roll them up (*without* the cheese filling in the previous recipe) and put them in a frying pan with the sauce, and heat them slowly, spooning the sauce over them. When the sauce has become a little syrupy and the blintzes very hot, sprinkle a little sugar over them, warm some cognac or Curaçao in a spoon, and light it with a match, and pour it over the blintzes, which are now called *crèpes suzette*.

WAFFLES

If you don't own a waffle iron, it's probably for the same reason that you don't keep an ironing board in the closet. However, while it's tough to press a dress shirt, it's easy to make a waffle. If you scrounge around a thrift shop or the Salvation Army second-hand store, you might find an antique *round* waffle iron, which will make your brunch look really special.

Just remember a few simple ground rules. "Season" the iron regularly with a little butter or corn oil. Let the iron get hot enough, so that a little butter will really sizzle on contact, before you put the batter in. Pour one tablespoon of batter into the middle of each little compartment (it will spread once you've closed the lid). Don't lift the lid until the outer edges of the cooking waffle stop steaming. A cooked waffle is golden brown. Lift the lid gingerly: if the waffle looks as if it's going to split or stick, gently pry it loose with a fork. Let the first waffle cook longer than the others, to lessen the chance of making an adhesive mess that you'll have to scrape off the iron while Betty Lou's stomach growls. Resign yourself to the fact that the first waffle is never the greatest, anyway. If you're chivalrous, serve her the second.

Variations on the waffle can see you through many weekends. Away you go, with . . .

> Waffles and maple syrup (real syrup, no sugar-and-caramel-flavored cheap substitutes), with a blob of butter on top, bacon on the side
>
> Waffles with sour cream and imported Swiss cherry jam or Swedish lingonberries
>
> Waffles with vanilla ice cream and Grand Marnier liqueur
>
> Waffles with "super fine" sugar and fresh lemon juice
>
> Waffles with butter and cinnamon sugar (¼ cup sugar with 1 teaspoon powdered cinnamon)

Waffles can be made from packaged pancake mix (see instructions on the box), but homemade batter is easy to make. Mix 1½ cups of flour, 3 teaspoons baking powder, 2 teaspoons sugar, ½ teaspoon salt. In a large bowl, using a rotary beater, beat in 1 cup milk, 2 already beaten eggs, 3 tablespoons corn oil or bacon fat (from the bacon already frying slowly on the stove). If she's not a big eater, though, you may want to halve this recipe. If the batter gets thicker than heavy cream add a little extra milk.

COUNTRY FRIED APPLES WITH BACON

Buy:

Apples, hard, green (2 or 3 medium-sized)
Bacon

Lemon
Bread for toast, or muffins

KNOCKOUT BRUNCH MENU

Fresh Orange Juice with Vodka
Broiled Grapefruit Halves with Brown Sugar and Sherry
Eggs Florentine Benedict
Chilled Moselle or Rhine Wine
Toast and English Jams
Coffee with Dark Brown Sugar and Dark Brown Rum
Several Copies of the Sunday Papers

Clearly, this is the ultimate brunch, but don't be daunted by it. Once you break it down into its component parts it becomes manageable. It does, however, require a good deal of preparation the day before, and probably a trip to the liquor store just for the brunch drinks! I'll give you two shopping lists, one for food and one for drink, and the recipe for Eggs Florentine Benedict. The rest of it, you will find, is a question of assembling and organizing rather than cooking.

Buy:

Vodka
Sherry, medium
Rum, dark

A good Moselle or Rhine
  wine (1 or 2 bottles)

Buy:

Orange juice, frozen,
  concentrated (1 can)
Grapefruit (½ per person)
Cherries, fresh (¼ pound)
Eggs
English muffins
Spinach, fresh (1 package)
Milk

Cream, light (1 pint)
Butter (1½ pounds)
Lemons
Bread for toast
English jam or marmalade
Coffee (a particularly good
  brand)

Eggs Florentine Benedict has four separate elements, each of which has to be cooked separately and then combined: buttered toasted English muffins, a first layer of spinach cooked in a rich Béchamel sauce, a second layer of poached eggs, and a third layer of Hollandaise sauce. Of these, you can prepare one the day before: the spinach.
For the recipe for spinach with Béchamel sauce, see p. 190. Make it the day before and store it in the refrigerator. Take it out in the morning and

warm it up slowly over a very low heat. If it seems very thick, add just a little milk.

For the recipe for Hollandaise sauce, see p. 148.

For the recipe for poached eggs, see p. 235.

The Day Before:

Make the spinach and Béchamel sauce.

Make the orange juice.

Put the wine in the refrigerator.

Set the table.

First Thing in the Morning:

Make the Hollandaise sauce, and keep it warm on the back of the stove.

Make coffee.

Lace the orange juice.

Slice the grapefruit and turn on the broiler.

Toast muffins and store them in the oven.

Ditto toast.

Boil water for poaching eggs—heat up the spinach and Béchamel sauce.

Drink orange juice—broil grapefruit.

Eat grapefruit—poach eggs—and so forth!

Chapter 11

Canebrake Cookery—
Getting Away from Them All

"A WOMAN IS only a woman, but a good cigar is a smoke."

Truer words were never spoken. For when Rudyard Kipling wrote that phrase, he captured the inner feelings of all men, the universal masculine need for something more than just the female of the species.

You see, all males share a special and innate sense of priorities—something like a conscience, only better. Whereas the conscience tells us what is right and moral, the sense of priorities tells us what is good and satisfying. Now unquestionably, women rate highly on this ladder of libidinous longings, but they are not the only rung, and they may not be the top one. For there are certain subtler yet grander desires that reign strong and long (not just until age 55 or 60) in all masculine souls. And when one of these urges surfaces, women might just as well not exist.

The good cigar, a simple yet totally pleasurable experience, epitomizes this male need. Another of man's requirements is solitude, time for quiet contemplation and a few good (undisturbed) nights of sleep. Tied in with this idea is the concept of wanderlust, the need to bathe one's head in other climes, to get away from it all—and them all. Sure, the loaf-of-bread-jug-of-wine-and-thou-beside-me-in-the-wilderness routine has its appeal, but most men will agree that there are times when nothing can compare with that good cigar, a jug of Scotch, and Old Blue beside me at the campfire.

And even the most ardent womanizer will admit that from time to time he has to recharge his batteries. There are weeks when everything just gets too complicated, when there are too many women, too many hassles, and it's impossible to keep everything straight.

Marie is coming for dinner on Thursday. And then there's that weekend at the ski lodge with Margo. Or is it Jane? You promised to phone Emily last Tuesday evening and forgot, you dog, winding up in a singles bar with Carol instead. So now everyone wants to cut your heart out with a dull knife, when all you were trying to do was keep all hands eager and happy.

That's when it's time for a change of pace—and scene. Time to get away from women and the predicaments that surround them, time to follow your sense of priorities and head for the hills for some fishing, hunting, hiking, or whatever else in nature turns you on.

And *don't* weaken by asking some honey to come along. Feminine campers are only a drag. Being women, they simply can't keep up with you. When Kate's boots begin to raise blisters on her pretty little feet, it will probably occur on a mountain top at least 25 miles from the nearest hamlet. Result? You and a couple other suckers will have to blow an otherwise promising trip by carrying her back down to civilization. While this is going on, Kate will be cringing every time you flush out a brown thrasher, all of which will strain relations with everyone on this particular detail.

Women don't belong in the woods—at least not for more than an hour or two of dalliance. They can't even use an axe or carry a pack, and they're a veritable menace with a fly rod. Even if they're lucky enough to catch a fish, they'll make you take it off the hook while they giggle and shriek, then they'll sneeze all night long as a result of catching a chill in the cold mountain air. Yes, old Shakespeare hit it on the nose when he said, "Frailty, thy name is woman." So leave her behind with a fond farewell and a promise of anything up to and including Arpège. She'll be much better off—and so will you.

"Don't worry, Marie darling. It's only for a few days."

"But you promised to take me to hear The Who, you rat!" This will be followed by one of those classic pouts.

"What in hell is The Who?" you'll ask her, stalling for time as you edge toward the door. "Oh yeah, the rock group. Well, I'll take you when I get back. That'll give you enough time to finish darning my socks. And Marie baby," you'll conclude as you weasel out of her apartment and into the hall, "kiss me so I won't forget your softness and warmth . . . and don't forget to sew the buttons on my shirt, like you promised. You know, the blue one. There's a dear."

So much for Marie. For now. But before heading off into the canebrake, plan your trip carefully. You don't want to arrive 30 miles north of Elk Breath, Wisconsin, and discover you forgot to bring matches or a frying pan or a first-aid kit, which is an absolute must. If Henry gets bitten by a copperhead or falls off the edge of a 20-foot cliff, you can't just leave him there to die, even if you still haven't forgiven him for making a pass at your maiden aunt that time he got bombed at your family reunion last year. And all those canned goods you backpack into the foothills beyond East Ringworm, Arkansas, will be about as nourishing as a hod of bricks if Lester forgets to bring along a can opener. You've got to watch that Lester because he has some rather strange moments. He's the yo-yo who asks for a demi-tasse every time he eats in a diner.

If you're planning an elaborate trip involving bush pilots, guides, and canoes, you'll probably be in the charge of someone like Tonto who will see that you've got everything you need in the way of food and equipment. After all, he has his professional standing to think about, and it wouldn't do at all to have a covey of greenhorns stumbling around in the dark praying that someone from Traveler's Aid will show up. But if you've got a more simple scene in mind, make a list of everything you think you'll need, keeping in mind that each surplus item will add weight to everyone's load.

How many of you are going on this junket? How long will you be away? Will you be able to purchase some of your supplies from time to time or will you have to take everything with you? George has this weird thing about Animal Crackers. He eats about three boxes of them a day, exulting with a robust growl every time he finds the effigy of a bear. (Bears, apparently, are much scarcer than geese and pigs, so it's one huge event when he finds one. All of this, of course, can be traced back to a childhood which was somewhat less than normal.) The point is, however, that George will have to stock up at the front end of the journey, since Animal Crackers are not a big item at the average Hudson's Bay Company trading post.

Can you count on catching fish for some of your meals? And how about shelter? If you're planning to use a cabin, you won't have to worry about tents and the mosquito netting that may also be necessary. Operating out of a base camp will be a lot different than being on the move to a new campsite every day or so. If you're canoeing, will there be any portages around rapids? This can make a difference where Bill is concerned because his bad back means the rest of you slobs will have to assume his share of the load. Face up to these problems now. You won't be able to solve them later when necessary compromises may turn your woodland wanderings into something like a death march.

When it comes to cooking, plan on incorporating what you catch or shoot into as many menus as possible, a number of which follow. The advantages of this approach are obvious. But don't get carried away by anticipation. You'll also have to carry along plenty of canned goods and dried foods. The latter offer the benefit of being light.

By organizing your trip properly, you'll enjoy yourself more. Oh, yes, you won't be gone very long before you'll miss Marie and Margo and Jane and Emily and Carol, but they'll still be there when you get back. And just think how much more you'll enjoy them after a week or so in the midst of grimy clothes, unshaven faces, lukewarm beer, and poker games in the light of a Coleman lantern that attracts every mosquito in North America. Getting away from them all has rewards that won't be completely evident until you feel once again all the softness and warmth of Marie or Margo or Jane or . . .

QUICK SPAGHETTI

Buy:

Spaghetti (a 1-pound package)
Chuck steak, ground (½ pound)

Tomato sauce (8-ounce can)

Check Cupboard for:

Olive oil
Butter
Oregano

Basil
Parsley
Garlic

Find a good-sized pot and melt 2 tablespoons of butter in it. Add the chuck steak and mix it around and fry it until it begins to brown—try to persuade it to separate into small particles. Then add the tomato sauce, 2 cloves of crushed garlic, 1 tablespoon of dried parsley or two of fresh, and a pinch each of basil and oregano. Mix well and let simmer over very low fire for about 15 minutes.

The sauce tastes better if you allow it to cool for several hours and then rewarm it when you are ready to eat.

Optional: add a chopped onion with the tomato sauce.

To Cook the Spaghetti:

Find a big pot, fill it with water, and bring it to the boil. When it boils add 1 teaspoon of salt and 1 tablespoon of olive oil. Throw in the package of spaghetti, and stir it well so that it doesn't stick to the bottom or remain in clumps. Boil it for ten minutes until the spaghetti is *al dente*, (cooked but firm to the bite). Then pour it out into a colander and run hot water over it. Put a lump of butter on each plate before serving the spaghetti, and stir the butter into the spaghetti. Serve with the sauce.

Sprinkle with grated Parmesan cheese if you have any on hand.

WIENERS AND KRAUT

Buy:

Sauerkraut (2 1-pound cans)
**Hot dogs (1-pound pack or
   can)**
**An apple, fresh, or
   equivalent dried slices**

An onion, medium
Beer (1 can)

Check Cupboard for:

Cloves, whole (optional)

Caraway seeds (optional)

Drain the sauerkraut well and rinse it thoroughly in cold water. Put it in a heavy saucepan with the chopped onion, the chopped apple, 2 whole cloves and a pinch of caraway seed. Cover it with the beer and let it simmer for an hour. Then add the wieners and cook them long enough to heat them through. If you want to stretch this a little, peel and quarter a couple of potatoes and let them cook with the kraut and apple. If there isn't enough beer to cover, add just a little water. If there is, drink what's left.

HOPPING JOHN

Buy:

Rice
**Black beans or navy beans
   or black-eyed peas (1 can)**

Bacon

This one will do nicely as a main dish if you add a few chunks of ham, or as a side dish if you have some fresh meat to grill.

Cook up 3 cups of rice (meaning you cook enough rice to provide 3 cups of cooked rice), and then stir into it the can of beans with its juice. Add a couple of tablespoons of crumbled, fried bacon. Heat it thoroughly and season with salt and pepper.

You can add all sorts of things to this dish. Use chunks of ham or any leftover meat instead of the bacon. Throw in any leftover vegetables except potatoes—tomatoes are a good choice. If you use canned tomatoes, drain 'em first or you'll end up with soup. Save the drained-off tomato juice, combine it with a little vodka, and drink it.

CORNED BEEF AND CABBAGE

Buy:

Cabbage, one medium-sized head

Corned beef (1 can)

Potatoes, medium-sized (2 or 3)

Carrots (2 or 3)

Check Cupboard for:

Beef bouillon cubes

Cut the cabbage in chunks, the peeled potatoes in quarters, and slice or halve the carrot (scraped). Put them all in a pot with a beef bouillon cube, a little salt and pepper, and several cups of water. Cook until the vegetables are almost done, adding a little more water when and if necessary. Then add 1 can of corned beef, mix it through the vegetables, and continue cooking until vegetables are done. You may want to add a little fat and/or a little vinegar according to personal taste.

NAVY-BEAN SOUP

Buy:

Navy beans, dried (1 package) or canned (1)

Salt pork or canned bacon (1 pound)

An onion, large **Tomatoes (optional), (1 can)**

This soup can be made with dried beans or canned beans. Dried beans must be soaked in water overnight, but they are a lot lighter to carry.

Wash the beans and let them soak overnight in enough water to cover them. Next morning, fry up the salt pork or bacon in a large pot, add the diced onion, and fry it until it turns golden brown. Add the beans with the water they were soaked in, and if necessary add a little more water so that the beans are covered. Let the soup simmer on the back of a camp-stove all day very gently, keeping an eye out in case the soup boils too fast or runs low on liquid. If you use canned beans, the whole process is telescoped. When it's nearly dinner time, throw in the can of tomatoes if you want to add it, and add salt and pepper to taste. If the soup is too thick, you can add water and warm it up again.

HABITANT PEA SOUP

Buy:

Dried yellow split peas (1 **Onions, medium-sized (1 or 2)**
package) **A carrot (if you have a**
Salt pork, fat (2-inch cube) **grater)**

This very thick soup is a meal in itself and will really stick to your ribs.

Read the directions on the package of split peas to see whether they need to be soaked or not. Boil 1 quart of water in a large soup kettle, and then add 2 cups of peas. Put the soup aside, cover it, and let it stand for an hour. Then add the cube of salt pork, 1 or 2 sliced onions, the grated carrot. Simmer the soup for an hour or two until the peas are soft. Remove the lump of pork and add salt and pepper to taste. If you find the soup too thick, dilute it with milk. (This may mean using dried skim milk reconstituted with water.)

FRESH-FISH CHOWDER

This depends on what kind of fresh fish you have on hand. If it's trout, forget the chowder and pan-broil it instead. If it's catfish go ahead. And if it's saltwater fish, by all means go ahead. The chowder works best with lean fish such as pickerel or sea bass.

Catch:

**Some fish (you need two or
 three fillets)**

Buy:

Salt pork (a 2-inch cube)
Potato (a couple)
Onions, large (2)
Evaporated milk (1 can)

**Tomato paste (1 small can),
 or ketchup or tomato sauce**
Curry powder

Chop the salt pork as finely as you can and fry it until it turns golden brown. Add the onion and cook it but do not let it brown. Add a teaspoon of curry powder and mix it into the fat. Dice the potato and add it to the pot with just enough water to cover it. Cook until the potato is done but not mushy. Then add the fish fillets and let them cook until they are just done, i.e., white and beginning to flake. Finally add three tablespoons of tomato paste (or ketchup or whatever) and the milk. Allow the chowder to heat, but do not let it boil again. Season to taste with salt and pepper and serve it up.

POACHED FRESH-CAUGHT FISH

Catch:

**Some fish. Cook them whole
 if they are small enough;
 cut fillets if they are not.
 Dig a few clams if there
 are any around.**

Poaching a fish is very much like boiling it, except that you can do it in a skillet and you use very much less liquid. Poached fish is particularly good when served cold.

The principle of poaching is as follows: put enough water in a skillet (size depending on how much fish and how many people) to surround your fish. Having used the fish in order to measure this quantity, remove the fish and bring the water to a boil. Add the fish and let it cook without reboiling for ten minutes per pound of fish. Chuck in a few clams to cook with the fish if you have any. When the fish is done, drain off the water, add seasonings, and serve.

If you have a piece of cheesecloth, wrap the fish in it before cooking.

If you can find the following ingredients or some of them, put them in the water before boiling it and they will give the fish a fine flavor: sliced onion, peppercorns, sliced carrot, a bay leaf, a pinch of thyme, a slice of lemon, a little salt.

If you are poaching the fish at home, boil the water with these ingredients for about half an hour, strain it, and then cook the fish in it. The water is then called a court bouillon, and is traditionally used for cooking good fish.

WHISKEY VENISON

Catch:

A deer

Buy:

Whiskey (1 bottle)
**Orange juice, concentrated
(1 12-ounce can)**

Garlic, a lot
Celery seeds

Check Cupboard for:

Peppercorns

Make a marinade as follows, combining all ingredients in a large pan: 1 cup whiskey (drink the rest), the can of orange juice, 4 or 5 crushed cloves of garlic, 6 whole peppercorns, ½ teaspoon of celery seeds.

Marinate a hind quarter of the venison in this mixture with a cover on it for 24 to 36 hours in as cool a place as you can manage—a refrigerator if you can find one. Turn the meat occasionally.

Cook over coals for about 1 hour, basting with the marinade.

PAN-FRIED VENISON

Catch:

Venison steaks, about ¼″
thick (4)

Buy:

Currant jelly (1 jar) **Beef bouillon cubes**
Burgundy or Burgundy-type **Butter**
wine (1 bottle)

Fry the venison in a skillet with a little butter. When it is done, remove it from the pan and into the drippings which remain add 1 cup of currant jelly, ¾ cup Burgundy, 2 beef bouillon cubes, and 1 tablespoon butter. Let this come to a boil, stirring constantly. Season with salt and pepper. Pour it over the venison. Drink the rest of the Burgundy.

RABBIT ABBOTT

Catch:

Rabbits, a couple (cut them
in pieces)

Buy:

Bread crumbs (1 package) **Eggs**

Check Cupboard for:

Flour **Garlic powder**
Oil

Mix together in a bowl 2 eggs, 2 tablespoons water, salt and pepper to taste, and a little garlic powder. Beat lightly with a fork or wire whisk. Put half a cup of flour on a plate, and ¾ cup bread crumbs on another. Dip each piece of rabbit into the egg mixture, then into the flour, then into the egg mixture a second time, then into the bread crumbs. Salt and pepper the pieces lightly again, and add a little more garlic powder if you like. Put the pieces away on a flat platter, covering them, in as cold a place as you can find—a refrigerator if possible. This will allow the coating to set. Remove them from the refrigerator ½ an hour before cooking.

Find a big frying pan and fill it with oil ¼ inch deep. Warm up the oil and brown the rabbit on each side until it has a golden color. Add ½ cup of water to the pan—being careful about spattering fat—cover it with a lid, and cook over a low fire for about 25 minutes. Then remove the cover for the last ten minutes to allow the coating to get crisp. Serve with a jelly if you have any—apple or currant or cranberry—save the strawberry and grape for breakfast.

CAMP STICK BREAD

Buy:

Biscuit mix (1 package)   **Milk**

This is just about the world's simplest way to make bread.

Add ⅔ cup milk to 2 cups biscuit mix, and stir it around with a fork to make a soft dough. Put flour on your hands and roll bits of dough into shapes as thick as a fat pencil and about six inches long.

Find some green sticks and peel them. Wind some dough around the end of each stick as a spiral, and pinch the ends to secure them to the stick. Bake them over hot coals, turning them so that they cook evenly. When they are nicely browned, slip them off the sticks. Eat 'em with bread and jam, or with hot dogs, or anything else you fancy.

HUNTING CAMP RED RICE

Buy:

Rice, long-grain (1 package)   **A pepper**
Tomatoes, (2 20-ounce cans)   **Celery**
An onion

Check Cupboard for:

Ketchup   **Tabasco**
Worcestershire sauce   **Garlic**

Open the cans of tomatoes and drain 2½ cups of juice out of them into a saucepan. Bring the tomato juice to a boil.

Put some oil in the bottom of another saucepan (3- or 4-quart size), heat it a little, and add a cup of rice. Stir the rice in the hot oil for a minute or two until it is well-coated. Then add the 2½ cups of tomato juice which you have heated. Put a tight lid on the rice, and simmer it until all the juice is consumed and the rice is cooked. Watch carefully to make sure it does not overcook and start to burn.

In the saucepan in which you heated the juice, combine 1 cup of the tomatoes from the cans, 1 small chopped onion, 1 green or red pepper chopped in small pieces, 2 celery sticks sliced thin, 1 clove of crushed garlic, a couple of shots of Worcestershire sauce, a shot of Tabasco, and salt and pepper to taste. Cook this mixture over medium heat until the onions, peppers, and celery are soft, adding a little water if necessary. Then fry up a couple of slices of bacon, let it cool, and crumble.

Combine the cooked rice, the sauce, and the bits of bacon, and serve.

This rice is particularly good with venison steaks or deer livers. It becomes an excellent perloo if you replace the bacon with fresh shrimp.

BRUNSWICK STEW

Brunswick stew is one of the great traditional stews that originated in the American South, most of them based on small game. These stews, such as Jambalaya and Kentucky Burgoo, have undergone all sorts of modifications and supposed improvements, but the traditional ingredients are still the best. A Brunswick stew is not a Brunswick stew unless it contains: squirrel or rabbit and ham, corn, okra, lima beans, tomatoes, and rice. The ham should be hard-cured, smoked, aged country ham. To these basic ingredients you may add others—a chicken for instance, or other vegetables such as potatoes, fresh peas, and green beans.

Catch:

Rabbits, a couple

Buy:

Ham, ½ pound
Corn, fresh if possible (buy a lot and use the rest roasted)
Tomatoes, ripe
Okra, fresh if possible, if not, a can

Lima beans, (1 frozen package or 1 can)
Rice
Butter

Check Cupboard for:

Bay leaf
Whole hot chili peppers

Parsley
Thyme

Cut the rabbits into serving-size pieces and dice the ham. Put them into a large pot with enough water to cover, and add salt and pepper in moderation. Make a little cloth bag out of a small square of cheesecloth which you can tie with a bit of string. Put into it a hot pepper, a bay leaf, a sprig of parsley, and some thyme (a sprig of fresh thyme if possible—it often grows wild). Tie up the bag and add it to the pot. Put the pot on the fire and bring it to a simmer, not a boil. Let it simmer until the rabbit begins to get tender.

The next trick is to add the fresh vegetables at intervals so that they won't overcook. Add a cup of fresh corn first (and a cup of lima beans *if* you have *fresh* ones). Wait for 5 minutes and then add ¾ a cup of rice. Wait 10 minutes and then add 1 cup of sliced okra and 2 tomatoes, quartered. Cook for another 15 minutes and then add a tablespoon of butter and stir it in. *If* you have no fresh vegetables, and are using canned or forzen ones, put the rice in first, and add the vegetables about 10 minutes later.

Do not add water unless absolutely necessary. The stew should be very thick—thick enough to eat with a fork. But be careful not to burn the bottom of it.

This recipe should serve five or six people.

STEBBINS' BAKED BEANS

Buy:

Baked beans (two 1-pound cans)

Bacon

Brown sugar

Brandy or rum

Check Cupboard for:

Garlic

Bay leaf

Dry mustard

Load the beans into a pot. Add ¼ cup brown sugar, 1 tablespoon of dry mustard, 1 bay leaf, 1 crushed garlic clove, 4 to 6 slices of bacon cooked and crumbled, and ½ cup of brandy or rum.

Let it cook slowly for 30 to 45 minutes, adding more rum or brandy as needed.

This dish is better warmed-over, so let it sit for several hours before eating, and then heat it up.

Index

SCORECARD

Menu	Guest	Comments

SCORECARD

Menu	Guest	Comments

SCORECARD

Menu	Guest	Comments